AGENDA

ATLANTIC CROSSINGS

50th Birthday Celebration for

Greg Delanty

Greg Delanty teaches at St. Michael's College, Vermont. For a part of the year he lives in Derrynane, County Kerry, Ireland. His recent books are *The Ship of Birth* (Carcanet Press, 2003), *The Blind Stitch* (Carcanet Press, 2001) and *The Hellbox* (Oxford University Press, 1998). His *Collected Poems 1986-2006* is out from the Oxford Poets' Series of Carcanet Press.

He has received many awards, most recently a Guggenheim for poetry which is assisting the writing of his next collection – a selection of his own poems using the template of the sixteen books of *The Greek Anthology*.

AGENDA

CONTENTS

CELEBRATIONS IN POETRY FOR GREG DELANTY ON THIS SIDE OF THE ATLANTIC

CELEBRATIONS IN POETRY FOR GREG DELANTY ACROSS THE ATLANTIC

REVIEWS/ESSAYS

POEMS

Front cover: Drawing of Greg Delanty by Eamonn O'Doherty, Paris 2003.

Eamonn O'Doherty is an artist best known for his large-scale public sculptures, more than thirty of which are sited in Ireland, Britain, Europe and the U.S.

Sequence in pencil and watercolours: Johnny Marsh

Johnny Marsh was born in 1961. He lives and works in Sussex. He studied Fine Art at Goldsmiths College and has recently qualified as an Art Psychotherapist.

Editorial

Welcome to this special bumper double issue of *Agenda*, *Atlantic Crossings*, a large part of which celebrates the 50th Birthday of **Greg Delanty**, the Irish/American poet published by Carcanet Press, who has received too many prizes and awards to mention both in the United States and Europe, including, as long ago as 1983, the Patrick Kavanagh Award, considered Ireland's most prestigious poetry prize. Currently he is honoured to be the holder of the Guggenheim Fellowship in the US. In addition to writing his own poems, he has also been involved in many editorial and translation projects.

We wish to thank Saint Michael's College in Vermont where Greg Delanty teaches. We wish, also, to thank Eamonn O'Doherty for the portrait on the cover of this issue of Greg Delanty sketched in the Centre Culturel Irlandais, 2003.

Many thanks also to all the contributors, both well-known and lesser known, on this side of the Atlantic, and across the Atlantic, who partake in the celebration of poetry with Greg, as well as in the other sections of the journal. Thanks also to all our readers who are as important for the survival of poetry as the poems' makers.

It is a pleasure to include poems in the Irish language, some of which are Greg's own poems translated into Irish by Liam Ó Muirthile, others of which are written in Irish as the first language by Colm Breathnach and Liam de Paor. An unusual piece of translation is that of a poem by the well-known Irish poet and Arabic scholar, Desmond O'Grady, into Arabic.

Contributors hail from the UK, the US, Canada, Australia, The West Indies, including St. Lucia and Trinidad, and also from Egypt, The Czech Republic, Poland and Hungary. Some of the Irish/Americans are represented as being 'across the Atlantic' while others are 'on this side of the Atlantic'. Here definitions are blurred and it was probably down mostly to where the poems were sent from. American spellings are kept when they are in the original work.

The essays on Delanty, which cover both personal, literary and academic angles, illuminate his work for the reader less acquainted with it and, hopefully, encourage the reader to seek out his *Collected Poems* (Carcanet). The general essays/reviews, too, by poet/novelist/essayist William Bedford, poet/retired teacher Tony Roberts, highly-regarded Faber novelist, Duncan Sprott, and poet-essayist Sam Milne, relate to poets in this issue, such as Paul Muldoon and Galway Kinnell, and/or to poets promoted by *Agenda* such as Geoffrey Hill, James Harpur, Anne Beresford and, of course, the ever-supportive Grey Gowrie.

The anthology of poems towards the end of the issue represents fresh, exciting voices emanating mainly from the UK, including the two young chosen **Broadsheet poets**. This time, the **Notes for Broadsheet Poets**, part of an ongoing series both in the magazine and online, comprises an essay by an actual young **Broadsheet** poet who was represented in the last, *Lauds* issue of *Agenda*.

I hope, therefore, that this issue, *Atlantic Crossings,* will strike a chord with all of you. The *Atlantic Crossings* of many of the poets here, particularly the Irish and American ones, link most obviously to the theme of exile which permeates this issue. Other crossings underlined in these pages of *Agenda* are of birth/life to death, of moods – from Mr Down to the 'upbird', of one register to another register, of the literal to the metaphorical, of one language to another, of themes, forms, identity and voice, and of the writer to the reader and back.

Please do not forget to visit our increasingly vibrant **website**
www.agendapoetry.co.uk
with its compatible mixture of poems and paintings and much more.

Please, also, **do not forget to subscribe and/or to renew your subscription** as we rely on the support of each one of you for our flourishing. Subscription lists are the vital backbone of literary journals such as *Agenda* in an increasingly materialistic, cut-throat world. And a subscription, come to think of it, is no more than, say, a few cappuccinos a year or a couple of bottles of good wine!

A final thank you goes to Marcus Frederick (known to many of you via emails as 'Fred'). To run an international poetry magazine is a big job for two people, but Fred keeps it altogether consistently and unfailingly.

Patricia McCarthy

Nota Bene: **Agenda's 50th Birthday** falls next year, 2009.

Contributions, suggestions, donations, including new and renewed subscriptions are all welcome for a bumper issue and launch to mark this special, forthcoming anniversary.

NEW TEAR–OFF SUBSCRIPTION FORM
at the end of this issue.

WALKING

Johnny Marsh I

Introduction

Few poets have their *Collected Poems* published before they are fifty, but Greg Delanty, being the Irish/American globetrotter that he is, the self-confessed 'cocky young cleric at St Brendan's door, / refusing to leave till I've played the music of the world', who eschews elitist 'angelic harping' in favour of plucking 'the common note of an open harp', is one of them. His *Collected Poems 1986-2006* (Oxford Poets, Carcanet, 2006) demonstrates his considerable innovative achievement in form, emotive power, range, original use of language and metaphor, and shows him emerging as an important voice for our own day, as well as for the past and the future.

Tom Sleigh, the highly-acclaimed American poet, whose work is featured in this issue, writes most articulately of Greg Delanty's work:

> A tone at once profane and bracing and heartbroken – that's what I hear when I listen in on the secret frequencies of Greg's work, the frequencies that underlie his comedy and irony and penchant for satire. You can see it at work in *The Hellbox* and *The Blind Stitch* especially, in which the language wants to elbow aside any conventional lyric sentiment. It's as if Greg has set out to wring the neck of what Derek Walcott (whose work is also featured here) once called, "the standard elegiac", while remaining in touch with the bedrock griefs and disappointments that spur his poems on.
>
> But that's not the whole story: on the spiritual front, there are many poets who have great spiritual hunger, but little gift for spiritual perception – and by perception, I mean a credible language for things of the spirit. Greg's poems are marvels of having it both ways: for every gesture of faith the poet makes, there's an equal and opposite reaction of a recusant conscience: he's sincerely praying, but with crossed fingers. This kind of split in his sensibility, and the way he embodies it in his mastery of demotic speech, slang double-entendre, and sheer raconteurish vitality, make him one of the few poets now writing who can show 'an affirming flame', and not get burnt in the process.

The following tasters show that Delanty is indeed very much his own man. In starkly realistic poems whose end rhymes are often death 'knells' with their monosyllabic thump that mocks the insistent, unrealisable hope, he is the son watching his 'Ma's protracted killing by 'Mr Mort' from cancer. He is a husband who watches tenderly over his wife's pregnancy – 'all the cordial choir are Noah-calling you now' - and invokes the unborn 'little lambkin, waxwing, luckling' who at times turns 'large and despotic, a parody / of a mad medieval king.' What male poet has sung so keenly about the birth of a child since Jon Silkin's memorable lament for his newborn? Delanty's highly accomplished villanelle, 'The Language of Crying', 'We're still learning the language of crying, / its parent-boggling irregular grammar'....'Surely the future's not teething yet. We stammer. / We're still learning the language of crying. / Anybody would think you were dying' haunts the reader but simultaneously shows the 'Christ-child''s equal power to haunt the parents: 'such a caterwaul's parent-petrifying'. In 'Circus' he parodies himself at the birth as 'the whistle-blowing clown, / the huffing and puffing red-faced Bozo father / of fathers, wearing a lugubrious frown, / cracking side-splitting sideshow banter / and flat-footed jokes, a sidekick to your mother.' He is also the terrified, awe-struck new father, the 'doubting Thomas' withdrawing from touching the 'unbelievable hole' of the fragile fontanelle and excusing himself as 'a nut', or elsewhere as 'a fool'.

He can be the wayward husband in 'the conjugal hall of mirrors', a womaniser 'loopy about women', who has even 'a wandering eye for flowers' and who fantasises about playing around, thereby becoming 'everyman'. In the nitty-gritty poem, 'The Family Man and the Rake', he is 'like a character in a movie with a doppelganger/carrying on with some looker, promising to ditch my family / but for the kids' sake the affair must be undercover…' Dashing home, he goes through a red light 'and wonders / if it's an omen, slipping eternity back on his finger'. It's a recognisable cliché, the persona of the poem as elusive as the defined adulterer:

> You know the story. At this stage nobody can tell
> the doppelganger from the doppelganger's doppel
> in a hall of mirrors, or which one is writing this now.

Yet in the delicately moving poem, 'The Blind Stitch', he is also the reconciler, who makes it up with his wife and demonstrates his deep love as they sit together, symbolically regaining a unity. He remembers her sewing a vest for him while he sews a button on this old vest now. The move is from the literal to the metaphorical and recalls Heaney's poem from *Seeing Things*, 'Markings'. There, the boys, having marked out a home-made football pitch with their jackets on the grass, started to move into another world: …'by then they were playing in their heads', as dusk fell, with the ball that became 'a dream heaviness'. 'Some limit had been passed'. Here:

> Our hands, without thought for individual movement, sew in
>   and out, entering and leaving at one and the same time.
> If truth be told, the thread had frayed between us, unnoticed,
>   except for the odd rip. But as we sew, love is
> in the mending, and though nothing's said, we feel it
>   in a lightness of mood, our ease, our blind stitch.

An unusually self-analytical man, he owns up to his moods and manic-depressive tendencies as he seeks a balance between his two selves, 'the upbird and the off-yellow / downbird' in 'Sightings'. He is not afraid to laugh at himself, for his 'general depression shot' is given to him by 'the roller-coaster / god of humour, doctor Mood-Swinger himself.' And he communes with his 'old faithful companion', 'Mr Down, Mr Nightday':

13

No sooner did I shake hands with Squire Black and we get
    all chummy, inseparable even…

The poem ends with a kind of a soliloquising mantra, the repetition of 'Soon enough' and 'That's alright' reassuring him that he will get over this blackness.

In the remarkable poem, 'To my Mother, Eileen', he is the 'likely lad' with the 'eye' and the 'knack', the 'Prince Threader' who threads his 'camel of words' through the needle for her. On one level, this poem recalls Seamus Heaney's beautifully delicate sonnet, number 3, from 'Clearances', about himself as a boy and his mother peeling potatoes together 'While all the others were away at Mass'. At the 'pleasant little splashes' of the peeled potatoes into the cold bucket of water, he and his mother, heads bent towards each other, 'Her breath in mine', were 'Never closer the whole rest of our lives'. Delanty's poem, however, describes more than a unifiying action. The thread is an extended metaphor for the son/poet's language: 'I raise the needle to the light and lick the thread / to stiffen the limp words…' In the act of threading the needle he learns the beginnings of what is to become his concentrated craft: 'I / peer through the eye, focus, put everything out of my head.' And yet the simple familiar action is graphic also: 'I shut my right eye and thread'. After a realistic miss and more concentration – 'Enough yaketty yak', he returns 'the threaded needle' to his 'Ma'.

He is also the 'likely lad' friend, the one who goes for the 'craic', who, with one pal or another, can 'talk poetry blue / in the face', can rant and rave or tenderly lyricise, and, like Yeats, can make mythological figures of those in his circle. In the entertaining narrative of 'The Speakeasy Oath', Liam Ó Muirthile borrows a kimono from Delanty 'its script more readable than the serif characters of our / tattered Irish primers'. The kimono's 'druid sleeves' catch fire upon which Liam utters 'a veritable string of swear words right out of the lost / lexicon of old Irish oaths'. Ó Muirthile 'like some stepdancer gone bonkers' and Delanty, 'in me scald, dancing buff' dousing the sleeve, dance a weird jig together, taking it as 'a thumbs-up from the muses, / after our night before's oath to set the poetry world on fire.' In 'Opening Up', to Anthony Cronin, he makes a clever pun on 'ink': 'I chance sending you these inklings of how much / we think of your inked life'. In 'The Ink Moth' – introducing Seamus Heaney at the Katharine Washburn Translation Memorial – he recalls time spent with Seamus, and wonders where is Katharine.

Her company like yours, Seamus,
    was the spring touch that released in us
      the woolly bear moth,

the love moth I translate it to here,
    stuttering into the air,
      winging it here and here
              and here.

The repeated 'here's almost fly off the page fittingly and demonstrate the different types of wings that are a recurrent motif in Delanty's poetry. For example, in 'The Great Ship', the 'crickets, cicadas, grasshoppers and frogs', with their 'song and wing-music', comprise the 'quartet / that comes out on deck and plays away / as the great ship goes down.' The irony is that they become 'brave, noble souls' who must 'Play on' in the words of a traditional hymn: *Nearer, My God, / to thee. Nearer to thee.* The love moth 'stuttering' in the Seamus poem brings to mind Paul Celan who claimed to possess a 'true-stammered mouth' and saw the world 'as a thing to be stuttered after.' Another poem on moths is 'The Skunk Moths' in which Delanty compares skunks, with their backs to him, to big black and white caterpillars who will turn into giant moths. Here the 'wing' image is extended and deepened:

> Imagine the Luna's gossamer tulle wings, the tippets
>   brushing us, fanning us tenderly, wrapping us in a veil,
> bringing us gently to our knees in a gathering humility,
>   brushing aside our mortification, finally at home, natural
> in the natural world – their wings our cocoon – becoming
> ourselves, pinioned resplendence, at last the human mothfly.

'In Times of War', a sonnet in the last collection of his represented in *The Collected, Aceldama*, Delanty very cleverly knits the 'wing' image into the theme of language and poetry. Over a poet 'flies the spindly-legged bird, Longevity, / croaking in the mind's ear all will be "Okay, Okay"'. Another poet is praising 'geese flying in fair formation / to Inchicore...' The following wonderful alliterative statement: ' how their wings will outwing the war' proves the strength of 'wings' to outlast and even overcome human violations. The internal rhyme within the one line of 'Inchicore' with the end rhyme 'war' emphasises this. Then, invoking 'the two poets I steer by' – Yeats and Patrick Kavanagh – he states humbly, 'I know my station', before rounding off the poem with a resounding rhetorical question in the rhyming couplet: ... 'but what of the mother stooped over her child, / the wild pen over the limp cygnet, the pen defiled?'

This sonnet represents an important aspect of Delanty's poetry in general: its strong political focus. Delanty uses the sonnet form as a statement of implied complicity within the Western tradition. This is mostly concealed within the poem's construct, just as it is mostly concealed within the construct of our lives. Delanty himself is a political activist who engages in civil disobedience, and stands in vigils and demonstrations weekly. He disagrees with W.H. Auden who claimed that poetry makes nothing happen. Delanty believes that poetry does make things happen and states: 'I think of art and life more as a kind of palindrome'. He writes both overtly and implicitly about war, hunger, the misuse of power, including nuclear power, the homeless, the murders of innocent children, women and men; and about the death of nature. However, his poems are not all negatively critical of political systems. They also try to find new ways of looking at the world which society has not, as of yet, turned to. He is aware of the dangers in writing overtly political poetry and admits: 'There is a sense in contemporary poetry that to purposely write poems in an overt way about politics lessens the authenticity of the poem and the poet. This is only true when the poetry is coming from the shallow waters of overt didacticism in the poem and produces poor poetry.' 'Metaphor is important throughout my work and acts in a political way. Metaphor and simile imply sameness and unity perceived beneath the skin of seeming difference, that beneath the skin of difference we are kin.'

The final rumination on wings in *The Collected* occurs in 'Behold the Brahmany Kite' where the poet wishes, at his death, to become 'the grub of the Brahmany Kite' which has the name of a god and 'mighty' wings. In a series of instructions he delivers himself up:

> Keep your elegy eye on the bird a day or so. Watch the kite
>   make nothing of me.
> Then, as I have now, give the Brahmany an almost
>   imperceptible nod and turn and go.

This premature epitaph is an original one, linked whether consciously or sub-consciously to the epitaph Yeats wrote for himself at the end of 'Under Ben Bulben'. Both Yeats and Delanty use imperatives as if they want to be in charge of their own deaths. Yeats talks in the third person, as opposed to Delanty's first person, of the inscription he wants on the ancient limestone cross on the road by Drumcliff churchyard: 'Cast a cold eye'. This 'cold eye' that Yeats commands to be cast upon life and death relates to the 'elegy eye' Delanty orders which will watch the kite reducing him to insignificance. Yeats' urging of the horseman to 'pass by', emphasised by the exclamation mark, is echoed in Delanty's urging of the onlooker to give a mere 'imperceptible nod', then to 'turn and go'. Both poets wish to make a clean cut, it seems, between life and death.

Delanty is often the traveller, as in the aforementioned 'Behold the Brahmany Kite', never the mere tourist. He doesn't have the problem D.H. Lawrence encountered, for example when the latter was temporarily in Mexico, and felt he was merely skating over the surface of civilisations and cultures. Foreign places are absorbed into Delanty's sub-conscious and become part of him and of his place of origin. The collection, *The Blind Stitch*, contains a sequence of poems set in India and Sri Lanka. For example, in the moving 'Elegy for an Aunt', the poet is in India watching a funeral-procession. He identifies this Hindu funeral with the recent human details of the Christian funeral of his aunt that he attended, as one of the pall-bearers, back home. It appears that, to the poet's friends at the funeral and to himself, the notion of reincarnation, though alien to Catholicism, was in fact a possibility back there amidst intimations of mortality, irrespective of any creed:

We all copped another of the old world souls was cut
    from us, as Rosy was and Noel and

and and, and with each *and* a subtraction as if we're
    disappearing ourselves
limb by phantom limb. Soon we'll be nothing but air.

In this sense, Ireland becomes India and India is Ireland: he refers to 'the ghats /
of chemical factories lining the Lee, our Ganges'.... At the end of the poem, while
monkeys cavort on the balcony outside his room, he is as always the conscious
poet, whose eyes 'strain / to follow / my pencil, this jotting the leaded shade of
smarting smoke / and ashes below'. Smoke and ashes are the same whether in
India or Ireland or anywhere and reduce everyone to a common denominator.

    In another of the 'Indian' poems, 'Ululu', the poet and his partner have a row,
and after this 'latest tempest', the poet imagines his soul has entered the trapped
and hurt 'monkey of these parts', 'this creature high in the trees, 'ululating to
the emptiness of the night'. Again the identification, this time between man and
animal, Christian and Hindu, is complete. Similarly, in 'The Stilt Fisherman', the
poet berates himself for wanting fame and learns a humility from the fisherman.
Whereas he, the poet, has 'wasted so much time.... Fishing to be known', the
modest stilt fisherman is celebrated even though oblivious to this. He gives
humble thanks at catching a 'shimmering seerfish', and it is significantly not just a
small wave that washes in around him, but 'The ocean in the swell of a wave'. What
the poet deep down knows is that fame is hollow and he should be content, like
this fisherman, to have a kind of anonymous acknowledgement:

Combers furl and fall
around him, the boom
of tall drums played in the Temple
by bowing, anonymous men.

The 'pounding' of 'two-sided' drums, this time belonging to Buddhist monks,
continues in 'Prayer to Saint Blaise'. Since dawn they have been chanting and
playing their drums 'in the Temple of the Sacred Tooth, praying to the molar
/ of Buddha.' Hearing them, the poet transports himself back to his Catholic
upbringing, with its confessions ('of impure thoughts'), candles, Latin blessings
and stock prayers that he starts to mumble again now that 'the candle of middleage
gutters down to / a malaise of disappointment'. His guilt about wanting fame re-
appears: 'I've lingered too long in the underworld of the poetry / circle, another
jostling jongleur jockeying to sup / from the blood of fame, or rather the ketchup,
my ailing / throat desperate to be heard.' And he decides on a fresh start: to 'chance'
coming again 'to poetry pax. / I'll kneel before my childhood's sacred tooth.' In
this last line he characteristically turns the 'Sacred Tooth' in the Buddhist Temple
into the 'sacred' tooth of his childhood religion, so that, again, the Buddhist and

Catholic images unite, different religions stemming from the one impulse.

There is no doubt that Delanty has the gift of the articulate updated gab of the genuine Bard as, along with straight talk and erudition, he subverts, inverts, parodies, mouths mongrel and traditional lingos and even makes up his own words into a kind of Delanty Esperanto, furthering what James Joyce achieves in *Ulysses* and *Finnegans Wake*, adding allegorical figures reminiscent of Bunyan. Inventive and often cheekily outspoken, he daringly mixes Cork slang, American drawl, classical allusions, mythological references, Biblical and liturgical language, Gaelic Irish and straight English, as well as puns and clichés, into a linguistic hotpot whose bubbling has an orchestrated, compulsive chant of its own. His poems roll off his tongue deceptively easily. Hovering in the ear in their own virtuosity, with very distant mini-echoes of John Donne, Hopkins, Blake, Dylan Thomas, even Jean Genet, they engage the reader's depths, sense of irony, humour, and of belief in humanity.

He speaks of his need to write poetry as of his need to breathe in air. Without it, he says, 'I would have been a more destructive person. I would have been isolated and probably would have sought connection via some group – say a religion, or even sport, or worse'. (He did, in fact, swim for Ireland, and was Irish champion for his age group for a number of years!)

In a recently published prose book, *Hiddenness, Uncertainty, Surprise: Three Generative Energies of Poetry* (Newcastle/Bloodaxe Poetry Lectures Series 7), Jane Hirshfield, who is represented with a poem in this issue, states: 'The making of good poetry entails control; it also requires surrender and a light hand. A genuine art lives somewhere between the divination bones and the dice. That is, it lives along that exploration line that has to do with which aspects of our lives we can know, which we cannot, and the spirit and tools with which we engage the question. We travel this line by taking aim with a whole life, and then letting go, committing ourselves to the toss.' Delanty surely fits the bill here. In a poem 'To Belarussians after Chernobyl', representing his overall concern with world traumas, and issues whether political, familial, societal, or ecological, he says:

And now more than ever I want handicapped

words to turn into such music that will recreate
a miraculous humdrum night such as ours
for you: with voices telling unbelievable tales;

with hurricane lamps, crickets, birds and trees…

It is these very 'handicapped words' owned by us all that Delanty metamorphoses into 'such music' which is never 'humdrum' but attached to the real and the daily, or to memory, both personal and communal, to such 'tales' and images while he takes risks with his own vulnerability and ours. As Jane Hirshfield claims in her aforementioned book: 'To feel is to be at risk, and to be at risk is to feel.' In his non-didactic questioning of our species, of himself, and of our multi-faceted world, Delanty also complies with what she says about being unsure: '... to be human is to be unsure, and if the purpose of poetry is to deepen the humanness in us, poetry will be unsure as well' while 'what lives in a poem lives in us'.

In the terrifically energetic long Joycean prose-poem, 'The Hellbox', full of wit, daring eroticism from a poet reared an Irish Catholic, and clever references, he posits:

> But outside poetry's ticker, if the power of suggestion,
> leaving so much to the imagination, is the chief attribute of
> a poem, then Delia of the delving cleavage you're *some* poem.
> Oh, when will the nine Delias descend and blow me?
> O *Jesus*, there's been enough ducking and deprecating.
> What about the Muses down on 42nd Street,
> the ladies of my blue fantasies that come to life
> in the confessional of peep-show booths,
> stripping the lingerie of suggestion
> slip by agonising slinky slip, dancing
> into the poetry nip? Please talk dirty to me.

Elsewhere in this poem, he utters: '...I want the other / side of the truth of this story: how since this sublunar life / of ours is such a pain, so imperfect in one way or another, / that the more imperfect words are, the truer they are / and greater. Thus spake a Grecian saucepan.' He concludes by stating his own aims in poetry from an exile's point of view:

> All I want is not simply to parrot American voices,
> reminding me of how immigrants learned
> a new tongue, mimicking gramophone records
> or following theatre stars from show to show.

Rather, he wants his 'words to become / the stuff of Temelcoff's dreams – trees / changed their names and their leafy looks; / men answered in falsetto and dogs spoke in the street.'

Language is a recurring theme throughout his *Collected Poems*. In the moving elegy to Peggy Kenneally, '450⁰F', he 'is word-stretched' to give her 'her due'. In 'Lepers' Walk' he has been 'doing a line / with your ersatz crush, Madam Words'. He finds on 'the islands of Academe and Literati', that were meant to offer promise, only 'strains not unlike the small-town class: fear / of other island enclaves, numb envy / among locals, immunity to the very spirit-vaccine / they themselves dose out.' And he dreads infection.

The whole of his important collection, *The Hellbox* (1998), shows Delanty using to his full metaphorical power his unusual heritage: that of his father's printing works. Until then, he had envied other contemporary poets and those of the previous generation for their agricultural backgrounds and how they used these in their poetry. In this sequence, printing terms and printers' argot serve as original extended metaphors for the theme of language, giving his work deeper levels of meaning beneath the surface structures. The hellbox, for example, was a container in which worn or broken type was thrown to be melted down and re-cast into new type. Delanty typically shifts this from the literal to the metaphorical in an ingenious way: the hellbox becomes a metaphor for poetry, the art of re-making and renewing out of what has gone before. It is also a metaphor for emigration and immigration in the melting pot of the US, and indeed in any multi-cultural society such as the UK.

In 'The Composing Room', one of the poems in this collection, the men in the room become more than 'ordinary / blokes trying to keep the devil from the door, // and with luck have enough left over each week / to back a few nags, and go for a few jars.' With their composers' sticks, they set 'inverse words and lines / of each page that could be taken for 'Greek scripture' and declare:

> In the beginning was the Word and the Word
> was made cold type and the Word was
> coldness, darkness, shiny greyness
> and light – and the Word dwelt amongst us.

The poet himself becomes one of them, hankering 'to know the quality / of each letter'. He wants to 'set the words up, / making something out of all this / that stays standing – all set as masterly // as the words those men set that reveal / something of the mystery behind / and within these letters and the wonder and / the darkness, but with the lightest touch.' He is aware metaphorically of the dangers in being a poet: of the possible foul-ups, of proofreaders missing mistakes, of the evil eyes of fellow composers, and of the 'bosses / writing on the composition: *Kill.*' But he knows:

> the real achievement will be that I tried to set
> the words right; that I did it with much labour
> and not without a font of love…

The old names for printing, he tells us, were *The Mysterious Craft*, or *Mystery*. His ultimate, humble hope (in which he sends himself up) is that *The Mystery* will be met 'if only / behind the characters of one fly-boy's words.'

> I want to home in on the newness, strangeness, foreignness
>   of everything, returning it to itself, its exile from itself,
> the perpetual simultaneous goings and comings of life,
>   while remaining always human, open, up front.

The 'hellbox', as a general metaphor for re-making oneself, permeates his work and illuminates the major themes of emigration and immigration which are, as he says, a metaphor for all of us since we are all exiles from the worlds we would like to be in, all metaphysical exiles 'trying to find home'. Delanty was brought up in the city of Cork and, as a boy, was at home, as we have seen, in that noisy printshop owned by his father. In 'The Lost Way' he muses:

I can still recall the forking-out, print-inked hands
of my father, setting gentle words in me, his impress,
and me swearing I'd set words like him some day.

In 'Film Directions for the Underworld', recalling Cocteau's black and white film, he sees Irish emigrants (himself included) in Manhattan as film extras who could any second 'step out of / the film' and 'feel at home again, cursing / the static screen of Irish rain'. In this same poem he suggests: 'I've a hunch the Irish underworld is the realm / of the emigrant. After exiles are waked, / they feel they've somehow passed on'. There are tinges of homesickness in some early poems. For example, in 'The Emigrant's Apology' he recalls sitting in the family pew, stifling giggles during the sermon. But now he is away, an emigrant, he cannot help thinking of his mother as an abandoned lone figure: 'Now all I would have to think of is you / wearing a black scarf alone in a front pew'. In 'Home from Home' likewise, he admits '…I'm in a place, but it is not in me / and could you zip me open you'd see…./ an island shaped like a Viking's bearded head…' He is not, however, like 'exiles over all the years' 'with only dolorous songs for company'. He resolves not 'to play the harp backward / any more' (in the poem of a similar name) nor to be like those who craved 'for the old country / and in our longing, composed a harp, / pipe, porter and colleen Tir na nOg'. No, 'like the Earl Gerald, ' who turned himself into a stag / and a green-eyed cat / of the mountain', the poet, along with others has 'learned the trick / of turning ourselves into ourselves, / free in the *fe fiada* anonymity / of America'. It is a dodgy crossing over. He admits 'Look / even me own poems are getting blasted bigger. / I'm cross-fertilising my regular, leprechaun-small strain / with the crazy American variant…' Ultimately maybe it is where we are inside ourselves that counts, and nationality and place shouldn't really matter as Delanty realised quite early on in 'Tracks of the Ancestors':

As we traverse our landscapes
    whether city, prairie
bush or bog, we are
    walkabout aborigine.

We can't identify where
    exactly we are from day to day,
but if we hold to songlines
    we shouldn't go astray.

In his *Collected Poems*, Delanty's work has a distinct shape. Through his different books, images and metaphors are repeated like different stitches in a tapestry, such as the 'wing' image already discussed, and they develop in context and meaning. There are many images pertaining to sewing, stitching, and threading. 'The Blind Stitch' has already been quoted. In the tender elegy 'The Memory Quilt', the poet invokes Mona Phillips as she is dying:

> Ah, my Yankee Doodle Dandess grandma, I promised you
> this crochet of words a decade
> and a day ago. Have I, Tailor Tardy, left it too
> late?.....

Chattily, he gives Mona gentle instructions for the afterlife: how she must talk to the spirits who have passed on – the ones he knows: 'Yodel an old Baptist hymn.' He shows gratitude for her quilt that he wraps around him when the weather is chilly – 'the quilt with your family history / that you outlined in the plain calico hands of Patti…. And all the other hands. / Each is stitched into the palmistry of muslin squares. / Certain life-line strands / unravel and tear. / You wave goodbye / from the embroidered emblems around.' And he ends with the haunting: 'Ah, Mona hardbye hardbye.'

In the soothing 'The Palindrome Stitch', the palm trees that 'could be the spines of local dancers' sway 'in time with the sea and your sewing hand'. The sibilance stresses the lulling peace, and the poem, being the clever palindrome that it is, having started with 'Now quiet is everything…' comes a full circle, with the initial sentence enunciated backwards: 'Everything is quiet now'.

Likewise, the 'hellbox' image that initiated the 'box' images throughout his work is extended. More boxes are opened up: the 'birth box', before his child is born: 'I knock on wood now for you / in your birth box / that we'll only have to welcome you / into the school of normal hard knocks', and the final box or the 'coffin dark' of his mother 'covered with such a posy / all the way from your roman nose to your pedicured toes.' Delanty prays that his 'voice box not fail' and, in 'White Worry', he talks of insignificant white noise, versus intruding black noise that we all experience:

> all my dear white noise switched habitually on,
> the reliable buzz in my head shrouding daily black noise.

In the poem 'The Malayalam Box', combining the box images and the sewing threads, the poet seems to be in love with the very sound 'Malayalam' (which is spelt the same backwards) and here again, he finds himself 'in the Cork and Kerry of India' – as if he can never really be in a foreign place, so strong is his national point of reference inside himself. Along these lines, he admits 'Maybe it's merely that we all / navigate the same waterways along with the security / of separateness. Is that all a poem is, a wave from a boat?' – the boat being 'a frail, rocky craft'. In this chatty poem, accompanied by poets Gerry Murphy and Gregory O'Donoghue, Delanty is the spokesman for the trio:

> We want to save ourselves also and write the *dán* of life,
>   endurance and muted celebration; poetry and life
> a kind of palindrome of one another like the word Malayalam.

He ends with the key to his whole approach:

>   how every blessèd thing is somehow
> threaded together; how local bards explain
>   Malayalam is a box of various petals: lotus, frangipani,
> cosmos; how any movement alters the words; how I shake
>   these petals for you now out of my own Malayalam box.

'Behold the Brahmany Kite' also links the 'box' and sewing images:

> And, in my way, I too believe in the kasti – the sacred
>   thread – of the elements
> stitching us all together, and would rather the kite pluck
>   the flesh from my bones
> than I be laid in the dolled-up box of the West....

Let us hope that he is a long way off from this!

   To conclude: it seems evident that Delanty's major voice offers the reader what Jane Hirshfield calls 'an enlargement of being, the slowed and deepened breath that comes with the release of fixed ideas for the more complex real.' It also offers that 'sense of connection with others that good poems both emerge from and forge.' After all, as Hirshfield asks, 'What is good poetry if not language awake to its own powers?'

Patricia McCarthy

I create my architecture from

an old suitcase...

Johnny Marsh II

Greg Delanty

To The God We Have Demeaned For So Long

Late, late in the early hours, scratchings
on the door wake us. Ah, it is the furtive god
who down through the ages has had to front
for Mort, for evil, for the frenzied Maenads
of Dionysus, for Bastet, for bad luck, for good
luck; the creature chosen to draw the chariot
of Freyja, who in this latest reincarnation
is the domesticated god of Happiness; the god
we have shunted aside, drowned in a bag,
the god we've cursed for such independent ways,
refusing to obey our every whim;
the sleek deity we often don't notice
in the room until abracadabra he's in our lap,
or binding us in coils of feline affection
round the ankles, making us his own; the secret god
who disappears again to patrol the palace
and temple of our house and the night.
                                        Oh
get up and let the poor creature in,
wait for him to leap up on our bed
and settle in the vales of our bodies:
a father, a mother, a snug child in the Kingdom
of Happiness – it is time we were responsible
to that god Happiness. Say his name again.
Happiness. Give this shy deity his due,
as we have given his bullying siblings:
Despair, Trouble, Melancholy, Depression.
Listen to him there in the dark. Listen
to the motor of Happiness, the God of fur nestled
among us in the dark. Listen to this curled God purr.

Introduction to *The Greek Anthology, Book XVII*
by Greg Delanty

The Greek Anthology is a collection of over 6,000 short poems written by over 300 authors and was compiled by Constantine Cephalas in the tenth century. During the twelfth or thirteenth centuries, Maximus Planudes re-arranged the work and added the poems of Book XVI, said to be a lost book of Cephalas's anthology. In 1918, W.R. Paton began translating the poems into English as part of the Loeb Classical Library series of the *Greek Anthology* which was published by Harvard University Press in the United States and Heinemann in England. A good account of the history of the anthology is given in Smith's *Biographical Dictionary*, under Planudes, as W.R. Paton tells us in his preface to the Loeb Classical Library series of *The Greek Anthology*.

Greg Delanty uses the template of *The Greek Anthology*, with its variety of voices and curious publication history, to add his own book. The poems collected in *The Greek Anthology, Book XVII* are attributed to poets like Gregory of Corkus, Danus, Adriennos, Honestmedon, Rakius and many others that Delanty makes up as he goes along.

These poets become the dramatis personae of Delanty, and allow him, as he says, 'to get at things in me that my regular self can't seem to. The personae allow me to use different registers and an attitude that may not be fashionable in contemporary writing. The poems are set in the Greek world, the place where democracy was founded, and the myth world that is a blueprint for the Western world.'

The Greek Anthology spans over a thousand years and countries. 'This suits me,' Delanty adds, 'as my life has been divided within different times and countries. Also, there is the element that all poetry, all of life is a continual translation, a connecting with the world and translating it into oneself and out of oneself. This is metaphoric of what we do every moment. It also connects back with a past that seems like a long time ago, but we find that it isn't so long ago and so different, which is both comforting and terrifying.'

*

From *The Greek Anthology, Book XVII*

The Road Workers

I only noticed them and then almost too late
        as we drove on, cursing the minor holdup:
the laborers in their lemon jackets
        pouring tar, working the orange dinosaur diggers,
one with a snout like a giant insect-eater. Maybe
        it was Handel, sung by Maria Callas,
on the radio that opened up the sacred in everything,
        brought me to my senses, the high way of art.
There they were, the Lares of the roads, the motorways,
        slaving away, laying out the ink-black tarmac
in the boiling sun. Sweating for us beneath their hard hats.

                              Melogue

The Land's Entreaty

Oh, the gasping straw-colored landscape
        of southern Crete, the parched mountains
– with modest adobe, ruby-domed chapels
        like weather stations on the mountain crowns –
come down to the sea, begging for water,
        just a drop, a sip to quench their thirst.
The Libyan sea sniggers and offers them salt
        as Jesus was offered vinegar on the Cross
while the soldiers played dice beneath,
        not giving a damn one way or other about the god
above them, beseeching his father
        to forgive them, that they know not what they do.

                           Elena, the Gnostic

Templenoe

The seine boats, colorful as jockeys, jockey each other
        at the starting line, with names like race-horses:
El Nino, Rainbow Warrior, The Liberator, Challenge,
        Golden Feather, The Kingdom. With a shot they're off.
The crowd lets out yelps, incitements subduing even
        the raffle seller, the ice cream van's jingle, the trinket stalls.
The gods of Tackiness, holy as they are, are beaten for now by local gods
        inciting each crew to win: the stocky helmsman of Waterville,
the shrewd one of Valentia, the determined one of Derrynane, the fierce one
        of Cahirsiveen. The silver trophy glitters on Templenoe Pier,
winking that the gods of antiquity are among us still. Make no mistake
        about it. On Iveragh. Which one will lift the cup today?

                                              Kerrius

Appreciation

How ignorantly we've treated the god of rain,
        cursing the drizzle, shower, downpour, the cats and dogs,
hailstone, torrent, the spectacular deluge that cleared the air
        accompanied by Lightening and his laggardly brother, Thunder.
You'd think such insults would be too much for the god.
        Maybe sometimes they are and the god throws a tantrum
and catches us without an umbrella in the open,
        at a football match or the seaside, no shelter in sight.
But this vexing god is kind by nature. We tend to forget without him
        we'd be sans the multitudinous shades of green,
the harvests of Demeter, the gifts, bounty he showers
        upon us. It is time to bow down to the god of the clouds,
the god of the sky. Pay him homage. Long may he reign.

                                              Pluvius

The Tug Of War

Right now the old conventional tug of war goes on.
        The Pheromones versus the Choice gang.
The thigh muscles bulge, faces strain puce.
        The sweaty heroic battle.
How exhausting. The best we can expect is
        the Choice team hold, not allow
the other pack – Boozing Bob, Delia Dope,
        Dusty Lust & co–drag them, the underdogs,
over the line till they lie beaten, grimacing in the dirt,
        the Pheromones doing a lap of honor, brandishing
the cup, cheering, gloating, through every cell of the body.

Silenus

Happiness

Forget happiness, perhaps the most elusive word
        in the language. Accept your lot
of misery, mundane discontent,
        love woes, family foibles and furies,
the doldrums of friendship, the megrim of the body,
        being in the dark with respect to the whole show,
the general epicedium since the human episode began.
        Unhappiness is our plasma. Consider
for instance, how you are more at home, wallow even,
        in Melpomene's sad songs. Consider the dearth
of happy emanation and say I'm wrong.
        Maybe only then will Happiness grace us.
When we let go of chasing Happy's shirt tails
        this deity will begin to feel ignored, left out,
tap us on the shoulder saying, remember me?

Melogue

In The Daily Planet

The gods are always at it, picking on each other,
Hera and Poseidon, Hades and Demeter; the gods more human
than the humans themselves, or at least
        that's how it seemed until today it struck me
        as the barman jabbed at a regular with a barbed remark
        and turned up the news, everyone glued to the latest Iliad,
that it's humans who put the gods in the shade,
being so expert in backstabbing, naysaying, killing, general disarray.
Too late even for a *populus ex machina* to save the day.

Danus

On The Second Coming

God's annoyed with Himself for having let things spin
        out of control. Now He's unable to send our Savior back
to live amongst us. Not even He could save himself today,
        the matrix beneath the surface of our daily lives being sewn
 so intricately by the crafty deity, tireless Complicity.
        His temples are heated by oil secured at the expense
of slaughter. The pillows we lie on at night are the down
        of the bird that saved Noah. Even a sackcloth would likely
have molecules of invisible blood in its stitches.
        What really gets His goat is that he cannot mosey
downtown and take in His creation, trees blossoming up
        from concrete, the hubbub of folk about their business,
a passing girl who reminds Him of Magdalene, the smell
        of coffee. How He envies the creature
created in his own image. How He longs to become His image.
        How He pines for this earth. How absurd the old God
feels now. Our Image. Pray for Him. Pity the poor Word.

Gregory the Theologian

The Grand Design

A renowned maker asks for a holy calm as he observes
        the third planet from the sun; how its superior animals
turn Phoebus, the day star, against even themselves,
        that all is part of the divine plan, that everything
will be alright. Let us cry out among the carnage, the melting
        of ice mammoths, the fossil fuels that'll turn us to fossils,
that what this ostrich-maker declares is too easy.
        Now turn the page of the renowned faker, the Grand Maker.
Verily I say unto thee, it's those who know, who act
        not, who are the generals of the darkness of our age.

Sidnius the Didact

An airplane over the sea...

...loops back

Johnny Marsh III

Paul McLoughlin

A Wave from a Boat? The Poetry of Greg Delanty

As a fifteen year-old at school, one of my GCE O-level Literature texts was *The Rover* by Joseph Conrad. I loathed the book so much that for years afterwards I avoided the entire C-section in my local library. Reading *Heart of Darkness* and then *Nostromo* (something a long-deferred degree required) I knew how Saul of Tarsus felt, and I read every word of Conrad I could lay my hands on. Many years later, browsing in Skoob, I somehow took an instant dislike to a couple of Delanty poems. I'd guess now the collection I dipped into was *The Hellbox*, and that the poems were from its middle section, perhaps, like 'The Printer's Devil' or 'The Broken Type', with their odd appearance, or 'Ligature', a thirteen-line poem beneath the banner of a six-line epigraph. More years later, against my better judgement, I paid all of £3 for the *Collected Poems* in a remainders-shop (almost before the thing had been properly released by Carcanet) and ended up carrying it around with me for weeks, finding treasure with every dive.

What changed my mind about Conrad was an intensity that made even abstractions like 'immensity' resound. I love his sentences, his painstaking and highly aesthetic control of complexity, qualities I had clearly been unable to respond to earlier. What changed my mind about Delanty was a voice I now felt immediately at home with. I love the playful seriousness with which he juxtaposes registers, the way his poems are driven by the variousness of what happens, and his determination to accommodate the world as it is, to 'sing the happy days as well'.

Here was a poet who appeared to find metaphors wherever he looked, and extended metaphors, too. This rediscovered Delanty was out to out-Martian the Martians:

> Skin-head pigeons strut in a gang
> Along the road's white line
> And fly under a fuming cop car
> ('Out of the Ordinary')

> A tourist waving a bee away
> is conducting a symphony
> ('Two for Joy')

> Loudspeakers welcome back soldiers
> who plug their gas pump salutes
> to their foreheads as generals cruise by.
> ('Backfire')

In a more recent poem, 'For the Record', from *The Ship of Birth* (2003), we look up to see a 'plane drawing a line of coke / behind it on the sky's blue counter', an image that might appear gratuitous were it not in a poem that celebrates achievement and 'how we somehow manage mostly / to live together – confused only by ourselves'.

There is nothing new in this highly visual approach, of course. Craig Raine's 'Wasps with Donald McGill bathing suits' comes to mind, as does his lobster 'scraping its claws / like someone crouched // to keep wicket at Lord's'; and his view from an aeroplane coming in to land: 'And then Belfast below, a radio // with its back ripped off'. No doubt it was Delanty's delight in this kind of imagery that led to his being described (by fellow Corkonian, Thomas McCarthy) as a Munster Martian. 'The Onion, Memory' is a poem of Raine's that Delanty admires. His own 'The Memory Quilt' might even issue from it. But he feels the so-called Martian poets (Raine, Reid et al) too often crowded out their poems with metaphors. Norman MacCaig had done it all before, and better:

> A hen stares at nothing with one eye,
> Then picks it up.
>
> ('Summer Farm')

> I love frogs that sit
> like Buddha, that fall without
> parachutes, that die
> like Italian tenors.
>
> ('Frogs')

For MacCaig the ordinary and the extraordinary were one and the same, and metaphor was a means of demonstrating this. What interests Delanty about metaphor and simile is precisely the emphasis they place on sameness in a world intent on foregrounding *difference*. He makes significant use of the extended metaphor as a result, sometimes informing whole collections with closely related images. Throughout an early poem, dawn is seen in terms of the Roman Catholic Mass, with the sun as host. In 'The Arrival', awaiting the birth of his son is like 'waiting for a train in India', the unborn child 'an unseen express / pistoning towards us through the monsoon rain / of monitor static'. And like the train, he's overdue!

Delanty's ease in finding connections is striking and a great number of his poems proceed from this facility. 'Elegy for my Aunt', a poem that links Ireland and India through their rituals for the dead, concludes:

> Now monkeys lumber and loaf on the balcony outside
>   above the cremation's glow,
> I still smell of pall smoke and my eyes water as they strain
>   to follow
> my pencil, this jotting the leaded shade of smarting smoke
>   and ashes below.

It is the sameness, the relatedness of things various, Delanty is keen to record:

'the world is all intimation of sameness / defining continual difference' ('Pathetic Fallacy'). In 'The Malayalam Box', he is speaking, seriously, familiarly, and punningly, with and to a pair of fellow Cork poets:

> I signal to you how I want to uncork this corker day.
>   You should have seen the teal sheen of the kingfisher;
>   the boats, not unlike currachs, laden with copra;
>   the fish owl miming stillness; the hammer & sickle flags
>   traipsed from huts – how they're linked to Vishnu somehow
>   in my head; how every blessèd thing is somehow
>   threaded together

The Malayalam is a box of multifarious petals and the word itself a palindrome. For Delanty, poetry and life are also 'a kind of palindrome of one another'. When he finds comparisons that provide the connecting glue for his poems, he is putting on stage what he believes is happening off. If a watched telephone turns into a bird – from a 'handset clamped like devouring jaws on the rest' to 'a sleeping bird with its head tucked / back on its wing' – that's because his mood has changed from one of anger and resentment to one of conciliation: 'If you call / I'll unfurl its neck and tenderly, tenderly, I'll sing'. That repetition of 'tenderly' is risky, too.

Delanty has spoken of how poetry has unified him with the world, how he doesn't know what he would have done, or amounted to, without it, so it isn't surprising to find poetry itself rearing its head in the poems. With all that's going on, it's the 'miracle of miracles: / poetry, shagging poetry, I kid you not' that saves, the demotic adjective a safeguard against solemnity. Poetry is something Delanty is grateful for. The memory quilt his grandmother crafted for him leads, tardily, a 'decade and a day' later to the 'crochet of words' that is the poet's reply, when she is dying. He asks that she excuse his 'fustian transmutations' of her 'domestic art'. But he wants both to keep his feet firmly planted in the real world, and somehow retain a belief in the transformative power of poetry, its potential to set in order. He turns a growing familiarity with baseball and its lingo into just such a quest. In 'Tagging the Stealer', he recalls seeing on television in a bar a catcher who was 'unknown, but no rookie' signal the pitcher from behind the pinch-hitter's back 'though no one copped until seconds later / as the catcher fireballed the potato to the first baseman, / tagging the stealer':

> It doesn't sound like much,
> but everyone stood up round the house Ruth built
> like hairs on the back of the neck, because the magic
> was scary too. Jesus, give each of us just once
> a poem the equal of that unknown man's talking hand.

(For those who cherish these finds, try comparing this to the close of Andrew Motion's fine poem, 'The Dancing Hippo'). There is no magic, except when there is. Delanty's gratitude for all that poetry has made possible for him (not least its capacity for helping him argue with himself) means that his is an art that makes little or no attempt to conceal its being artful. In 'Opening Up', he recognises that in order to achieve the genuine, one must foreground the risk of insincerity (whatever it is one is trying to *avoid*, the pleasure derived from giving).

If poets like Plath and Lowell were hell-bent on beating language into submission, Delanty is more forgiving. He is a political animal; he even stood for election in Vermont so concerned was he about environmental issues (and came too dangerously close to winning for comfort, he says!). But he doesn't preach. 'Homage to the God of Pollution in Brooklyn' takes us by surprise. 'Like so many', he tells us, 'I grew up in a town with a belovèd river the colour of slime', and 'couldn't / fathom why teachers made us paint / the waters of our colourbooks blue'. Brooklyn's river is no exception, but rumours of 'this mire's clean up' provoke a potentially awkward confession, that he'd end up:

> lonesome for the iniquity of fishless
> water slouching towards the putrid shore. But heaven
> on earth, I don't suppose I need worry on that score.

Humour and humility keep him from the pulpit of unctuousness. When a like-minded friend looks at the smog-snow on Broadway and complains 'That's what we breathe in every day', Delanty is reminded of how the nuns said 'every trespass soot-darkens' the soul, and laughs 'not without cynicism and apathetic stoicism, qualities / necessary these days to survive, or rather, to get by'. He wishes the world were a better place, too, but he is aware the self-evident may also be naïve. 'The Emerald Isle, Sri Lanka' is an example of a strife-torn land:

> I could risk prayer
>
> at the moated temple, not for the gift of words for myself ,
>   but that the Tamils and
> Sinhalese would risk talk, dumb and green as that sounds.

In later poems, this environmental and political concern has grown a little more urgent. Delanty believes all poems are political in so far as each is a personal response to a public happening (and poems turn public when published). One might argue that if all poems are political, then none are. Much more promising, and persuasive, are the poems that deal with large issues by treating the apparently minor. The paired poems, 'The West' (from *The Ship of Birth*) and 'Loosestrife' (from the Collected's *Aceldama*) repay attention. In County Kerry, the rhododendron is proliferating to such an extent it is suffocating all other plants and forms of vegetation, even if we are beguiled by its 'purple fantasy'. 'Loosestrife', in Vermont and elsewhere, similarly spreads its 'glory across the earth', eliminating everything in its path. County Kerry lies in the west of Ireland, but the title of the poem seems to imply a heavier significance. And the American poem ends 'Ah, our loosestrife, purple plague, beautiful us', the last word conscious that the previous poem in the final collection is called simply 'US'.

This concern with what we are doing to the environment and the world we live in is made the more telling by Delanty's acknowledgement of and increasing pre-occupation with what he calls complicity. We are all responsible for what happens around us, even the most saintly of us. And complicity shows up in the strangest places. Delanty, for example, makes great use of the sonnet form introduced to the Irish by Edmund Spenser and Sir Walter Raleigh, both of whom spent time in Munster and committed 'heinous crimes in that region, including killing women and children'. In a section of 'The Splinters', a long poem at the end of *American Wake*, the speaker, Spenser, chides those 'trapped' in a 'complicity' they can never 'quite break free of' And complicity goes even further back. 'Aceldama' reflects on the Field of Blood bought with Judas's thirty pieces of silver, a field that now houses the anonymous graves of those who lost their way. Driving past it temporarily spoilt a family outing, but the 'city below' still 'shimmered'.

It is this kind of painstaking honesty that makes Delanty such an attractive read. His is a transparent art – we can always see its workings. It is tempting to extend this to the man himself, to Delanty's being a transparently good man (though, doubtless, he will say this is taking a step too far). It is an art he worries over and always takes seriously:

> Is that all a poem is, a wave from a boat?
> Maybe. I'm waving now from my frail, rocky craft.
> Can you see me? If I pass on the street later without a nod
> take no offence. Is that you waving from a passing raft?
> ('The Malayalam Box')

I for one am pleased Delanty is there to be waved at.

David Cavanagh

The Hummingbird, the Cowbird, and the Brahmany Kite: Reflections on Greg Delanty and His Poems

> How often have we waited for the magic
> in the hands of some flipper throwing a slider,
> sinker, jug-handle, submarine, knuckle or screwball?
> … Oh, look, Davo, how I'm sent sailing
> right out of the ball park just by its lingo.
> But I swear the most memorable play I witnessed
> was with you on our highstools in the Daily Planet
> as we slugged our Saturday night elixirs.

So much of Greg Delanty appears in these lines from his poem, 'Tagging the Stealer': the playfulness, the love of 'lingo' and willingness to push it, the metaphors that grow so naturally out of the poem's situation, the music and, of course, the 'Saturday night elixirs.' I happen to be the 'Davo' addressed in the poem, and for two decades I've had the deep pleasure of sharing with Greg many poems, joys, woes, more poems, sport outings, and elixirs to leaven or launch us. There has been great jawing and slagging, as Greg might say. The relationship has given me many treasured things, among them a close-up view of a poet completely dedicated to poetry, living his life as a poet more fully than most seem to manage in this distracted age.

The exuberant strings of imagery and lingo, whether about baseball, the printing business (as in *The Hellbox*), or the mysteries of a child's birth (*The Ship of Birth*), involve much more than playfulness and love of language. They seem to represent a search for a language equal to the wonder of the situation. His unborn child's ultrasound 'is chockablock with quarks & squarks, / gravitons & gravitini, photons & photinos' that somehow add up to 'Our alien who art in the heavens, / our Martian, our little green man' and, ultimately, 'our friend' ('The Alien'). The search for the right word often spins the poet into a new situation, which in turn requires another string, another search-and-name mission. Like the ultrasound or, rather, like a whole nursery of newborns, Delanty's poems are full of insistent, emergent life.

His focus on writing poems and ability to concentrate in almost any setting are extraordinary. I've found him writing in crowded bars and restaurants, on the beach, at the tennis court sitting down by the net, in cars, at the grocery, hunkered in the corner of a locker-room at the YMCA. In fact, he is a famous nude at the YMCA in Burlington, Vermont. He can often be found there, standing buck naked outside the showers, working on draft poems strewn across a shelf used for towels and soap, wearing only a pair of reading glasses and a pencil, while naked men move past him in and out of the showers. Usually, they take no notice, having grown used to this poet man with his pile of papers; or, if they notice, they glide silently by, hesitant to break into, or perhaps even intimidated by, the force shield of his concentration.

If he goes on a bike ride he brings poems with him. If he has to wait a few minutes on a street corner, he pulls out his drafts. He carries small pencils and books in various pockets. And he reads poems by others. Voluminously. Daily. Ubiquitously. An Irish poet who lives in America and travels quite extensively, he has avoided the trap of allegiance to a particular school or national sensibility. He has read widely and deeply among Irish, British, and American poets, but also Norwegian, Greek, Chinese, Australian, French, you name it. Delanty is that rare wonder: a poet who reads and who feels himself part of a global tradition of poetry, not just a writer of the moment or a national exemplar.

Although many of his poems, especially earlier ones, have an Irish connection or flavour, he has become a poet of global interests. In the long, freewheeling lines of 'The Hellbox' one can hear Whitman and other American voices even as he plumbs the mythology of an old world Irish printing business. In his sonnets and other formal poems, one can hear and, more important, feel the depth of English and Irish tradition cutting against contemporary situations. In the sprawling yet controlled poems of *The Blind Stitch*, one feels the influence of the western world, old and new, colliding with the long, raucous history, traditions, and colour of the east.

He has often said, only half joking, never mind prestigious prizes for poets – there should be prizes for *readers* of poetry. And never mind MFA programs for poets. He says there should be MFA programs for critics, people who know how to read poetry and can spread the word about good poems. When he teaches his poetry workshops at Saint Michael's College in Vermont, the courses are as much about reading poetry as they are about writing it.

Another side of Delanty that is perhaps not so well known is his political activism. In the days when I first met him, he was a regular demonstrator for peace at the General Electric plant that made the high-tech Gatling guns used on attack helicopters in Vietnam and elsewhere. He began demonstrating against the war in Iraq before it began. He has participated in poetry readings against the war. Once or twice a week, he joins a peace vigil by demonstrators who have held up peace signs for passing motorists every day since the war began in 2003.

His main political focus now concerns the environment. He has participated in and organized readings with an environmental focus. He has worked with Step It Up, the American nation-wide group founded by Bill McKibben that has involved many thousands in demonstrations, rallies, and other activities. Closer to home, he ran for office in the Green Party during a campaign to help raise the party's profile. (With serious political intent but an amount of tongue in cheek, he ran for the position of high bailiff; no one was quite sure what the role entailed.) He has organized an environmental council at Saint Michael's College, where he teaches, to help make the college greener in a variety of ways and to foster an atmosphere of political purpose and empowerment for students, faculty, and staff. He has said that his political involvements are very important to him, not only for their intrinsic worth but because their outward, social focus balances his much more inner and private work as a poet.

In the poems, of course, the outer and inner worlds coalesce. In 'Loosestrife,' we hear the voice of the political Delanty who sees in the invading plant an image of 'us' as a beautiful but imperialist killer:

> Voices praise your magenta spread, your ability
> to propagate by seed, by stem, by root
> and how you adjust to light, to soil, spreading
> your glory across the earth even as you kill
> by boat, by air, by land all before you....
> You'll overtake the earth and destroy even yourself.
> Ah, our loosestrife, purple plague, beautiful us.

On a more personal level, the man loves animals, plants and, especially, birds or, as it so oddly sounds with his Cork accent, 'the boards'. Finches, chickadees, hummingbirds, grackles, doves, and many more appear at his backyard feeders. They also appear in his poems, as themselves and as images to depict love, the passing of time and of life, as in '(The hummingbird)', 'The Phone Bird', and 'Behold the Brahmany Kite'. In 'The Birds', the narrator 'admitted a fondness/for the cowbird' that lays eggs in 'foster birds' nests, the cowfledgling killing the other brood.'

It's a complex, disturbing image. The narrator goes on to reflect that the cowbird adopted its parasitic habits…

> …since following
> bison across the plains, without any time to nest:
> What else could these creatures do? We survive
> rightly or wrongly. And who are we to talk, us American flock?
> The birds might ask – even the cowbird – who is
> any person to talk? Where are the great bison herds now?
> Ah, don't be so hard on the cowbirds. And, besides,
> I like their silly finch-beaks stuck on their crow heads
> like those characters in that Greek comedy
> about a better world, with bird beaks stuck on their pates.

This notion of complicity ('who is / any person to talk?'), that we are all connected and all responsible in various ways for the problems of the world, is an important motivation for his political activism, and it appears more and more often in his recent poems. So does compassion for the human plight and the struggle to make sense of it all. In 'Ur God', he ponders the marvelous variety and oddity of gourds, then sees in them our own commonality and search for the numinous:

> ...And the name,
> the concealed god within; our
> gourd whispering we're all the same
> beneath the rind, the god we scour
> the earth for on our knees.

A more private aspect of Delanty is that of the restless wanderer, at times the bemused observer, and at times the lost soul. The beautiful 'Elegy for an Aunt' begins in the streets of a city in India:

> You'd not credit it, but tonight I lost my way and there
>   wasn't a sinner to direct me
> in the maze of alleys narrower than the lanes off Cork's
>   norrie quays, and as manky,
> when around one corner trots a funeral of Hindus
>   with fanny-all on but their dhoti baydinahs.

The speaker follows the mourners through streets toward 'the burning ghat' and into his memories of funerals back in Ireland. His isolation deepens but eventually connects us all with an image that is pure Delanty:

> We all copped another of the old world souls was cut
>   from us, as Rosy was and Noel and
>
> and and, and with each *and* a subtraction as if we're
>   disappearing ourselves
> limb by phantom limb.

The poem ends:

> Now monkeys lumber and loaf on the balcony outside
>   my room above the cremation's glow.
> I still smell of pall smoke and my eyes water as they strain
>   to follow
> my pencil, this jotting the leaded shade of smarting smoke
>   and ashes below.

Lines from a man whose life is thoroughly entwined with his poetry. Each feeds the other, and we are, with gratitude in my case, fed as well.

Terence Brown

Greg Delanty and North America

It has been one of the curiosities of the modern Irish poetic tradition that experience of the North American continent, of exile there and of lives lived in its actual and psychic weathers, has so rarely been registered by our poets. And this despite the fact that many of them have spent long periods of time there, some like Padraic Colum and more recently Paul Muldoon, settling in the United States and others occupying academic posts that involved lengthy transatlantic sojourns. It is striking indeed how little North America has impacted on the work of Seamus Heaney, for example, despite his Harvard professorship and continent-wide reputation. Which is not of course to say that Irish poets have not been influenced by American poetry. Heaney himself in the nineteen seventies allowed immediate personal experience to enter his work in *Field Work* in a Lowellesque manner; John Montague's experiments with the short line in the 1960s and '70s owed something to Black Mountain metrics, while Paul Muldoon's enigmatic early lyrics probably derive in part from his reading of Robert Frost's troublingly multi-levelled short poems. When North American experience does get addressed directly in Irish poetry as in Derek Mahon's 'The Globe in North Carolina' and in his New York reflections in *The Hudson Letter* or more indirectly in Muldoon's 'The More a Man Has, the More a Man Wants' in *Quoof* , it serves to highlight how little Irish poetry had engaged with the relationship between Ireland and America that has been a crucial part of the nation's historical destiny.

In the 1980s economic crisis in Ireland provoked a new wave of Irish emigration to the United States, which took many well-educated young Irish men and women to 'undocumented' posts in such cities as Boston and New York and other more fortunate individuals to jobs in various East Coast universities and the possession of a coveted 'green card'. For both these groups the experience of emigration was markedly different from that of the many millions who before them had left Irish shores for the new world, when departure from Ireland marked a fundamental fissure in their lives, the forsaking of one reality for another. Since the 1980s ease of trans-Atlantic travel, communication (e-mail accompanying reduced phone charges) and a common popular culture has made emigration an ambiguous experience with the Irish and American worlds superimposed upon one another as it were in a globalised set of cultural referents in which places can seem simultaneously present in the mind and permanent residency both a mere legal fiction and a documentary necessity.

Greg Delanty's poetry has been markedly alert to this new Irish-American condition of life as he has made his own experience of migration to the US a major theme of his verse (he holds an academic post in a Vermont college). In 'The Land of the Eagle' indeed he rebukes Ireland, with a nod to Yeats, as 'that country for old men' that abandoned 'its young' casting them up in the Bronx and, as he puts it in another poem entitled 'America', in a 'landscape without voice or memory'. But this has not meant that he has sought to compose a poetry of exilic regret and lament in the traditional manner of emigrant ballad and song, but as he puts it in 'We Will Not Play the Harp Backward Now, No', to acknowledge how North America can be an escape from an over-determined history and a culture of control and complaint: 'Here we would flap the wings of our singularity and not have to fear...' having learnt 'the trick/of turning ourselves into ourselves'. Not that the call of the old country does not have its tenacious grip on the affections, as he implicitly admits in 'The Lost Way', (dedicated to fellow Corkonian Robert Welch) that a few of his poems are 'hearkening back/a kind of grappling for the life buoy's O/ of the roads, streets and life of the drowned city/ we both hail from'. And the cost of a life lived as a trans-Atlantic commuter is a source of anxiety for the poet who, as he puts in 'The Hellbox', 'when push comes to shove, more than anything' did not 'want to feel a foreigner' in his own 'what would you call it, homeland'. And this anxiety is not only because migration involves absence but also increasing alienation from a home territory that itself in a provoking irony is undergoing an intensifying process of Americanization, that had begun in his youth:

> My home city emigrating from itself, changed
> so hell for leather, even if it was for the better,
> that some of us felt oddly abandoned
> ....
> And I'll say little of how aliens like Burgerlands
> and McDonald's took over main streets and buildings
> in the continuous sci-fi movie of our century....

In this state of ambiguous being which is not quite exile and is by no means assimilation in a new culture that supersedes the old, poetry offers itself as compass and consolation; for in 'Tracks of the Ancestors' he advises a fellow emigrant.

> We can't identify where
>   exactly we are from day to day,
> but if we hold to songlines
>   we shouldn't go astray...

and in 'The Lost Way' on a journey through the American winter:

> The snow fell in the silence that poetry
> falls with as it drops a beneficence of
> white calmness around us in the darkness.

However migration involves risks for the poet as poet beyond those associated with nostalgia and the hackneyed stereotypes of the exile's bitter moods. Most dangerous is that he should simply become an ersatz American poet, parroting 'American voices', as he puts it in 'The Hellbox', the poem where he addresses at length, the problematics of his bi-located imagination and social experience. By contrast he wishes as poet to retain a vibrant authenticity of felt life in his work :

> I want to home in on the newness, strangeness, foreignness
> of everything, returning itself to itself, its exile from itself,
> the perpetual, simultaneous goings and comings of life,
> while remaining always human, open, up front.

A sense of vital, actual experience is in fact wonderfully sustained in Delanty's verse in its notable linguistic energy, product of a distinctive fusion of a literary lexicon (even Latinate at times) with contemporary demotic, Cork argot, Irish language phrases, place names, craft cant and North American slang (baseball lingo in one poem, 'Tagging the Stealer'). The language of his verse functions indeed as the verbal equivalent of the printer's hellbox (subject of one of the finest of Delanty's poems), which the poet tells us 'was a container in which worn or broken type was thrown to be melted down and recast into new type'. For in Delanty's work a world in constant transition (the 'simultaneous going and comings of life') is realized in a vocabulary and variegated tonal register that displays language itself in the process of being re-made. The effect is to suggest how the experience of migration, journeying and return are inscribed in the very diction of the poetry, where the exuberantly-shaped stanzas and the buoyant rhythms of the verse itself disallow any indulgence in deracinated sentimentalities.

All of which is not to say that Ireland does not remain an unquenchable imaginative source for Delanty. His poetic precursors are evoked in 'The Splinters' as 'dark icebergs', whose hidden depths must be acknowledged. The national mythology and propensity for mythmaking, the constant call of memory are things he could not shrug off even if he wanted to. He is in thrall furthermore to a genius loci, which, in a poem entitled 'Spiritus Hibenicus', he conjures in images of ghosts 'waving handkerchiefs of whitethorn/from gaping windows across the eternity/of the spangling Atlantic'. And above all there are the unbreakable bonds of family, forged in childhood.

Delanty often writes movingly of the intimacies of childhood and familial domestic life. His peripatetic experience makes poems about family members studies in fragility and transience in which tenderness and vulnerability are openly admitted. There is a sense, unusual among Irish poets, that the male is properly at home in the domestic sphere, amid women's business (though Heaney has some memorable poems in this mode, as does Michael Longley). In 'The Sea Horse Family' the poet urges 'Today I would have us become sea horses, and I,/ being the male, would be the one in the family way', and in 'The Hanky' the adult poet remembers his mother at her housework, as adept and masterful as any man abroad in the world:

> You'd reach up, unpeg the clothes,

take in the great and the small sails
one by one: towels, trousers,
the spinnaker shirts blowing in your face.
You worked by touch down the line
with the urgency of a sailor hauling sheets
in a storm.

It is in his collection entitled *The Ship of Birth* (published in 2003) that Delanty's poetic intimacy with the domestic sphere has its fullest and most moving expression. The coming to term, birth and infancy of his child and the mortal illness of his mother are set in haunting apposition. The settings of these tender, moving poems are alternately Irish and North American (as befits a Vermont poet, the volume is snow-filled), as if in the face of the absolutes of birth and death home is truly where the heart is. The migrant recognizes where he has settled, where the future beckons, even as he knows the past will always be with him. Strikingly the North American settings seem as natural to the poet in these intense times as the Irish. They are now where his life happens. It is fitting therefore that the volume concludes with 'The Skunk Moths' in which a North American suburban garden provokes a vision of at-homeness and of transcendent human self-acceptance:

Imagine the Luna's gossamer tulle wings, the tippets
    brushing us, fanning us tenderly, wrapping us in a veil,
bringing us gently to our knees in a gathering humility,
    brushing aside our mortification, finally at home, natural,
in the natural world – their wings our cocoon – becoming
ourselves, pinioned resplendence, at last the human mothfly.

Christopher Ricks

The Voice of Greg Delanty

The voice of Greg Delanty broke happily in upon my life more than twenty years ago. He was reading some of his poems to me. When he gives this further voice to his poems, he never foists in things that he has somehow failed to write in, and he always elicits his own understanding without coercing the rest of us, his hearers, who are delightedly at one with his humours.

The opportunity for me, in a handsome room at Christ's College, Cambridge, all that time ago, had come about through a friend of mine who was acting on behalf of a rich widow. The American poet Allan Dowling ('Business executive, man of letters, motion picture producer, poet') had left to her not only money for her to give away but a prompting that she give it to the young so that they might see the world of the arts, particularly in the new world. Hitherto Mrs Dowling had been the patron of young musicians; now she was to be good to poets, and I was asked if I'd help in the choosing.

The previous year, the award – a handsome one for travel in the U.S.A. – had gone to Andrew Elliott. This year, it was to go to Greg Delanty. The next year (a fact that stays blank), it would no longer go to a poet. I never learnt why. Perhaps it never went to anyone. Perhaps the musicians had returned as the first love for Mrs Dowling. Perhaps (a dark thought) her decision had something to do with the fact that my first two poets were both from Ireland. Perhaps the money had run out. These are all doubtful; what is certain is that I have never regretted my recommendation first of Andrew Elliott and then of Greg Delanty. I like the thought that I may have changed his life. I very much like the knowledge that he has changed mine.

You don't have to have heard him read the poems to be able to hear them for yourself and in themselves. But the English hearer is inveigled into the comedy of their language both being and not being his or hers.

> Having long since chucked testing such love, doing a line
> now with your ersatz crush, Madam Words, you switch
> to tell with a lover's ardour how Lovers' Walk
> was Siúl na Lobhar in the Gaelic days, but the Sassenach,
> anglicising street names, mistook the Irish v sound.
>
> ('Lepers' Walk')

At the very end of *Collected Poems 1986-2006*, there are Notes. 'These annotations are mainly for non-Irish readers'. This is put to us in accents that are drily endearing. For one of the many good things about the poems proper is that they are mainly for Irish readers, mainly for non-Irish readers, and mainly for human beings. Greg Delanty's way of writing political poems, for instance (or, even better, of writing poems politically), may be very different from the way followed by a friend of mine from the old days, but Greg has heeded the warning that is Adrian Mitchell's gnome:

> Most people ignore poetry
> because
> most poetry ignores people

(Heart on the Left: Poems 1953-1984, 1997)

Which is one reason why Greg Delanty's is not like most poetry.

Liam Ó Muirthile

Natural Tongues

'I want to home in on the newness, strangeness, foreignness
  of everything, returning it to itself, its exile from itself'.
                                                    ('The Hellbox')

We are likely, in Greg Delanty's work, to encounter images of home making
way from any and all points of the compass as if on some voyage or *imram,* that
genre of imaginative sea-voyage which the Irish described with such gusto and
exhuberance. Or as rather, indeed, images of apparent otherness which, when
they come into sharper poetic focus, turn out to have emanated from home, or
issue from their own selves which may well be home in another guise.

This hold on home, and the hold of home on the self, is remarkable for its
groundedness in the idea of the English language of his native Cork city as being
not only 'the closest ding in English to Irish, but as nare to Elizabethan English
freisin...' *Ding* in the Irish language is a 'wedge' and while he does not imply or even
connote the Irish-language meaning in his poem 'The Lost Way', his consistent
working of Cork slang, local dialect forms, and phrases from the Irish language
itself, gives his poems a tonality which could only issue out of that particular and
resilient mixum-gatherum, hocus-pocus and sure-tonguedness of the English
language of Cork. It is, of course, much more than that. It is an uncovering and
rediscovering, a displacing and resettling of the self. And even if Greg Delanty's
statement about the Irishness of English in Cork is questionable on scholarly
grounds, this is in itself irrelevant. His statement rings true, because he says so.

'The Lost Way' itself is dedicated to the Cork poet and scholar, Robert Welch,
himself an Irish speaker, and it is in many ways a pivotal poem. It probably
allows Greg Delanty to finally get a fix on the questions of language in his work:
'They turned us away from our natural tongue/ with their regime, more than any
tallystick'. The tallystick was the brutal notched stick worn around the neck by
pupils who spoke Irish in the National School system of Ireland, or even in the
home, during the nineteenth century, each notch representing a word of Irish
for which physical punishment was duly meted out. The tragedy was that many
parents connived in the abusive system.

Greg Delanty's acknowledged difficulties within the school-system, in an era
when the Irish language was abused as a tool of social engineering and control,
were paradoxically and gratifyingly the making of him as a poet. In many ways, the
recovering of that 'natural tongue' characterizes his whole journey into poetry and
into language. It would be a gross misjudgement to view Delanty's usage of local and
dialect forms of the English language as mere local colour or artifice. This working
has anchored his Corkness, his perceived authentic self, and allowed him to shade
and phrase his English as a world language, much as Derek Walcott's work too is
a *pot-pourri* of his own Caribbean identity. In the open tuning of poems wherever

they are set, the Cork riff – 'what was once laden with melancholia, heebie-jeebies, willies,' ('Homage to the God of Pollution in Brooklyn') – is clearly present, either as background accompaniment or full-frontal foreground ('Elegy for an Aunt'). The Cork riff is tuned to the key of American speech and poetry, specifically, and oddly enough, seems to lose its force and fade out in other poems which may have a more English-English timbre. In the masterly poem 'Homage to the God of Pollution', he successfully integrates both registers, keeping the riff down low, as if that organic integration were in itself a key to the resolution of the poem's dynamic. What the implications of this are, is another matter. Whatever they may be, there is an enduring toughness in the sensibility, in the emotional intelligence of the poems which allows them to belong in their own place like weathered standing-stones.

For all that, Greg Delanty is a neo-classical poet who is acutely conscious of literary form. His craft has never been in question, whatever about the craftiness! It is reasonable to view the Irish-language tradition as classical in its essence, and that its late survival in his beloved Cork and Kerry region left a tidal mark at least on the nature of the literary and oral cultures in both languages. Where else on the island of Ireland would we find, in three neighbouring urban streets, the actual place of composition of the eighteenth-century text *Parlaimint na mBan* (The Women's Parliament) as well as many poems, the birthplace of Frank O'Connor and James Joyce's grandfather's stables?

The city had an open backdoor to the southwest and the feeling of being a European crossroads-on-sea. Nowhere else in Ireland had the written text of the Irish language been worked so late into the nineteenth century by dairy farmers, tradesmen, tailors, stonecutters, teachers, Catholic and some Protestant clergy, and professional scribes with commitment and playfulness, and with an enduring sense of regional and local identity. Frank O'Connor too, was a fluent Irish speaker who mediated the world of poetry in Irish through his translations. All this, the strong oral storytelling and *seanchas*, and much more, contributed to zones of feeling and thinking which could be construed as alternatives to the predominant culture. Greg Delanty, in many respects, draws from that well. A generation of students slightly older than Greg Delanty, but who had come through the same school-system, chose the Irish language as a medium for poetry with the founding of the journal *Innti* in University College Cork in 1970. Some of those poets, at least, are the closest of all, both in terms of recovering their own 'natural tongue' and in the open tuning of their poems, to Greg Delanty's work. The image of the two-headed Janus is appropriate, the keeper of gateways and doorways and much else. The backdoor is more than likely the way of the Irish-language poets.

Greg Delanty is a dedicated, single-minded poet, generous in spirit, encouraging and pressing forward the work of fellow-poets. He, more than most, insists that the Irish-language experience be given a wider context as a metaphor for the general destruction of endangered cultures and species. It is appropriate, therefore, that some of his own work be given an airing in Irish. In their Irish-language guise, they could well have found their home on the pages of *Innti*.

*

The following poems, from Greg Delanty's *Collected Poems 1986-2006*, are translated into Irish by Liam Ó Muirthile, and printed in English by kind permission of Carcanet Press:

An Máistir-Chlódóir

An Bhealtaine, an chéad lá den earrach.
Táim ar thrasnán do rothair ag dul ar scoil.
N'fheadar an dtógfaidh Adolina Davy nó Lily
Walsh ceann díom im chéad threabhsar fada?
Gearraimid bearnaí trí charranna ag puthaíl,
ag glamaíl, agus sinn ag breith barr bua
ar an trácht am lóin.
Tá ár roth tosaigh nua ag gathú na gréine.

Fiafraíonn tú díom an bhfuilim ok.
Deirim leat go bhfuil pian im thóin.
Gáireann tú, á rá nach bhfuilimid ag dul i bhfad.
Ach ní theastaíonn uaim ceann scríbe
a bhaint amach go deo. Fágaimid slán.
Cuirim díom ag rith chun Bull's Eyes a cheannach,
ag éaló ón gclog sa chlós ag bualadh im cheann.

Tá na milseáin i bhfolach faoi thobar an dúigh.
Sceitheann m'aghaidh faic-le-ceilt orthu
le súile uile-fheiceálach an Bhráthar Dermot.
Sméideann sé. 'Sín amach do lámh' ar sé go grod,
'Agus anois an lámh eile' á cánáil
go dtí nach bhfuil im bhosa
ach taos bog,
loisceadh a tugadh go minic cheana
do na céadta eile,

ag cur ding i ngach cinniúint ar an bpointe boise.
Ar thug an bráthair úd drochbhuille duitse leis,
nuair a ghlaoigh sé isteach ort á rá,
go rabhas-sa, do mhac, *beagán* mall?
Bhí sé dall laistiar den ghruig, níor thuig
go raibh léamh an mháistir-chlódóra agat ó bhonn,
                    droim ar ais & bun os cionn.

('The Master Printer')

The Master Printer

Though it's May, it is the first spring day.
You are giving me a crossbar to school.
I'm wondering will Adolina Davy or Lily Walsh
notice me in my first long pants.
We weave through fuming, hooting cars,
outwitting lunchtime traffic.
Our new front wheel is answering the sun.

You inquire am I okay.
I confide my behind's a bit sore.
You laugh, say we haven't far to go.
But I never want to get there.
We wave each other off. I run pell-mell
to buy a pennyworth of Bull's Eyes,
escaping the thought of the line-up bell.

I hide the sweets beneath my inkwell.
My nothing-to-hide look reveals them
to the all-seeing eyes of Brother Dermot.
He smiles, orders me to put out one hand
and then the other, caning until
both my palms are stinging pulps,
as he has beaten so many, so often,

distorting each palm's destiny.
Did that brother harm you too,
summoning you in to declare
that I, your son, was a *bit* slow?
He did not know, blind behind a frown,
that you had the master printer's skill
of being able to read backwards & upside down.

Ní raibh an ceart ag Williams

Tagaim ar an suaimhneas i ngach aon ní anois im thimpeall;
sa choireán modhúil mara agus sa solas méarnála
ag léim thar an bhfarraige long-a-dánach
agus sna faoileáin ag faoileoireacht sna spéartha.
Sileann tonnbharra carraigeacha sa sáile
agus déanann rónta díobh.
Buaileann siad a mbosa le ríl anamúil
halla rince an chuasa,
agus ligeann sceamhanna áthais os cionn ceol na mara.
Seo isteach, seo amach le bosca ceoil an aigéin.
Tá méaranna súpláilte as radharc ag seinnt
ar shreanganna áthais ala na huaire seo amháin.
Seo iad na rónta, ag druidim, ag scaradh, ag druidim athuair.
Leathann a gcuid eití tuathalacha ina sciatháin.

('Williams Was Wrong')

Williams was Wrong

Now I find peace in everything around me;
in the modest campion and the shoals of light
leaping across the swaying sea
and the gulls gliding out of sight.
The tops of wave-confettied rocks
slide into the water and turn into seals.
They move to the lively reel
of the cove's clapping dance hall,
raising blithe yelps above the sea's music.
The ocean draws in and out like an accordion
and unseen little fingers play the strings
of joy on what the moment brings.
The seals close and part and close again.
Their awkward fins have turned to wings.

Ulailiú

Tar éis traslámhach na bhfocal shíneamar sa leaba.
　　Ceapaim gur tháinig tromshuan ort féin.
Bhíos-sa ag éisteacht le hulailiú mná sí – meascán ait
　　de ghlamaíl chait agus de chaoineadh *loon* –
dheineas amach gurbh é moncaí na háite seo é
　　go rabhais ag caint air, i ngaiste
gonta, ag saothrú an bháis b'fhéidir.
　　Im chodladh, thaibhríos gur chaith
mórshiúl an aigéin mo chorp ina raic i dtír tar éis
　　dul amú sna tonnta i ndiaidh na stoirme,
agus go raibh m'anam imithe i gcréatúr seo na gcrann
　　ag ulailiú le folús na hoíche.

　　　　　　　　　　　　　　('Ululu')

Ululu

After the crossfire of words we lay in bed.
　　I think you dropped into an obliterating sleep.
Hearing the banshee sound – a curious mixture
　　of a crying cat and the keen of a loon –
I figured it was the monkey of these parts
　　you told me of, trapped
and hurt, perhaps in its final throes.
　　Asleep, I dreamed my body
was washed up by the ocean's procession of waves
　　I'd lost myself in after our latest tempest,
and my soul had entered this creature high in the trees,
　　ululating to the emptiness of the night.

Fiona Sampson

Spirit-Whiff: Greg Delanty and the Icon

> Though you're standing, there's something kneeling
> Within you.
>
> ('Dawn')

Now that *icon*'s the name for a symbol on a screen, that word itself – and the world it speaks to – seems curiously flattened and deadened. Until its slippage into metaphorical currency, after all, an *icon* wasn't simply a representation, or representative, of something admirable. It was what funnelled the incomprehensible absolute into the world of sensory apprehension. Through this funnelling, which was therefore both transposition and transformation, the untouchable could be touched, seen, held, or kissed. An icon *was* that part of the immanent which was also *ours*. To turn this about face, as symbols do: it was that part of our world which didn't stop there but opened into the infinite.

'Dawn', Greg Delanty's early and perhaps his most explicitly liturgical poem, shows us this symbolic action of opening-out as it extends its own metaphor:

> something kneeling
> Within you, beneath a wafer-like sun,
> Raised in the red-raw hands of morning,
> Hypnotised by the sky's rose chasuble,
> The mists's wandering incense
> And the decked-out altars
> Of fishing trawlers.

This opening-up of possible meaning beyond the given world is of course the very action of liturgy – the *enactment* of the Mass – itself. 'Dawn' mimics this action – if liturgy were an art-form, we'd call that ekphrasis. But liturgy is not art; and the Catholic Mass is not purely symbolic, but centres on bringing the Real Presence into the place where it is conducted. It too performs both transposition and transformation: that old distinction Julia Kristeva makes between the symbol, which does both, and the mere sign. When, at the end of Delanty's poem, 'You take the host from pink fingers […] / And turn in the risen sun's glow', *you* have been caught in that glow too.

There are no icons in Protestantism, where the immanent remains necessarily *beyond* what it presses up to – kept out by our own human faculties, our Original Sin. In churches crammed, in Britain at least, with signs inherited from a Catholic symbology, *nothing changes* during the process of Communion, despite its optimistic name. The music and the surroundings may be beautiful, but these are dead signs, liturgically speaking. They have, apparently, no Living Presence. So far so clear – yet so profoundly counter-intuitive, too. Particular kinds of experience, other than the strictly ecclesiastical, *do* seem to open onto meanings beyond themselves. A beautiful sun-rise is just one example. And here we come upon a fundamental problem of poetics. In Wittgenstein's famous conclusion, 'That whereof we cannot speak thereof we must remain silent'. But our strong human sense of the unspeakable *within* experience – whether or not we are religious, but including for example moments of intense emotion – seems to entail a human compulsion to draw that unspeakable within range of language. It's a paradox; but paradox itself is after all a fruitful poetic trope – not least in metaphysical verse – yoking together what seems unyokeable with criss-cross parallels.

Another way to say this, with the great metaphysician Emily Dickinson, is that poetry does best when it can 'Tell the whole truth but tell it slant'. It can only be by going *beyond* an Aristotelean grid of direct correspondence that language might hope to speak of what it cannot say. One way to do this is when rhyme asserts a correspondence between two words which *overtakes* their apparent semantic discrepancy. Delanty, who in his first book can show us the inner logic of 'run pell-mell', 'line-up bell' or 'a frown', 'backwards and upside down' ('The Master-Printer'), riffs wonderfully on this subversive capacity in the punning 'Ur-God', which closes on the transformative rhyme-pun: 'Our word, / which art on earth, hallowed be thy gourd.' Earlier in the poem he poses this question, to which its own rhyme is the answer: 'dolphin, pumpkin, / or the serpent inciting sin / and knowledge. How could they be kin?'

Another 'spirit-whiff' – to use a Delanty phrase from 'The Soul Hunter' – finds its way through transformative workings of metaphor. Delanty very often makes the shape-shifting work of metaphor explicit by showing us the actual narrative moment of transformation. Thus, when 'The tops of wave-confettied rocks / slide into water and become seals' (a retroactive metaphorical transformation), 'Their awkward fins have turned to wings' ('Williams Was Wrong'). In 'Opening Up', human motivation makes us 'each a bit like one of those Russian figurines / [...] our actions / often arising out of something smaller'. In 'The Coronation', taking its title from the baby's final presentation for birth, 'You make, at best, a willing but much-pressed / subject and servant of your loyal queenmother'. Knowing itself to be active, the characteristic Delanty metaphor embraces *action* as its moment. It is, in other words, profoundly advertent: actively *turning* what's been given towards something Other.

The iconic turn, that funnelling an icon performs, which by means of a *greater-than* sign, >, allows the infinite to find a place in the finite world of experience, is one possible view of the way symbols and vocabulary work in poetry. At such points, poetry accommodates something disproportionate to its prevailing formal system. Or perhaps, inversely, a poem is made up of such funnels, or icons, which open into disproportionate intensities and complexities of meaning; the arguably infinite variety of possible readings. These openings into infinities which occur below or beside the surface of versification offer poems another life – not exactly secret but, like the crinolines those *greater-than* signs so closely resemble, at the same time both hidden and displayed. An icon works in this way, to both step in front of and to step up in place of the numinous (or, on the Orthodox iconostasis, to conceal and stand in for the priest busy in the sanctuary). Similarly, a poem does not acknowledge, yet doesn't conceal, its own sources of power. The poetic trope – whatever it may be: image, rhyme, allusion – is simply present within the line of poem, neither transcribed nor advertised in any particular way (*pace* the metrical positioning of rhyme).

Delanty's own most straight-forwardly 'vertical' imagery often draws on collective knowledge, including collective knowledge of Christian imagery, re-activated through allusion or, occasionally, paraphrase. Driving past an unconsecrated burial ground, after a family outing to the beach, 'shrouded our bright time. Our world, / the city below, shimmered like the silver pieces / scattered on the dark floor of the temple.' (*Aceldama*). This poem's epigraph reminds us that Judas's blood money was eventually used to buy an equivalent burial ground for 'strangers'; but only someone with some Christian background would know whom Judas betrayed and the fundamental nature, therefore, of the symbolic freight of that betrayal.

Dialect also trips open doors into resonances of place and time, the stronger for being re-mouthed from exile – like the 'lexicon of old Irish oaths' in 'The Speakeasy Oath'. Sometimes collective knowledge is local to the book or sequence in hand. The reader is co-inhabitant of this local context of particular concerns. By the time we read the villanelle, 'The Language of Crying', in 2003's *The Ship of Birth*, with its couplet 'We're still learning the language of crying, / Anybody would think you were dying', we know that the book, whose title we recognise as an allusion to D.H.Lawrence's 'The Ship of Death', deals with both the birth of a first-born and the death of a mother, whose lives overlap by only a few months and whose paradoxical meeting therefore compresses this poetic material – which is as it were 'book-ends'. We understand, too, that Delanty is a poet of resonance and multiple register. This readies us to hear within these lines the further dark paradox, which is that even the new-born *is* in fact, dying – because we all are. And that unevenness of resonance, which is a sign of *how much* is being funnelled into this poetry, extends with subtlety to the phrase by phrase gestures which act as intensifiers within a line: 'Christ child' is both a transcription of an exasperated parent's outburst ('Christ, child!') and an acknowledgement that this infant 'king' is both sacrifice (he is born to die) and guarantee of some life after death for his parents.

Delanty's strategies here and elsewhere are both characteristic (of his own work and, to a degree, of contemporary Anglophone poetics) and profoundly *unusual.* This most Catholic of poets uses the touchstones of Real Presence, over and over, in his work. He does so by taking us beyond the surface grid of language – those interlocking and parallel streets which are the lines of the poem on the page – and he achieves this transition by asserting the *quiddity* of the printed word. Not for nothing was Delanty's sixth collection, in 1998, titled *The Hellbox* – a term both Catholic in is cosmogony and part of the professional jargon of printers, from whose tribe this son of 'The Master Printer' comes.

How does this work, beyond the level of suggestive association? In 'Live', a poem from a couple of years before this book, Delanty reflects on a photo of a propaganda photograph of a Belarussian cornfield after Chernobyl:

> I can't
>
> decipher the black banner's Belarussian.
> The white letters look jumbled, words back
> to front, reminding me of what live becomes
>
> when spelt backwards and what's hidden
> behind everything that these men live for now

The word *live* functions much like a rune here: as a (compound) mark whose *physicality itself* entails a set of meanings additional to those of the unwritten word. In poem after poem in *The Hellbox*, it's the written word which is reified. 'In the beginning, typography was denounced / as the Black Art' is the apparently paradoxical start to 'White Spirits'; while 'The Broken Type' and 'The Printer's Devil' play fast and loose with typesetting conventions although they 'read' like conventional poems. In 'The Composing Room':

> In the beginning was the Word and the Word
> was made cold type and the Word was
> coldness, darkness, shiny greyness
> and light – and the Word dwelt among us.

And, although these are elegies to a way of life – and *i.m.* the father whose way of life hot metal printing was – this poem makes clear their deep-level debt to the Judeo-Christian idea of the word as the original icon. In that tradition, the Word of God is both news and the truth that news retails: it belongs to God both in the sense of being his possession and through being part of him; is both what God speaks and the spoken being of God. In other words, it performs the paradox of being both in and beyond language; both concrete and immanent. At every point, and every level, Delanty refers us to the word: to the play in language, the pleasure of poetic beauty and precision, and to the word's mysterious ability to speak of that whereof we cannot speak.

So we're left with this. Into a body of work, to date, which is sensitive to every twist and turn of the human condition – dealing explicitly with death, loss, birth, family and love's highs and quieter lows – and which is as warm-blooded, and frequently vernacular, as any you'd be lucky enough to come across, Greg Delanty manages to insert *that whereof we cannot speak*. In poetry marked by tremendous clarity of surface and meticulous semantic control he nets a high degree of immanence. There is a kind of not-losing-faith with the word and all its possibilities which enables this. Delanty is a rarer poet than we imagine – because he is at the same time so approachable, musical, *legible*. We would do very well to listen to his iconic use of language; since it may just be the way 'that down-to-earth angel' – who, Delanty suggests with characteristic modesty in 'the Hellbox', 'is sooner / rather than later going to turn up to give poetry the kiss of life / and "blow us all out of the water"' – learns to speak.

Avenues and Arcades

Cities merge in the memory -
PARIS, FLORENCE, BARCELONA.

Johnny Marsh IV

CELEBRATIONS IN POETRY
FOR GREG DELANTY

On this side of the Atlantic

Colm Breathnach

Dá gCífeá í Tar Éis Fíon a dh'Ól...

(do Mhicheál agus Michelle)

Dá gcífeá í tar éis fíon a dh'ól,
an cineál craorag sin ón tSile a mhiceo,
í ag pramsáil romham tríd an gceantar gnó
i lár na hoíche agus loinnir ina snó
mar nár fhágamar an tábhairne 'dtína ceathrú chun a dó.
Á, dá gcífeá í tar éis fíon a dh'ól.

Dá gcífeá í tar éis fíon a dh'ól,
cineál na Gearmáine ar a dtugaid Hoch,
a lámha amhail éin bhána ag gabháil gach treo
is a glór ag breith bua ar challán an tsló
i gcaifé súgánach san ardtráthnón'.
Ó, dá gcífeá í tar éis fíon a dh'ól.

Dá gcífeá í tar éis fíon a dh'ól,
sútha talún faoi uachtar agus Beaujolais Nouveau
ag cóisir ghairdín i dtosach an fhómhair
a rothar le hais an gheata is é ag brionglóid
faoin mbóthar abhaile is an ghrian ag dul fó.
Á, dá gcífeá í tar éis fíon a dh'ól.

Dá gcífeá í tar éis fíon a dh'ól,
bán ón nDomhan Úr, ó fhíonghoirt Chalafóirn',
i lár halla ag hapáil tríd an nGoirtín Eornan
ina bróga gorma svaeide nua.
Dá gcífeá í mar a chímse í tar éis fíon a dh'ól...

If you could see her after drinking wine...

(to Micheál and Michelle)

If you could see her after drinking wine,
Wine from Chile of the berry-red kind
Prancing ahead of me in the middle of the night
Through the business district with her face alight
Having left the pub late and a little tight.
Ah, if you could see her after drinking wine.

If you could see her after drinking wine.
Wine called Hoch from Germany's Rhine
Her hands like birds fluttering in flight
In a sugawn café when the day is high
Her voice louder than the crowd's by just a mite.
Oh, if you could see her after drinking wine.

If you could see her after drinking wine,
Beaujolais Nouveau, strawberries and cream
At a garden party under autumn's gleam
Her bike by the gate lost in a dream
Of the road home as the sun goes to sleep.
Ah, if you could see her after drinking wine.

If you could see her after drinking wine.
Wine from California's grape-fields fresh and new
Hopping through the Stack-of-Barley a bit askew
In her oh so new blue suede shoes.
If you could see her, as I see her,
                                    after drinking wine.

A translation of the previous poem by **the author**

Paddy Bushe

At the Blueberry Barrens of Maine

Blueberry Barons, I misheard,
And I imagined dark men
Oozing power and greed.
But the barrens were just expansive
Fields in the cleared forest,
Lucent now with a twiggy gauze,
Russet and purple after winter snow,
Waiting for the surge of sap.

Blueberries in Greenland, remember?
Their powdered skin swollen with juice,
Rampant with foliage that clung
Like springs on the ice-cleared rock
In the lovely, fragile summer.
Across the expanse of the Atlantic,
Well south of the floating ice,
I tender you their memory.

Maine Birds

for Jerry and Carol

On your veranda, elated by the cold
And passion of the dawn, I read Frost:
Scatter poems on the floor;
Turn the poet out of door.
The blue jays flickering through the alders
Screech approval, downy woodpeckers
Nod vigorously in affirmation, and geese,
Passing overhead towards Canada, honk
And beat their wings in applause.

Anthony Cronin

Love Fills All Spaces

Love fills all spaces,
Not only
Rooms where the curtains float
Gently in its aura,
But squares where you have been lonely
Among the happy diners
And lovers enrapt in each other,
The concrete stretches under amber lights
Where cosmic worry strikes,
Even the Parks,
Even on Sundays
Where a boredom, worse than familial
Seemed once to still the leaves.
Nowhere is unfilled
Or pointless, empty and apart,
Love in all places
Even in the desolate spaces
Of the long unvisited heart.

John F. Deane

Corrie

Winter light on the corrie hill,
darkling-gold of fallen fern, brown flush
of dying bracken;

a heaven-beam moves over the mountain-side
like a slow fire, dreaming;
Genesis-feet, the everyday exodus of time

shifting between cloud and cloud;
gulls in the next-door harbour at their disputations
speaking their histories of calamitous events:

of the tarnished china of a sheepskull,
the windy acres of its eyes, the gawp of its mouth that the gales
have gnawed over, rains have cleansed;

death, say the gulls, is the dark province
where we scavenge behind the trawlers' arabesques,
where the human dead are taken down

into the heaving, unlit corrie
of the waves, where they fall, dreamlike, and slow,
down, and down, like seeds.

The Bedroom

They had spent their years avoiding
the big words, like love, avoiding the public embrace,
display of affection, or even closeness;

now she lay in the narrow bed, her mind
long gone wandering, her body nursing
the enemy, that is the friend, within;

he sat at the bedside, his old hands moving
dryly over against each other, his lips
trembling, eyes restless; certainly the last hours,

no chance left of offering the words, or gestures
that had by being absent held them together
their own way. Afternoon sun threw the room

listless, leaf-shadow shiftless on the back wall;
her breathing harsh, eyes closed, her fingers
twitching against the thick red eiderdown; he wondered

if the weight on her now was just too much, he wondered
on what abject voyage her mind had foundered and where
who? was she now? His love. His meaning. She.

And then the breathing eased, the twitching, her eyes
opened slowly and gazed towards him. She smiled
and it was she again, she was home, and glad, her fingers

shifted towards his old dry hands and as he reached to her
she sighed, so much at peace, and was gone. He sat on
a long while, knowledge filling him, and all the words.

Overture

Freude, Tochter aus Elysium

The Joseph lilies sway, in choir, a silent chorus
of white-coifed nuns; you stand, distant from them,
child of God, suffering God. On sodden fields
a flock of chittering starlings shifts; the eye is never worn
with seeing, nor the ear filled with hearing.

Freude, the poet wrote, *trinken alle Wesen*
An den Brüsten der Natur; all things
nourish themselves on joy from the breasts
of Nature. Here: the field. Its wet-daub acres
ragged as a famine-smitten family. Only the rushes
flourishing, their knot-rooted stubborn uselessness,
the matted shivering of scutch grasses, persistent
betrayal by the rains. Bitter
as the ribs of hounds :

though we hold in our hearts rich meadows
of the mercy of God, all of us,
forgiving and forgiven, riveted

by the outstretched arms of the Christ-man.

Made light by sorrows. By astonishment.
By the gold-flush blossoming of the furze-bush
around the edges of the field. Swallows

flew low over the wild meadow;
already the summer symphonies were giving way
to the organ-fugues of the fall; child of God,
suffering God, I have moved so many years
across incertitudes, listening for that slow
basso profundo, our sustenance of grief, and joy.

Freude!

I have been remembering that old cantankerous composer, deaf
as his podium, how he waved his hands about and heard
his Ninth Symphony's call of joy; and wondering that he stood
gazing out across the blurred and many

faces of death's company (full
orchestra, full chorus) who sang : *Brüder, überm Sternenzelt*
Muss ein lieber Vater wohnen! Brothers, there must,
above the canopy of stars, a loving Father live!

*

Father walked the kitchen floor
evenings, hands clenched behind his back;
mother held her head down, there had been disputes
and the air was dense
from withholding presences; she prayed
Legion of Mary prayers, whispered militancy, the sibilances

irritating. There sank within me,
down to irretrievable depths, habits
of pleading and the rusted anchor of guilt.
When mother had whispered her way into her heaven,

father sank into his depths, telling sins
on the ambit of his rosary,
bead after bead, a slow circuit.

I have been down to the shore again;
I hold his old brown chaplet,
crucifix dangling; each fine-wrought bead
fingered to a dull smoothness, chain tarnished from handling
but holding firm; I tell my own
blithe and sorry histories, bead after bead,
walk the length of the pier, hands clenched behind my back.

Brüder, überm Sternenzelt
Muss ein lieber Vater wohnen :

Eamon Grennan

Border Country

What to make of last night's dream –
bulging suitcase, church pews, genuflections,
soft murmurings of friends and strangers,
all the rites and ripples of familiar action

until one walks by in black,
head bowed, stately pacing,
and I have to leave the building
by the back door? Then

the hedged country opening
under a chop of helicopters
and half our hill blown skywards
suddenly in a thunder of smoke

and broken limestone
and nothing to do but duck down
where the wren and its brother dunnock
are sheltering, wishing myself

small as one or the other
so the eye-level knot-hole in the sycamore
could be the hiding place
I'll shiver to silence in

till smoke thins
and their mild, shy voices start again
and it's time to come out – all
clear into the clear air –

and not be any more there
where the bright-frocked, head-scarfed
village women are counting over
and over the bones of their dead

children, the men only sitting and staring.

The Shivers

A full-fledged sou'wester
makes the stove smoke, spoils the soup.
One forlorn chaffinch stands up
to the storm. Lookabout ruffled darling,
it's a wet windswept world, no other.

As for bleeding into song – what else
are servants for? Imagine imagining
you'd venture now another vow or voyage
in fog and doldrums. A reckoning
is nigh, she reckoned, beckoning him.

Nigh or nearer even. So your need
is simple: rain gear. Is it salt-sodden air
or poison at the root has turned
all the sally trees between here and Mayo
a dirty ash-brown?

No matter. If this coming storm storms,
it will leave in its laundered wake
no new leaf unturned, no heart not back
to the wall, no depth not unplumbed –
nothing, in a word, not in shiverbits.

James Harpur

Unborn

from 'Goldworker', in 'Voices of the Book of Kells'

Another day to dedicate to God;
another day of active inertia.
The page implores me to paint something
but my fingers are so cold, my nose-tip frozen,
my nipples sore; heart numb.

Colours lie powdery in crucibles
awaiting liquefaction by egg white:
chalk and red lead, copper green,
white lead and lapis lazuli
and orpiment that makes me the envy of Midas.

Sun breaks out and swamps the window,
washes the page the palest gold.
I'm awestruck by the gleam of absence:
no form, no line, no pattern. Just light.
How can I enhance *nothing*?

The blankness holds me: a virgin beauty
the slightest brush-stroke will despoil.
I revel in untold freedom, uncommitment,
the luxury of space, its depth of stillness;

what lies there, waiting to be born?

Ávila

The wind from Salamanca
brings dust heat sloth
and goats lick anything
for moisture;
within the granite walls
shadows of the convent garden
make imperceptible stations
and all is sharp and quiet;
in a cell of cool dark air
a woman lies on a bed
her thoughts evaporating
to extinction
the whites of her eyes
blind as yet
to the angel with a face of sun
waiting for her will to die
patient
its hand raised high
and spear with burning point
poised

Anne Haverty

I Mourn The Funerals

I mourn the days
   of the rare and important funerals.

The long drives,
   fooling in the back, to the event. Its object remote,
   we could be trivial, light. I could
   tell myself she had never, unlike us, quite lived.

And death was a zero.
   Some kind of a yellow belly, locked out,
   keeping himself to hidden fields and distant places.
   He was afraid of our father, of the car, our house.
   The whole town was safe.

How I could look
   unbelieving on his deed – as if he could steal a person
   and leave her face intact. If he had the person's family
   was superhuman – to see him close in and still stand.

These days he owns the town.
   Has a skeleton key for all the cars, steals people
   who were certainly alive; he has unlatched our gate,
   a soldier whose looting is salaried by the state.

And I don't live in wartime; this is normal life.

Seamus Heaney

Sweeney Outtakes

For Greg Delanty

i

Otterboy

'Eorann writes with news of our two otters
Courting all yesterday morning by the turnhole.
I can see them at their shiny romps

And imagine myself as the otterboy
Kneeling where Ronan stands in cleric's vestment,
His hand outstretched to turn a bordered page

Of the massbook I hold high for his perusal,
My brow inclined to those unseemly feet
Protruding from the alb. Then shake myself

Like a waterdog bounding out on the bank
To drop whatever he's retrieved and gambol
In pelt-sluice and unruly riverbreath.'

ii

Sweeney on Lynchechaun

'That three-leggèd, round, cast-iron pot
Deep in the nettle clump, cobweb-mouthed
And black-frost cold

After its cauldron life of plump and boil,
Reminds me of the cool, considered style,
The comely charm and outed hollowness

Of Lynchechaun; and its heaviness
When I'd lift it off the crane,
Its lightening when I'd tilt and drain it

I now see as premonitions
Of my seeing through him, the dizziness
As scales fell from my eyes.'

Eye-level

'Full face, four square, eye-level, carved in stone,
An ecclesiastic on the low-set lintel
Vested and unavoidable as one

Approached head on the full length of the aisle –
Unready as I was if much rehearsed
In the art of first confession.

What transpired next was meltwater,
A little trickle on the patterned tiles,
Truthfunk and walkaway, but still

In the nick of time, heelturn, comeback
And a clean breast made
Late and ruefully. The pattern set.'

Brendan Kennelly

Promise

Under the reeds and intellects
    The machines spin and throb
The lights are ever restless
    As money in the hands of Job

The goddess on her bicycle
    Surpasses the diving swan
The artist in her lonely room
    Knows what's going on

The chaos cries for structure
    The writer cries within
The goddess and the sun don't cry
    They love the setting sun

They drift with the changing clock
    Making way for long dark hours
Deep as the earth with hidden seed
    Promising spring flowers

May be, may be not

How come, she wonders, my most
exciting moments
happen by accident

while my shrewdest plans
tend to buckle at the knees?
It's as though

there's a playful spirit at work,
a mischievous, good-natured anarchist
laughing at calculation.

May be we'll meet sometime. May be not.
What must it be like to chat
with a laughing spirit in a busy street?

Would that laughing spirit make me
indiscreet?

Michael Longley

A Bouquet from the West

For Greg Delanty

Otter Cubs

As I listened to their gasps and sneezes,
They reappeared in memory out there
Among the reeds, and at my feet milkwort's
Sapphire glimmers seemed retina-born.

The New Window

Sitting up in bed with binoculars I scan
My final resting place at Dooaghtry
Through the new window, soul-space
For my promontory, high and dry, Fairy
Fort the children called it, rising above
Otter-rumours and, now, the swans' nest
Among yellow flags, a blur of bog cotton,
Afterfeathers from a thousand preenings.

Marsh Cinquefoil

Unanticipated here
In this Mayo boreen,
It brings back her long
Hair and her laughter
As she shares the Irish
For flowers and the chough
Closing its red toes
Above our heads twenty
Years ago in windy
Macha na Bo, marsh
Cinquefoil, the purple
Sultry out-of-the-way
Entangled bog-berry,
Her favourite flower.

January

The townland is growing older too.
It makes sense to be here in the cold:
Fuchsia's flowerless carmine, willow's
Purple besom. We are lovers still.
Mistiness and half a moon provide
Our soul-arena, a tawny ring.

Proofs

I have locked overnight in my antique Peugeot
At the channel, close to stepping stones, the proofs,
Uncorrected, of my forty years of poetry. What
Would I add to the inventory? A razor shell,
A mermaid's purse, some relic of this windless
Sea-roar-surrounded February quietude?

Greenshank

When I've left Carrigskeewaun for the last time,
I hope you discover something I've overlooked,
Greenshanks, say, two or three, elegantly probing
Where sand from the white strand and the burial mound
Blows in. How long will Corragaun remain a lake?
If I had to choose a bird call for reminding you,
The greenshank's estuarial fluting would do.

Catherine Phil MacCarthy

Migrant

Will I see you one day soon, a beautiful man
I hardly know, walking, in the zone?

Will the nonchalant face of a lone figure
shine in the headlights one evening

as I slow down – stubble neat, hair
crew – long limbs aching for sleep?

Will I be stilled by vigour in the pace,
in the step something effortless and light?

Will you go from me as swiftly
as you came, into the world one stormy

September morning, hunger cries
causing milk in my breast to leak

and stream, rain after thunder
and lightning? Will you as freely return?

Orchard

Under the floorboards when we first moved in,
three foot below on foundation clay –

of the red-brick, built in 1904, M A N O A H,
white enamel letters on the glass frame above the door
missing the O of a Hebron city –

lay the dun and blue wave-pattern
notebook of accounts disclosing
pages of translucent sepia, butterfly wings,
numbered, ruled and dated,

an inventory of garden produce:
red currants, peaches, Victoria plums,
tomatoes, and lettuce, sold in pound boxes
by the dozen to Alex Findlater & Co of Sandymount,

and Fletcher Sons of Smithfield or W.H. Cole,
the stylish hand-writing of H. F. Poole
flowing from July 1930 to March '33,
detailing a universe

that had not yet seen Krystallnacht,
or the night of the long knives,

while before us on that sunny afternoon in June –
a concert in Croke Park given by U2 –

the slow ravages of time,
gnarled stumps of apple and pear,
an orchard, overgrown with brambles,
honeysuckle, nettles, a butterfly's paradise,

ready to be reclaimed and re-sown
along with west-facing green houses strewn,
terracotta, and glass shards

sunk in loamy earth unseen,
that would turn up for years.

Patricia McCarthy

Visitation

For Greg Delanty

They came before you: the crows,
silencing the dawn chorus
of garden birds while drilling
their own thug language of caws
in our ears, filling each day
with the storm-clouds of their wings.

Our minds became monochrome.
Their bossy, babbled beak-speech
proselytised down chimneys.
Their fundamentalist claws
jammed open every front door.

We thought them evil omens
as their young wheezed out and in
like accordions from the flue
in fallen nests, reared to count
disasters and deaths, do stunts
in formation that straight-flew.

When you arrived from the best
of love-made nights, you noted
their black academic gowns
on the lawn where they waddled,
their dubious theses modelled

on gang-warfare and carrion.
You gave them Professorships
instead in arpeggios and scales
that they learnt, in your presence,
from silences in bush, tree
and shrub, and from ancient tales

of crow-paths from the south west
at sunset granting wishes
of the heart. Like the Norse God,
Odin, you balanced two crows
on your shoulders whose shadows

watched memory, logic and word.
Undoing Apollo's curse –
you stripped satin ebonies
from their feathers to reveal
silver-white full-throated birds
jousting in bardic colonies.

Thomas McCarthy

A Descendant of the Khans of Yarkand Speaks his Mind

Having heard so much at the Sultan's *divan* in Istanbul,
It is peculiar to see again Western adventurism
On the eastern marches of the Ottoman world –
                Oil is hardly the problem.
'It's something else', my uncle Abdullah said,
As he took leave of his ten thousand janissaries
                On the shores of the Caspian.
'For us, as always, it is a mere question of freedom,
Freedom of passage for all pilgrims to Mecca.'
                    'It could be fish',
My own father suggested, 'there is a shortage of cod
                Among the maritime powers.'
'Don't be a donkey', said my uncle, 'I recall
                When the Lesser Nogay Horde
Were prepared to attack all Astrakhan from the East.
                It is all madness
When you think of the long resistance of Turk and Persian,
                Three centuries of it,
With Shah Abbas, Nadir Shah and the great Shamyl.
                What a joy it was
To learn such dignity, leadership and quiet cohesion'.

We ran the gauntlet of coffee, pipes and sherbet,
                The choking tumbec
That is smoked through a green stem of the rose tree;
My uncle muttering *Alhumdolillah, Alhumdolillah.*
                It is fortunate for all
That adventurers blow away like the sand of March,
                Leaving a broad canopy
Of grief, that is true, but leaving us intact once more,
                And secret as a Druze merchant,
As unspoilt as borders of gold, as elephants of crystal.

They were friends of Colonel T. E. Lawrence

Or so they claimed when we met them at the railway junction,
The fuse already lit and dynamite hidden in the sedge,
A troop-train of the Turkish Empire fast approaching,
Our own Sheikh screaming at me to get down, get down,
You absurd Assyrian shepherd, get down or die like a fool:

But I was distracted by the two strangers on camels,
Two poets of the far Oceans, Irishmen, volunteers from the West,
Like the catastrophic *Munster Fusiliers* of Baghdad –
Captain Desmond O'Grady and Lt. James Clarence Mangan,
Who, dismounting, grumbling like their far-travelled camels,
Wanting to be sure, they said, sure of the Arabic word for 'home'.

Andrew McNeillie

Commemoration

And how far is it, the other journey? –
to resurrection day, the reception committee
in attendance at the pierhead,
reciting to the air in sure and certain immortality
verses on a newly unveiled plaque.

Here lies one whose name is writ in stone
who set sail decades back in cloudy weather
at the heart's funeral, some words
under a cloud, grief for a reckoning,
a balancing of books, the verdict open.

Night Snow

wee song for Sydney Graham

The real poem never ends.
The blizzard beneath its last footprint
is where we search in its memory,
the blizzard that is also night
as fresh on your face as snow.

Night-snow the ultimate
a body must weather, body I say,
but I mean soul
out on the manhole sea
where the littoral-minded sail

beyond Cape Metaphor to be.
And Sydney Coastguard keeps his watch
ticking on course for Greenock,
with Alfred Wallis at the wheel
aboard the good wreck *Alba*.

For who but a blind one can't see
Scotland from Cornwall? –
every small hour of the year
with the heart in the right direction
and a glass to his eye.

John Montague

The Wild Irish Goat

I have met a bearded billy in the heather
Horns curving back like scimitars, and
Once high on the flank of Mweelrea
I came face-to-face, to our surprise,
With one of Ireland's rarest females.

Through the amber embrasure of her eyes
The she-goat surveyed me, then leaped
Away down the rocky mountainside,
Snorting. To warn her flock to move on:
She had seen and smelt a human.

Gerry Murphy

Capaneus

For Greg Delanty

Who is that, stretched out yonder, all rippling muscle,
gritting his whole body against the constant flame,
as if the fiery hail would merely glance off him?

Lowering his voice, Virgil turned to me and said:
'That is Capaneus, one of the seven kings who invested
Thebes, he held and obviously still holds

God in some contempt and flaunts it ceaselessly,
but, as I told him, his frothing blasphemies make
a fitting badge for such an obdurate breast.'

A Difficult Guest

(after Cicero)

For Greg Delanty

What a relief,
to speed so formidable a guest
on his way without a wisp of trouble
on the horizon.
Caesar proved altogether most affable.
Need I say more?
We behaved like human beings together.
However, he's not the sort of person
to whom you would say:
'Be sure to call again on your way back' –
once is quite enough.
We talked mainly about literature
and the weather, this weird weather of late.
What did you expect, politics?
In short, I would venture to say,
he was entirely at his ease throughout.

Desmond O'Grady

Alexandria

You, Alexandria, shine now my last city
of all, last of the many I've waxed
and wasted in, wandering. Some of us
go through arrivals, lives, departures
while others dread to move for downfall.
Witness of so much dazzle and destruction
in wounding and curling time; yet still today
sustainer of any prodigal with your achieved,
apparently innocent, serenity. I realize now
you're the city I've journeyed to all the time.
In you I begin again, not end, city of imagination.

سكندريه

الان تألقى سكندريتى
انت آخر المدائن
التى جبت ورحلت فيها هائما
انت انت مدينتى الاخيرة
بعضنا يخوض تجارب المجئ و الحياة والرحيل
و آخرون ساكنون يهابون الانهيار
شاهدة انت على البريق وعلي الانكسار
فى وقت الجرح و الاندمال
والى اليوم مؤيدة انت لكل معطاء
بهدوئك الوديع
ادرك الأن انك انت المدينة
التى طالما رحلت اليها
فيك ابدا ولا انتهى
يا مدينة الخيال

'Aexandria' translated into Arabic by **Maysa Abdel Aal Ibrahim**

Leanne O'Sullivan

The Dancing Rooms

Then they called 'Malodeon Jim' to play,
and I heard through the sets of dancers
his gathering the chord notes in the box,
a riddled mounting to the tune-path.

The sound strikes against the frame
of the room and you take my hand gently
into the gleaming middle of the music,
the cross-stitch of movements in lamp-light.

All night the bay foams in the rock pools
like a thousand fallen swan feathers,
secretly as young girls arranging their hair,
something seen in the backward glances.

Our feet and bodies batter on the boards,
an enunciation of language on skin,
more breathless and luminous than the currents
of words lost upon the tongue.

Those who came from the island bring
the taste of salt and shingle on their lips,
and hear the music as a net cast out.
You and I hear it as a crystal hung

over the sea, the petals of light falling
on the crest of each small wave,
falling everywhere and everywhere lost.
The names of moths come clear to me now –

Swallow-tail, True Lover's-Knot, White Ermine
marbled against the lamplight. When we first
danced together you were poised perfectly,
turning the steps and half said words

into my body's rhythms, the grain of things done.
Again I follow you into your summer moods,
holding the last echo of a beat within a beat.
Here is my hand held out. Give me another.

The Wanderer

Would you walk with me, woman?
The cold is in for the night now,
and the mountains quiet. It's scarce
the sun rolls around her face
or walks out in the fields. The cold is in.
Would you walk with me, woman?

The night makes a blaze of my grief,
my only soft and finest love.
Her long hair is flung out before me
like moonlight on the sea.
All the memory of her is me.
Would you walk with me, woman?

I have no talk of war or song,
I have no ready ear to the earth
or words in passion for their work.
Sooner comes the dark engrained
on summits, and the ocean louder.
Would you walk with me, woman?

One more road in a whirl of roads
opens before me like a ritual of place.
I remember the foreign lightness of her touch.
I loved her soft and undecipherable notes.
The mountains are dark now. The cold is in.
Would you walk with me, woman?

Louis de Paor

Sméara Dubha

Priocann sí braonta fola den sceach,
súile daite chomh glé
leis an am le teacht
nár dhoirchigh a hóige go fóill.

Más buan mo chuimhne, adeir sí,
bliain tar éis filleadh ón iasacht,
níl na sméara chomh blasta in aon chor
le sneachta na bliana seo caite.

Tá gile na taoide
chomh hard leis an ngrian
a líonann gach cuas dá cuisle,
is dealg sa chaint i ngan fhios di
a réabann craiceann mo mhéar.

Ba mhaith léi go mblaisfinn
den mhilseacht dhubh
atá chomh searbh
leis an bhfírinne ghlan
ar bharr mo theanga.

Ó thabharfainn an lá seo
is na laethanta gearra go léir
a tháinig roimhe dem shaol
ach greim scrogaill
a bhreith ar an uain,

go mblaisfeadh sí arís is arís eile
de sholas an lae seo ag dul as
chomh ciúin le sneachta na bliana seo caite
nár bhuail (is nach mbuailfidh)
urlár an tsaoil seo go deo.

Blackberries

She pricks blood-drops from a bush,
eyes lit bright
as time to come
that hasn't yet darkened her days.

If I remember rightly, she says,
a year after coming back from beyond,
the blackberries aren't nearly as sweet
as last year's snow.

The white of the tide
is bright as the sun
that fills every cave in her heart,
and a thorn in her talk, unknown to her,
skins the tips of my fingers.

She wants me to taste
the black sweetness,
that is bitter as truth
on the tip of my tongue.

If I could take this day
and all the little days
of my life, now gone,
I would, take time by the throat,
and choke it until it stopped

so she could taste time and again
the leaving light of this day
silent as last year's snow
that never fell (nor will fall)
to this earth.

The above poem 'Sméara Dubha' in English, is translated by **Kevin Anderson, Mary O'Donoghue** *and* **Louis de Paor**.

Cranndacht

Chuir sí crann caorthainn
sa ghairdín inniu

chuimil a préamhacha
sular neadaigh i bpoll

méara chomh slim
le duilliúr an chrainn

a roghnaigh sí
dem bhuíochas.

    Fiúise, ar ndóigh,
    a bhí uaimse,
    cloigíní fola,
    deora Dé.

Is fada léi, a deir sí,
go bhfásfaidh an crann
go dtí an fhuinneog i mbarr an tí
mar a gcodlaíonn sí,

smearadh cré
ar a lámha leonta cailín
is iníon rí Gréige ag siúl
na hallaí bána laistiar dá súil.

    Tá rian fola
    ar stoc an chrainn
    ina diaidh
    nach féidir
    le máthair na báistí
    a ghlanadh ná a leigheas.

Nuair a éiríonn an fhuil
i ngéaga an chaorthainn
dem bhuíochas, braithim
an chré ag análú go trom
sa seomra codlata in aice liom.

    Go domhain san oíche
    ionam féin, goileann Dia
    racht fiúisí os íseal;
    ní féidir a thocht a mhaolú.

Trees

She planted mountain
ash in the garden today

teasing the roots
before easing them
into the earth

fingers as slender
as the leaves of the tree

she chose herself
in spite of me.

> I wanted fuschia,
> of course,
> bloodbells,
> Godtears.

She can't wait, she says,
for the tree to grow high
as the topmost window
where she sleeps,

earthstains on her torn fingers
and a Greek king's daughter
walking the white halls
behind her eyes.

> She's left a bloodstain
> on the bole of the tree
> that the rain's mother
> can't clean or heal.

When the blood rises
in the arms of the mountain ash
in spite of me, I feel
the earth breathing heavily
in the bedroom next to mine.

> In the dead of night
> in me, God cries
> buckets of fuschia
> so quiet that no one
> hear his grief without end.

This poem, 'Cranndacht' in English, is translated by **Kevin Anderson, Mary O'Donoghue** *and* **Louis de Paor**.

Maurice Riordan

Epilogue to the Pastoral Care of Gregory the Great

from Old English

Here is the water which the Lord of all
Pledged for the well-being of his people.
He said it was his wish that water
Should flow forever into this world
Out of the hearts of generous men,
Those who serve him beneath the sky.
But none should doubt the water's source
In Heaven, the home of the Holy Ghost.
It is drawn from there by a chosen few
Who make sacred books their study.
They seek out the tidings they contain,
Then spread the word among mankind.
But some retain it in their minds.
They never let it pass their lips
Lest it should go to waste in the world.
By this means it stays pure and clear,
A pool within each man's breast.
Others pour it freely over all the land,
Though care must be taken lest it flow
Too loud and fast across the fields,
Transforming them to bogs and fens.
Gather round now with your drinking cups,
Gregory has brought the water to your door.
Fill up, and return again for refills.
If you have come with cups that leak
You must hurry to repair and patch them,
Or else you'll squander the rarest gift,
And the drink of life will be lost to you.

Fiona Sampson

Noumenon

Eye and attention leap the skin,
the same motion the spring hare makes

leaping as if to leap out of herself –
kicking away her hind-legs,

their kangaroo weight,
to make herself light and pale like air

silked over pale ploughland,
light-fringed as her pelt –

cold air that seems to brace and knock her
each joyous jump:

Which hurries blood in your ears
while you watch her freeze and rise, as if to sing –

straight-backed leaper of furrows
raising a black-smudged, gilded profile –

Accusation, annunciation? All of you leaps with her
in the blind spring.

The Rapture

That *pew pew*'s a buzzard –
rags in wind.
Its call throws down a line

of perfect pitch,
sweet and sharp,

plumb
through blue afternoon –
the way a salmon,
cooling itself,
          surrenders
to the rapid brace and flux
of water,

immersion wholly chosen
yet without desire,

as if to live were something straight
as this gaze –
          not hard hover
but dive –

eye and wing
one single muscle
beating through air

till both are snatched-up
to rapture:

leveret screaming
in the monstrance
          of claws –
a creature struggling
towards the light.

Peter Sirr

Whalefall

Every so often a windfall whale will blow through the depths
and where it lodges the pitchblack waters begin to stir,
specialists in their brilliant bodies to wake and move
towards their reward: a slow devouring, months of it,
the hagfish and rattails, crabs and sleeper sharks
picking the carcass clean until the bones collapse
but now the bone-world begins: *osedax*, the bone-eating worms
with their feathery plumes, blown like bubbles from the last whalefall
lock on and feed, generation after generation
until the place is empty again, a sulphide nothingness
the eggs have already fled, riding the currents for the fall
that takes it on, the endlessly resisting life, the whale pulse. . .

Le regret de la terre

(*Jules Supervielle, 1884-1960*)

One day we'll look back on it   the time of the sun
when light fell on the smallest twig
on the old woman the astonished girl
when it washed with colour everything it touched
followed the galloping horse and eased when he did

that unforgettable time on earth
when if we dropped something it made a noise
and like connoisseurs we took in the world
our ears caught every nuance of air
and we knew our friends by their footsteps

time we walked out to gather flowers or stones
that time we could never catch hold of a cloud

and it's all our hands can master now

Enda Wyley

Bird

For my mother

Whoever says the world
cannot be stilled
by a bird,
has not been here
in this dark gallery,
not knelt on the late
afternoon floor
and gently pulled
frames forward,
seen images
speeding by
like the old flick books
we loved as children –
the head of a dead poet,
those dark shawls
of Markey's women
in the West.
Until suddenly
your world
is stilled
by this bird –
quirky, tufted thing
proud in charcoal,
flown over forty years
from studio to home
and now landed
in this city gallery.
Such faded wood
frames him,
and his cover
is such chipped
and mottled glass.
And yet your world
is stilled by this
that flapped from
Jan de Fouw's hand

when you were young
with your small children
and did not know how
you would make it to here
or that this bird would fly
forever in search of you,
his head flung westward,
his speckled heart beating
until there is no-one or thing left
only you and this beautiful bird –
quirky, tufted being
that stills this dusty place.

Johnny Marsh V

CELEBRATIONS IN POETRY
FOR GREG DELANTY

Across the Atlantic

David Cavanagh

It would be okay

if death were like these flaming fall
sumac leaves, orange-yellow prayer flags

the wind whispers through, or feathers
riffling on an elder's spear, and not
like the dragging, baffled cat.

It would be okay if death
were like the heron landing and not
the downed jay on a busy road.

It would be okay if death were not
a ragged curtain hanging off the rod
but a smooth wooden bowl of understanding.

Thirty Robins

My heart a red-poled saggy fence,
winter-worn, spring-heaved,
gappy and propped, but still a fence.

You with your laugh somehow
make latch, make creaky
gate of me, but still a gate.

Thirty robins wheel, a whoosh,
from black-branched crab and March's
mad berries, iced, unfallen berries.

Michael Collier

Among School Children

The boy with barbed-wire tattoos braiding his biceps
won't listen to what his classmates say
about Yeats and 'The Wild Swans at Coole',
and when I try to mediate, he interrupts me,
not with words but with his lunging head,
half shaven, half in dreads,
the face unequivocal with rage,
and then the mouth's abhorrence,
lips pressing like a strangler's thumbs
choking the words he'd rather kill than say,
'Swans, fucking swans', as if he knows precisely
what they are: sleek, vicious, stand-ins
for the sad, divorced, abandoned
heart's longed-for wrong.

Dale

You would love Dale not because
he's the only one in the Chris Ridge Care Center
who visits your invalid father
and not because his huge improbable body
is ferried gracefully on an electric cart
that's as stylish as a Vespa
but which he calls his *hog*.

You would love him not because
he has a voice that once sang
in music halls across the country
or that he continued to sing in choirs
until he could no longer stand.

And you would love him not because
he's put a hex on the dreaded physical therapist
and gleefully translates the cafeteria menu into French.

No, you would love him because unlike everyone else,
he says the center is not the worst place he's ever been.
He tells you about the nurses getting him up in the morning.
'Not all of them are gentle, not all of them are beautiful,
but look at me,' he says.

And then, of course, he visits your father,
who talks a kind of feeble gibber
and has to lift his body to lift his head.
Dale says, he likes his sense of humor,
and you can see your father likes him too,
and says something, perhaps his word for Dale,
when he hears Dale's cart entering his room.

Billy Collins

Continents Apart

We used to sleep close to one another,
sometimes facing away

as if guarding the bed
somehow with our eyes closed,

but more often looking
the same way, one body curved blindly

into the other, fitted together
much like the coasts of Africa

and South America were before
whatever dreadful force moved them apart.

How easy the geologist has it
who can speak of drifting without thinking of you.

Museum

I slid past a pencil drawing of a young girl,
a white marble statue of a warrior
as well as a vase that had managed to remain
unshattered for over three thousand years of history.

Then I stopped at a verdant oil painting
in a frame flecked with gold,
which I gazed at for such a long time
that the painting began to look back at me

which was especially odd because the painting
was not a portrait but a landscape
so what was doing the looking-back was a pasture,
a row of trees, and a light blue sky.

The longer we looked at one another
the more it seemed like one of those staring contests
you can never win, the kind you might
get into with a dog with bangs over its eyes.

But then the painting blinked,
or at least a tiny cow I had not noticed
changed her expression which was enough
to release me back into the vast world

that lay outside the frame of that painting,
which included the drawing of the girl,
the statue of the god and the unshattered vase
as well as the granite steps I descended,

the avenue of flags and gleaming yellow taxis,
the entire city and whatever was happening beyond
plus a sudden break in the clouds where two hands
were raising a blue chalice into the sky.

David Curzon

Correspondences

For Greg Delanty

Where have I found my correspondences?

In a spare landscape by Ni Tsan which shows
an empty pavilion on a riverbank
shaded by half a dozen slender trees –
each represents a friend, the Chinese scholars say –
all sketched with a dry brush, and on the other bank
are his low mountains and the vacant sky,

and in wet brushstrokes by the eccentric monk
Bada Shanren, 'the old man of the hills,'
who painted crazed black myna birds
and fish with eyes which seem to glare
in angry accusation at the blank
stretches of paper they are floating in,

and the vast landscape of Fan K'uan,
a distant cliff face towering over scrubby trees
and the tiny cortege, with a waterfall
pouring down the cliff in an unbroken plunge
far beyond the little wanderers
who head away from it to the scroll's edge,

and the meticulous Sung album leaves
of Ma Yuan, whose solitary scholars live
in one exquisite moment when the moon
shines through the branches of a plum tree just in bud,
or sit in contemplation far above
the torrent underneath them rushing on.

Rachel Hadas

The Vantage Point

All this hot anger will, I know, subside,
settle, clear. The world will open out;
those rooms that haunt my sleep,
low-ceilinged, with no trace of natural light,
will lose their walls, dissolve to pearl evenings;
the kindly ghost from his rare visit glide
gently backwards through the thick glass pane
not without a long look.

                  As the heat
and fever dissipate, where will I be?
Alert, detached, standing a little back
and to the side, unsure of anything
other than sunset, moonrise, cycle, season,
molten reaction cooling down to time.

Deplaning

To leave the city, the apartment; stray
from the well-worn tracks where no one speaks
for half a day, a week, two weeks
bestows – perspective, I was going to say,

as if absence were coterminous
with distance. As if I were on a plane
rising above the daily, the mundane.
As if flying cut me wholly loose.

Thinking clearly is so hard to do!
Do I mean pondering my situation
resembles flying? Or that aviation
opens a window for a better view?

Up in the air, this is all I can see:
little earthy patches, green and brown;
meandering rivers gleaming in the sun;
then fields of billowing cloud, then simply sky.

A bump; and we return to gravity.
I unbuckle simile, deplane,
trudge out into terrestrial life again,
that hazy realm where every boundary –

so sharp seen from the vantage of the air –
melts into mist. Cloaked like conspirators,
responsibilities, routines, and chores
beckon afresh, and choices disappear.

Jane Hirshfield

Chapel

The moonlight builds its cold chapel
again out of piecemeal darkness.
You who have ears and hands, it says, *come in;*
no need to stamp the snow-weight from your shoes.
It lifts another block and begins to chisel:
Kyoto, Vladivostok, Chicago, Perth, Beijing.
Huge-handed, working around you in silence,
as a cat will enter the silence where no dog lives.

Gail Holst-Warhaft

Wells

Why the clump of bare trees
on a hillside satisfies the eye
more than a single tree,
or a clutter of birds on the feeder,
a swath of spring bulbs,
a heap of oranges beside the road
near Argos, children in the schoolyard
gathered in what Greeks call
little wells, wells
of talk, teasing, gossip,
wells of women laughing,
old men drinking,
musicians passing notes,
cows sharing the shade
of an oak, wary cats
in the village square,
tombstones clumped by clan
on the cemetery lawn,
little wells of the dead.

Lia Hills

mythos

When I was a Myth I flirted with gods, courted favours of
wind and sun, one synapse in a world of thought, where
Logos and I performed a *paso doble* of shifting light. Passed
from mouth to mouth, I was spat and suckled by others'
whims, kissed to the snag of time, as perched on the
shoulders of blood-lipped nemeses, I soothed them into a
redeemable curse – corpses filing as lovers turned a loss –
warped to the scribed form, the triumph of syntax over chaos,
Homer, Heraclitus, Hesiod.

When I was a Myth, charred by the convexity of Reason's
lens, a fraternity of men in tailcoats deposed me beneath a
molecular stare, and I became a woman, the heathen's bride,
a tacit scream escorting the birth of the great divide. The
statesman's pocket my new cage, he called me a spectre then
stole my dialect to wrench the core of men, made me the
Braille, dots beneath skin, of a blindman's game.

When I was a Myth, I lay prostrate before a circling crowd and let
  them connect their
drips to me, till, blood brothers, we presented Poesis to a shackled world,
  our new
dialogue with Being creating man himself.

libretto

i

||: how to knit allegory | what is to be made
of the shift | news stories of a half-day an opus |
morning no longer fresh ||: who's plotting
this thing | *recitativo accompagnato* | two breasts
to sustain narrative | dead a fortnight & gone
to myth ||: who gets the prize | bel canto | the last
eliminated | or the most grievously grieved :||

||: there's theme like web |a spider's dangling |
before screen |of leitmotif | something Shakespeare
said | a bloodied king | or behind-the-wings fool
with more than his share | *coloratura* | of fancyflight :||

must we anagram | title letters | initials of the
forgotten bled |apply our DNA & there it is |
a transparent helix | words rank with design |
melding of lifted fable & the medium that fits :||

||: to celebrate | a confetti of mastheads |an aria
of *liebes und tod* | transfigured | 'til some new thing
confounds the mix | no melodic ending
just the perpetual stream of folly | and *reportage* :||

ii

it's a temporal game | the reigning of harmonics
Dasein finds its escape |Tristan's chord halts

before peak | climax spectral | it's seeking authentic
in its existence-towards-death | or not | just a cop out

a knit of allegory to sooth the bereft

iii

Wagner said:

Hör ich nur diese Weis(?)

Do I alone hear this melody (?)
…in the universal stream
of the world-breath –
to drown, to founder, unconscious –
utmost rapture!

iv

he has his final note
we go | libretto in comfortable fists

Galway Kinnell

Now That I Have Come Back Home

Now that I have come back home
and we have cried, and heard our cries,
and have fallen at last in love-sleep,
imitating each other body to body, I know
neither she nor I if we were to wake
in the middle of the night would be startled
to hear, besides our breath,
two parallel voices in the room
in harmony, love's and death's,
and to hear them in the darkness
cross over, and sing each other's part.

Holm Oak

Exemplary tree
be with your lost poets
be with Lorca,
with Hernandez,
with Machado,
be with those who stand and sing without shelter.

Adrie Kusserow

Sudan

What to do with the giant moth
      caught in our tent on the last night, dive bombing our headlamps.
I tell my daughter not to touch it,
      why, she says, you'll change them, I say,
trying to explain how our fingers are sponges
      for their blue and gold powders,
but we have no choice she says
      as we pull down the tent and begin our journey home
watching them fly into the night
      only to flock to the bright light of the generator
whose haggard lungs we pump each night,
      a throng of cell phones and computers
plugged into its one beleaguered but outstretched vein,
      this global vein, this electric river, with its flock of converts,
baptized in its current, this body electric
      that is just now beginning to twist like the Nile
through the sweet green fields
      of the post-war south.

Kathryn Maris

The Angels Wept

1 And it came to pass that the fountain of Bethesda flooded the land, for the angel stationed there wept through that long day.

2 A woman that waded among the multitudes held in her arms a box that she clasped like an infant.

3 She stopped at the foot of the angel, for she was tired. The angel said: 'Here was the path of the One Who Came Before You.'

4 The woman was startled, for she remembered that name, and knew that She once carried the box also. But the angel said no more and did not reveal that She had been a suicide and had left the box and her last quantity of gold with a plea that the Lord might find Her a successor.

5 But the woman who now held the box was wise, and though she knew not the One Who Came Before Her, she sensed her ghost upon her, and this ghost gave her fear, but also the ghost gave her strength.

6 She continued her path and faltered not, though among her trials were flood, sun, hills, cities, prison and sea.

7 And the Lord was pleased with her, though He did not condemn the One Who Came Before Her who died of her own hand, for He, like the angel, loved her with all His heart.

Paul Muldoon

Shrines

i

Small town after small town
I might easily have gone down on my knees
by each white cross or posy in its tin
and resigned myself to the fact
a cord of wood may yet be stacked
between two living trees.
Even those pigs had seemed content
in their profound disgruntlement.

ii

Had I had more than a glimpse of a lake
through a break in a plateau,
had I not suddenly had to brake
for Apollo wrapped in polythene,
I might have been emboldened
and gone with the flow.
Even smoke may rise with next to no fuss,
calm above the calamitous.

iii

Now as gas prices soared
yet another billboard had held out *Injured?*
before it all but implored
1-888-WE-CAN-HELP.
I caught the yelp
from a clothesline of a plaid work-shirt.
Even a storm-window took a stance
against what it could barely countenance.

Thomas O'Grady

Mythology

i

They All Laughed

Imagine vulgar Vulcan hammering
two-fisted in his forge, muttering 'Venus,
Mars . . . ,' his genius a spite-fired furnace
sputtering, his twisted tongue stammering.

Razor subtle, his knotted cords of discord . . .
rage-wrought wire netting, binding as a buckle.
Yet, once embedded, we heard the gods chuckle
one by one. Then the entire heavens roared.

ii

Straighten Up and Fly Right

What if I had succumbed to some gaudy
Gorgon's will-withering get-hither gaze
and thus whiled away the rest of my days
a sculpted hunk . . . just one more hard body?

O Andromeda! O scandal of scandals . . .
the way, rockbed-bound, you thrashed in the clutch
of wave after wave, summoning my soft touch:
O Perseus, come in wingèd sandals!

iii

Night and Day

By day I dream of life's dozen labors,
my Herculean hazards: the push-and-pull
of Hydra-headed crowds; the usual bull
(load after massive load); the smiling neighbors'

120

Dog of Death; and – truly colossal in length
and breadth – ungirdling sturdy Amazon thighs.
By night, tossed and turned, uplifted to black skies,
I, Antaeus, cry: '*Mother . . .* give me strength!'

iv

(Let's take it) Nice and Easy

Down that rutted road again, our fast-track route –
fleet Atalanta, flat out, setting the pace,
brash Hippomenes giving mad-dash chase,
rationing (gifts from Venus) gilt globes of fruit.

Then – as always, bittersweet! – that aftertaste
of bridled bits beasts gnaw and gnash against . . .
just desserts hand-picked by a goddess incensed:
lush laurels trimmed with the pitted spoils of haste.

v

What is This Thing Called Love?

How dared we, dear, go so against the grain,
grafting to your pure basswood trunk – that straight shoot –
my knotty oak . . . bole and branch, burl and root?
Were we – Philemon, Baucis – daft? Or vain?

Or just plain blessed by the gods' delightful whims?
None but guests from above could yield us this:
out standing in love's bright field, our bower of bliss,
each year's new growth more than a tangle of limbs.

Harvey Shapiro

Caedmon's Hymn

A translation from the Anglo-Saxon

Guardian of heaven whom we come to praise
Who mapped creation in his thought's sinews
Glory-father who worked out each wonder
Began with broad earth a gift for his children
First roofed it with heaven the holy shaper
Established it forever as in the beginning
Called it middle kingdom fenced it with angels
Created a habitation for man to laud his splendor.

David Slavitt

Pedro da Ponte

by Alfonso X of Castile

Pedro da Ponte has committed a very grave
sin, stealing Coton's poems. That man
labored long upon them, but this knave
and thief will stop at nothing and, if he can,
will steal the work of men who are better than
he is. Nervy? Ah, but he calls it *brave*.

Not so good for Coton though, who had no
luck, for Pedro has his poems: they're all
arranged in a fine leather portfolio
too rich for poor Coton, whose means were small.
Better for him had he let his quill-pen fall
from his hand and let the writing business go.

And Don Pedro? He should be hanged. After he stole
Coton's poems, and after Coton had died,
he would not give a soldo to save the soul
of the man he'd robbed – and who'd lent him money that I'd
say he still owed. Gratitude? Honor? Pride?
If he had these, he would crawl into a hole!
He is a traitor, a murderer, and a thief
who can give up any hope of his salvation.
He killed his friend (this is my firm belief)
in a drinking bout. It wasn't mere recreation;
he wanted him dead and it was premeditation.
He wanted the poems to add to his own thin sheaf.

Since nobody else will publish this accusation,
I take it upon myself, and I wish him grief.

Tom Sleigh

Canto IX,

lines 1-63, from Dante's *Inferno*

Fear went wild inside me at the thought
That he, my guide, on turning back, had felt
Afraid – though the sight of my face drained white
Brought back the color into his. He called a halt,
His ears straining to hear, for mist ravelling
Through darkening air was like a whiteout.
He began, 'If we don't win this fight! – what's taking
Them so long – the help they promised...'
I saw right off by how his tongue kept tripping
Over his words, trying to cover what he'd
Almost said, that maybe my fear was right –
Though into his stumbling I might have read
A worse meaning than he'd meant: 'Down here,
Deep as this, down in the depths of this dismal hole,
Does anyone descend from the first circle where
What they suffer most is hope cut off?' To my question
He replied: 'This road I follow? Would anyone
Make the journey here but those constrained
To go? But I was sent here once before,
Down to that deepest and darkest place
Not long after death saw fit to tear
Me from my flesh. The witch, Erichto,
Who forces the dead back into their bodies,
Conjured me to come to her: she made me go
Inside that wall and bring up into the sun
A spirit from the circle of Judas
Who lies in the depths farthest from heaven
That encircles all. So yes, I know my way
Down there – of that, you can be sure: the marsh
Exhaling that stench extends all the way
Round the city they won't let us enter
Without a show of anger.' And he told me more,
But my mind froze over – I couldn't hear –
For there, soaking through like a fresh blood stain,
Bodies shaped like the bodies of women,
Waists ringed by hydras twisting bright green,

Their hair of wriggling, baby snakes
And full-grown, horned serpents slithering across
Their temples, stood the three savage Furies
Staring down at me from their full height:
Handmaids to the Queen of unshakable
Pain and sorrow. My guide, who in his heart
Knew them all too well, turned and said to me:
'Steady on now. Take a good long look –
The ferocious ones...the Erinyes.
That one on the left, that's Megaera;
And she on the right, wailing, that's Alecto;
And there, between them, is Tesiphone.'
And then his tongue failed him: each scrabbled and clawed
With their nails their own flesh, they smote with
Their palms their breasts and cried out so loud
I huddled against the Poet in my fear.
'Where's Medusa? we'll turn that living one to stone –
Let her come around and let down her hair!'
This they shouted out at me, glaring down:
'When Theseus came to steal Proserpine
Back to the upper world, he got off easier than this one.'
'Turn your back – shut your eyes as tight as you can.
If the Gorgon comes looking for you, and you
Catch even a glimpse of her, never again
Will you see the light above.' Saying this,
Not only did the Poet turn me round,
But not trusting to my will, covered my eyes
With his own two hands: now, all who feel
They sense what lies behind these strange lines
Would be wise to peer beneath the veil
And heed the lesson that these words reveal.

Shrine

Shadow of a wing across the curtain.
The winter trees so bare the wood rings with light.
And sun keeps falling through plastic bags torn
To streamers in the branches and quiet

Multiplies long hours into the afternoon
And the paperweight with the brain afloat in clear glass
Gives back the slash and criss-cross of my workaday shrine:
A plastic baggie full of my father's ashes;

Three teeth pulled, blood dried on the roots; a hospital bracelet;
A vial of sand from the Sahara; a blown glass dolphin
Arcing across the sea from here back to Murano; and a geode split
In two, amethyst and space rock, bookends of the moon.

How long it takes a life to find its proper altitude:
And here it is, in front of you, emblem and inconsequence,
Concentrated into the paperweight's glass void,
There beside me, beyond me, afloat in pure transparence.

Daniel Tobin

Bitter Skin

As though his palms were a *mappa mundi*
And he the studied explorer, watchman

Looking back from the offing of his life,
He traces his course,
                          the embedded lines
Forked or flaring that elsewhere would be scars.

How he made it here, pilot of himself,
Flames in the hand's puzzled approximation

Of choices and years.
                       And where it begins,
The hectic parchment spreading up his arm,

Defines the boundary of each mulled regret –
No, his long stare affects the alchemist

Who would figure gold the secret of this rust,
The flecked skin like a fine dust sifting free,

In each flyblown cell a life he might have lived.

Smart Animal Gorilla

Koko, who calls herself 'Smart Animal Gorilla', has learned over
a thousand words. A CD of her poems sung by a human choir
is due for release.

News Wire

A thousand words, a thousand sonic baubles
Koko knows, more than most of us
or nearly, who are her hairless cousins,
who hardly savor the supple vocables

of the language (from the Latin, *lingua,*
meaning 'tongue'), as she sounds the silent
amplitudes, a flurry of pirouettes
from the soft pads of her hands, her fingers

shaping signs: her by now studied translation
from Modern Ape to Trainer's English,
while her kin diminish like Manx and Cornish
into the hellbox of extinction....

Koko, inscribe your elegies from the cage
for the lost forest, to the human choir
who've assembled in the studio's glare
to sing the primal notes of your name –

Smart Animal Gorilla, who writes on air.

Derek Walcott

In Amsterdam

i

The cruise-boats keep gliding along the brown canal
as quiet as prayer, the leaves are packed with peace,
the elegant house-fronts, repetitive and banal
as the hotel brochure, are still as an altar-piece.
We cruised it with Rufus Collins once, a white macaw
on his piratical shoulder. Rufus is gone.
Canals ring reflection, with calm at the core.
I reflect daily and how soon I will be going.
I want the year 2009 to be as angled with light
as a Dutch interior or an alley by Vermeer,
to accept my enemy's atrabilious spite,
to paint and write well in what could be my last year.

ii

Silly to think of a heritage when there isn't much,
though my mother whose surname was Marlin or Van der Mont
took pride in an ancestry she claimed was Dutch.
Now here in Amsterdam, her claim starts to mount.
Legitimate, illegitimate, I want to repaint
these rubicund Flemish faces, even if it's been done
by Frans Hals, by Reubens, by Rembrandt,
the clear grey eyes of Renée, the tree-shade on this side,
the chestnuts that glitter from the breakfast window,
why should I not claim it as fervently as
the pride of Alix Marlin an early widow,
as a creek in the Congo, if her joy was such?
I feel something ending here and something begun
the light strong leaves, the water muttering in Dutch
and the girls going by on bicycles in the sun.

A dragonfly's biplane settles and there, on the map,
the archipelago looks as if a continent fell
and scattered into fragments; from Pointe du Cap
to Moule à Chique, *bois-canot, laurier cannelles,*
canoe-wood, spicy laurel, the wind-churned trees
echo the African crests; at night, the stars
are far fishermen's fires, not glittering cities,
Genoa, Milan, London, Madrid, Paris,
but crab-hunters' torches. This small place produces
nothing but beauty, the wind-warped trees, the breakers
on the Dennery cliffs, and the wild light that loosens
a galloping mare on the plain of Vieuxfort make us
merely receiving vessels of each day's grace,
light simplifies us whatever our race or gifts.
I'm as content as Kavanagh with a few acres;
merely to lift our hearts to break with the surf's lace
or see how its wings catch colour when a gull lifts.

Eamonn Wall

Look at the Lake

i

Look at the lake.

Point out the lopped hemlocks.

A full moon hanging in the pine's curve.

ii

June on Lough Arrow. Two swallows
forage for flies. All of our origins dot,

breast-like & tomb-like, this old land:
Carrowmore, Lobby Rock, Cromlech,

an economy of sleep on the hillside, a
cloudburst popping the sheds at dawn.

iii

The fox turned its back to the lake.
The wind did not bother the slipway.

We debated the merits of turquoise.
The evening was gray and the water was cold.

Rain fell from the edges of sheds. The white
rabbit pounded the perimeters of its cage.

iv

The moon illuminated the lake. The trout were in motion.

I asked for your hand and the sound of your voice.

The love of your children, the moorhen's refrain.

Each street
is a farewell...

Johnny Marsh VI

William Bedford

The Fascination of What's Difficult

Paul Muldoon: *Horse Latitudes,* Faber, 2007
Geoffrey Hill: *A Treatise of Civil Power,* Penguin, 2007

i

Yeats was clearly wearing one of his masks when he wrote 'The fascination of what's difficult/Has dried the sap out of my veins', but the idea of 'difficulty' has plagued the arts ever since the arrival of modernism. 'We can only say that it appears likely that poets in our civilization, as it exists at present, must be *difficult*', Eliot wrote in 1921, his argument being that 'Our civilization comprehends great variety and complexity, and this variety and complexity, playing upon a refined sensibility, must produce various and complex results'[1]. Since then, his words have achieved the force of aphorism. But things have always been difficult. History is difficult. No doubt Wyatt and Surrey, Milton, and the Anglican poet-priests of the seventeenth century found their own times and circumstances just as pressing as ours. Psychological and aesthetic experience cause their own problems. Johnson found 'a kind of *discordia concors*' in the 'occult resemblances' and metrical practice of the metaphysical poets; the radical simplicities of *Lyrical Ballads* offended nearly all of its first few readers; Bridges simply could not *hear* the metrical effects Hopkins was after. In our own context, the notion of difficulty itself has become a political issue, a *bête noire* of the anti-elitism against which art pitches its essentially democratic understanding of reality. Both Geoffrey Hill and Paul Muldoon have been victims of this contemporary version of *la trahison des clercs*.

ii

Paul Muldoon has his own suggestion for dealing with difficulty, and it turns out to be a version of Eliot's contention 'that genuine poetry can communicate before it is understood'[2]. Trying to help a reader with the allusive texture of *Madoc: A Mystery*, he says: 'go with it. Read it as a ripping yarn . . . If you don't know who Burr or Blennerhasser is, well, you may have to go and find out. But that's okay. There are lots of things we have to go and find out. We have to go and find out, what red, what wheel and barrow are, at some level'[3].

With *Horse Latitudes*, the dustjacket offers immediate help with this kind of finding out, explaining that the 'horse latitudes designate an area north and south of the equator in which ships tend to be becalmed . . . and where sailors traditionally threw horses overboard to conserve food and water'. The title poem is a sequence of nineteen sonnets, each sonnet taking its subject from battles fought across history and geography, the common factor being that they all begin with the letter 'B'. From Bosworth to Bull Run, Beijing to Burma, the random brutalities of war are explored, though not with the 'florid grim music broken by grunts and shrieks' of Geoffrey Hill's 'Funeral Music'[4]. Muldoon is after something different. In fourteen of the nineteen sonnets, the emotional force comes from the death by cancer of the poet's lover, Carlotta. It is her 'battle' which moves. Several reviewers have drawn attention to the fact that *Horse Latitudes* omits any reference to Blair, Bush or Baghdad, as if their absence dilutes the obvious political message. But the 'obvious' is doubtless the point; if Muldoon has ever achieved anything it is to avoid the obvious. And yet there does seem to me to be an obvious reading here: Muldoon's list of battles beginning with the letter 'B' might just as easily have been created from the letter 'C' or any other letter in the alphabet. The randomness of evil is to be found anywhere, just as the randomness of cancer can strike anywhere. This is most clearly expressed in the nineteenth sonnet, 'Burma', where Carlotta remembers her grandfather in the Burmese jungles, cutting 'the vocal cords of each pack mule // for fear the mules might bray/and give their position away?' In a single poem we have the cruelty to animals signified in the sequence title, the 'swift excision' of cancer surgery and jungle warfare, and the characteristic Muldoonian stance seen in the final refusal to 'give *away* their *position*'.

The very best poems in *Horse Latitudes* work like that, as Muldoon has always worked. The technique does demand enormous skill, and there are a handful of poems that feel strained. The homonym in 'Bob Dylan At Princeton, November 2000' doesn't work because Dylan's name isn't 'Gym'; the wordgames in the much-too-long 'The Old Country' are irritating and add up to no discernible effect; the haiku of '90 Instant Messages To Tom Moore' are often banal – 'The butterfly sits/ another toffee-nosed toff/on a pile of shit'; and the repeated device at the opening of each stanza in 'Riddle' – 'My second sounds doubly in roar/but singly in oar' – is both uninteresting and in solution amounts to nothing, or nothing I could see. But these failures seem signs of creative tiredness, not an essential failure of 'method'. Some of Muldoon's finest poems are collected in *Horse Latitudes*.

As often with this poet, family stories generate some of the most powerful poems. 'Eggs' has the poet unpacking eggs and squeezing 'into a freshly whitewashed/scullery' of his childhood and previous eggs 'from any one of which I might yet poke/my little beak'; 'It Is What It Is' describes the unpacking of a new toy for a child, the protective bubble wrap reminding the poet of the bladder wrack of his childhood, his life now spread out around him with 'The fifty years I've spent trying to put it together'; 'Turkey Buzzards' moves from observations on these bizarre birds and their immune systems to another victim of cancer, the poet's deceased sister, Maureen Muldoon; and 'The Landing' takes us from a 'squid hauling itself through knee-deep shallows' to what I take to be a direct reference to the poet's own tactic of shining 'a beam on the seabed to cancel its own shadow'. Throughout the volume, surreal imagery makes contact with the profoundest losses and griefs, a new version of *discordia concors* that inevitably calls Donne to mind, not least because he is one of Muldoon's favourite poets.

Sometimes, the balance is not sustained. 'Sillyhow Stride' is one of Muldoon's most distressing personal poems, dealing movingly with his sister's awful death, but there are far too many direct quotations from John Donne, and Donne's voice is too strong for the poem. The quotations do not become part of the music of Muldoon's voice, in the way that Eliot's fragments do in *The Waste Land*.

But when the technique works, it is extraordinary, as in one of the finest poems Muldoon has written, 'Hedge School'. In the tighter form of the sonnet, we have the poet's great-great-grandmother outside a Hedge School 'with a rush mat/over her shoulders, a mat that flashed/*Papish* like a heliograph' to the poet's daughter in her 'all-American Latin class' where she may 'be forced to conjugate/*Guantánamo, amas, amat*' and learn with Luciana in *The Comedy of Errors* 'how "headstrong liberty is lash'd/with woe"' whilst her father is in St Andrews in Scotland, '(where, in 673, another Maelduin was bishop)', thinking about his sister and trying 'to come up with a ruse' for unsealing a dictionary and 'tracing the root of *metastasis*'. This astonishing poem draws together family history, imperial politics of the nineteenth and twentieth centuries, and personal bereavement, all expressed in the individual and political struggle to control language. It works in a way that Yeats would have understood immediately, 'the fascination of what's difficult' given poetic and emotional force by Muldoon's familiar, amiable and compelling genius.

iii

As his *Collected Critical Writings* (Oxford University Press, 2008) show, Hill has reflected upon difficulty and poetic technique more profoundly than any practising poet since Eliot. 'We are difficult', he observes somewhat irritably in his *Paris Review* interview. 'Human beings are difficult. We're difficult to ourselves, we're difficult to each other. One encounters in any ordinary day far more real difficulty than one confronts in the most "intellectual" piece of work. Why is it believed that poetry, prose, painting, music should be less than we are?'[5]. And of the responsibilities of poetic technique – the measure of the poet's seriousness – 'it is the precise detail, of word or rhythm, which carries the ethical burden' he argues in the 'Preface' to his version of *Brand*[6].

In the volumes published between *Canaan* (1996) and *Without Title* (2006), the moral complexities of the poet's vision are expressed in a fracturing of syntactical and metrical control which have been widely read as autobiographical – 'Shameless old man, bent on committing/more public nuisance' (*The Triumph of Love*, p.19) – despite Hill's well-known dislike of 'coy and prurient exercises in the "confessional" mode'[7]. But the description is used as a way of dismissing the 'public nuisance', as if Timon and Pandarus were nothing more than versions of Shakespeare's sour old age. We should be wary of misreading Hill's intentions, of seeing the personal as 'only' or 'simply' personal. What 'are poems for?' he asks in *The Triumph of Love*, his difficult *laus et vituperatio*: 'They are to console us/with their own gift, which is like perfect pitch'; and again, 'What/ought a poem to be?

135

Answer, *a sad/and angry consolation*[8]. What is the consolation being offered in *A Treatise of Civil Power*?

It is certainly not the 'Incontinent/fury wetting the air' of *The Triumph of Love*, but a reflective, syntactically and metrically controlled exploration of how 'that which is difficult/preserves democracy', not least by paying 'respect/to the intelligence of the citizen'. There is no doubt that the allusive texture is as challenging as in Muldoon's *Madoc: A Mystery*, the list of titles reading like an academic seminar: 'On Reading *Milton and the English Revolution*', 'On Reading *Burke on Empire, Liberty and Reform*', 'On Looking Through *50 Jahre im Bild: Bundesrepublik Deutschland*'. But surely this is Hill parodying his own reputation among the levellers and anti-elitists. The savagery of the irony ought to signal what is going on:

Getting into the act I ordain a *dishonoured*
and discredited nation.
Milton or Clarendon might well approve.
Can't say who else would. It smacks rather
of moral presumption. Things are not that bad.
H. Mirren's super.
   'On Reading *Milton and the English Revolution*'

From 'the seventeenth-century vision of harmony/that all gave voice to and that most betrayed' to the most recent political scandals where 'public apology ad libs its charter/well-misjudged villainy gets compensated', *A Treatise of Civil Power* explores that civil power which reaches down into every aspect of life, those private and public circumstances of '*homo sordidissimus*' which Hill studied so powerfully in 'The Absolute Reasonableness of Robert Southwell'[9].

Many of the echoes should have immediate resonance. From the 'scorched earth' of 'The Minor Prophets' where 'A fire devoureth before them; and behind/them a flame burneth' to the '*Devastated* is Estuary; *devastation* remains/waste and shock' of 'In Memoriam: Gillian Rose', *A Treatise of Civil Power* gives us the landscape of our daily lives. We live 'in the city that is not just, has never/known justice' – also in the poem for the Marxist scholar, Gillian Rose – a city where the poet recaps 'on words like compassion that I/never chanced in your living presence:/as empathy and empowerment', though in this instance out of human sympathy: 'I did not blunder into your room with flowers'. 'He was a realist in his providings' Hill says of Burke in 'On Reading *Burke on Empire, Liberty, and Reform*', and we know he is talking about himself and 'the ways decency erodes and you/can see the slippage, though still ideas like *firm/and precise judgement* seem to possess balance/and even redemptive value', though a value that demands 'more resources than I have exhaustion/to yield, pledge, dig up, borrow against'.

And yet there is a source of redemption, and as one might expect from Hill it lies in language, and the common culture. Poetry in 'Citations II' enacts 'the pitiless wrench between/truth and metre' and yet still in 'Citations I':

I think of poetry as it was said
of Alanbrook's war diary: a work done
to gain, or regain, *possession of himself,*
as a means of survival and, in that sense,
a mode of moral life.

This may be precisely the 'discord in harmony' of 'Johannes Brahms, Opus 2'
which takes us back to Johnson's unease with the metaphysicals, but in 'In
Memoriam: Gillian Rose' again, 'Poetry's its own agon that allows us/to recognise
devastation as the rift/between power and powerlessness'. If the 'rift' is politics,
and poetry at its most difficult the possibility of redemption, then the common
culture of E.P. Thompson's *The Making of the English Working Class* is where we
might find signs of hope:

The statute books
suffer us here and there to lift a voice,
judge calls prosecutor to brief account,
juries may be stubborn to work good
like a brave child
standing its ground knowing it's in the right.
Letters to the editor can show wisdom.
            'A Précis or Memorandum of Civil Power'

All of this may make *A Treatise of Civil Power* sound a dry read, but dryness is a
kind of passion, and in the face of our particular cultural and political crises may
be the most passionate and necessary response. And yet the poems collected here
are among the most emotional and vulnerable I think Hill has written. Certainly
one approaches 'On Reading *The Essayes or Counsels, Civill and Morall*' with some
trepidation, but the 'sterility' which C.S. Lewis found in Bacon's prose provokes
a personal anger in Hill, testing abstract reasoning against the judgement of
reality – 'whether the dispossessed figure at all/is a question unasked at my lord's
table' – when 'So many had, and have, nothing; and Bacon/speaks of *privateness*
and retiring'. It is the privileges of power that are being attacked here, and the
emotional force of the anger derives from the poet's own experience: 'My parents/
never owned a house. It could be said/that was their folly', but:

The poor are bunglers: my people, whom I
nonetheless honour, who bought no landmark
other than their graves. I wish I could keep
Baconian counsel, wish I could keep resentment
out of my voice.

The poet of the *Collected Critical Writings* remains in control – 'I accept, now, we
make history; it's not some/abysmal power/though making it kills us as we die to

loss' – but these abstract concerns are rooted in the personal life:

> I have a question to ask for form's sake:
> how that small happy boy in the seaside
> photographs became the unstable man,
> hobbyist of his own rage, engrafting it
> on a stock of compliance, of hurt women.
>
> *'In Memoriam: Gillian Rose'*

This is the 'small happy boy' who grew up in the Black Country of 'In Memoriam: Ernst Barlach', where he heard the common dialect captured in Kate Fletcher's translations of the Scriptures – '*All the children uv Israel blartid fer Moses'*, '*A thick clahd cuvvud the mahntin fer six days*' and 'folk *wuz frit on 'im*' – a dialect full of words such as '*glowery*' which has 'two meanings/if you crave ambiguity in plain speaking/as I do'. The affection is unmistakable, the loyalties obvious for anybody open-minded enough to read carefully. And the source is offered in all its vulnerability in the marvellous 'Coda' where we find:

> a taint of richess in the haggard seasons,
> withdrawing a Welsh iron-puddler's portion, his
> penny a week insurance cum burial fund,
> cashing in pain itself, stark induration,
> something saved for, brought home, stuck on the mantel

for the poet to remember and see 'how much is gift-entailed/great grandson, and son, of defeated men/in my childhood'. This is a powerful use of the personal, to illuminate the cultural and historical which so much of contemporary poetry ignores. In such poems, *A Treatise of Civil Power* explores 'the pitiless wrench between/truth and metre' indeed, and more deeply and movingly than any volume we have seen for a long time, even from Geoffrey Hill.

NOTES

[1] T.S. Eliot, 'The Metaphysical Poets', *Selected Essays* (Faber, 1980), p.289.

[2] T.S. Eliot, 'Dante', Ibid, p.238.

[3] Lynn Keller, 'An Interview with Paul Muldoon', *Contemporary Literature* 35.1 (Spring 1994), pp.1-29.

[4] Geoffrey Hill, *Collected Poems* (André Deutsch, 1985), pp.70-77.

[5] Geoffrey Hill, interviewed by Carl Phillips, *The Paris Review* 42/154 (Spring 2000), p.275.

[6] Geoffrey Hill, 'Preface', *Brand* (Penguin 1996), p.xi.

[7] Geoffrey Hill, *Collected Critical Writings* (Oxford University Press, 2008), p.365.

[8] Geoffrey Hill, *The Triumph of Love* (Houghton Mifflin, 1998), p.82.

[9] Geoffrey Hill, 'The Absolute Reasonableness of Robert Southwell', *The Lords of Limit* (André Deutsch, 1984), p.22.

Tony Roberts

Galway Kinnell: *Strong Is Your Hold*, Bloodaxe, £8.95

Galway Kinnell is a poet of celebration, as his master Whitman was. He is a significant American poet, one of a handful of fine talents emerging after Lowell, Bishop and Berryman, which included Donald Justice, Richard Wilbur and Anthony Hecht. Such anthologised poems as 'The Avenue Bearing the Initial of Christ into the New World', 'Flower Herding on Mount Monadnock', 'After Making Love We Hear Footsteps', and 'The Bear' testify to Kinnell's power and popularity.

Strong is Your Hold is his latest, life-affirming collection. The epigraph is from Whitman and immediately establishes the book's concerns

> *Tenderly – be not impatient,*
> *(Strong is your hold O mortal flesh,*
> *Strong is your hold O love.)*

Tenderness and mortality are the keys to the collection. The elderly poet hangs on to his world

> I, who so often used to wish to float free
> of earth, now with all my being want to stay
>
> ('The Stone Table')

It is not fear, but commitment that holds him, commitment and that same passion of which he wrote in the much earlier 'Body Rags':

> How many nights must it take
> one such as me to learn
> that we aren't, after all, made
> from that bird which flies out of its ashes,
> that for a man
> as he goes up in flames,
> his one work
> is
> to open himself, to *be*
> the flames?

As a preface, one must also celebrate the publisher, Bloodaxe, which has included a complimentary CD with the book. Here the poet reads all the poems from the collection in a warm, seasoned tone, which strongly brings out what is personal.

Part 1 opens with 'The Stone Table', where the speaker and his wife (One wants to call them Galway and Bobbie) sit out with their feet up on the stone 'cow pass' block, watching a young bear, reminiscing about other sightings of moose and coyote. Eventually the bear is disturbed, but the fact that it first

> peers about with the bleary undressedness
> of old people who have mislaid their eyeglasses

perhaps leads the two of them to simultaneous thoughts of their neighbour, who will be mourning his wife at her grave, or at his writing desk. That connection draws the speaker into consideration of his own circumstances, his changed views, expressed in his desire to live so as to repeat moments like these. Characteristically, the poem delights in the natural world, drawing analogies from animal and plant life. Man is never alone in Kinnell's poetry; he inhabits a world he shares with other animals. In fact each is often understood in terms of the other. The beauty of this particular poem lies in the conversational tone.

> As often happens, we find ourselves
> thinking similar thoughts, this time of a friend
> who lives to the south of that row of peaks

with which it celebrates enduring love in the face of finite time, but quietly, accessibly. One's opinion of the collection may well be formed by Galway Kinnell's tone, as well as by his attitudes. Fond reminiscences appear in other poems in Part 1, when Kinnell turns – as he often does – to anecdotes about his children, Fergus and Maud. He returns constantly to domestic moments that are meaningful to him as a human being, which is part of the charm of his work. This is in keeping with a comment he made in 1978 that 'One writes not about the spectacular events but about the normal events.'

In 'It All Comes Back' the reminiscence is unsettling: Fergus, at four, sat on his birthday cake; everyone laughed; the poet picked up the humiliated child, who then tried to 'rip my whole face off':

> And it came to me: I was one of his keepers.
> His birth and the birth of his sister
> had put me on earth a second time,
> with the duty this time to protect them
> and to help them to love themselves.

Ruefully, the poet wonders if the laughter was some sort of revenge that adults take on their own parents. He also feels his face has remained 'loose'. Then Kinnell does an unusual thing. He considers firstly whether he should retell the anecdote and then turns the decision over to his grown-up son. Presumably Fergus ticked the third option:

OK, publish it, on the chance that somewhere someone
survives of all those said to die miserably every day for lack
of the small clarifications sometimes found in poems.

The echo here is of another of Kinnell's masters, William Carlos Williams
(whose exact lines are quoted at the end of the book).

'Inés on Vacation', 'Hide-and-Seek 1933', 'Everyone Was in Love' are enjoyable,
but slighter anecdotes. 'Conversation' is a personal poem that is affecting in an
offbeat way. The poet is in conversation with his young daughter, Maud, who is
quizzing him about being old. Her questions are stimulating to him, artless but
astute ('Does the past ever get too heavy to lug around?'). Her sympathetic tone
gives free reign to both their imaginations. When he confesses he would like to be
at McCoy Stadium watching baseball, the exchange ends

> Me too. I like it when there's a runner on third.
> At each pitch he hops for home,
> then immediately scurries back.
>
> –   If it's a wild pitch, he hovers
>   a moment to be sure it's really wild
>   and then is quick – like a tear,
>   with a tiny bit of sunlight inside it.
>
> –   Why the bit of sunlight?
>
> –   It would be his allotment of hope.
>
> ('Conversation')

The ending exemplifies Kinnell's ability to accommodate the poetic image
naturally (the tear of sunlight) in language that is relaxed and colloquial ('bit of').
This is one of the poems which works particularly well on the CD, where the
delivery gains from the prosy rhythm and intonations of the American idiom.

In Part 11 of *Strong Is Your Hold* we return to the natural world and the poet as
observer. 'Ode and Elegy' (the former for the hawk, the latter for its prey, the jay)
depicts a one-sided confrontation, after which the jay's eyes 'shrink into beads of
taxidermists' glass'. The analogies, with Jesus and Judas, grape harvesters and jets,
bring the world of birds into our own. The poem 'Feathering' observes a woman
scattering feathers from an old pillow, in order to attract nest-building swallows.
The mood is playful, the woman at length off-balance:

> for she has been so long at play with these
> acrobatic, daredevil aerialists, she might
> momentarily have lost the trick of walking on earth.

In 'Burning the Brush Pile' the poet inadvertently burns a snake, while in 'The Quick and the Dead' he observes for hours the busy decomposition of a vole. To better evoke the activity in these poems, Kinnell breathes life into archaisms and dialect terms such as 'shinicle', 'clarts', 'prog', 'howk', and 'moil'. On Kinnell's part, this is a career-long attempt to stop 'so-called obsolete words' from 'falling off the back-end of the language' ('Conversation'). The former poem involves confrontation with an infuriated snake, who responds as a human being might:

> It stopped where the grass grew thick
> and flashed its tongue again, as if trying
> to spit or to spirit away its pain,
> as we do, with our growled profanities,
> or as if uttering a curse, or – wild fantasy –
> a benediction.

The vole, on the other hand, despite its seeming movement, is simply host to the creatures that drive life which, the poet tells us, 'is what we have for eternity on earth.'

None of the poems is more involving than 'Pulling a Nail', which deals with the poet's vexed relationship with his father, a man who built the house as he 'did/ everything he did, alone'. At the same time the poem celebrates the craftsmanship of the poet's father. It is a fine poem which imagines the father embedding the nail, then describes in great detail the process of extruding it, whilst at the same time passing on lore, as another father might to his son:

> A spike driven long ago
> resists being pulled – worse
> than a stupefied wisdom tooth,
> whose roots, which have screwed
> themselves into the jawbone,
> refuse to budge

The movement of the poem is from act to emotion, via memory, and 'the last heat/of our struggle' evokes the father and son's uncommunicative relationship. The bent nail becomes the bridge

> over which
> almost nothing of what mattered
> to either of us ever passed.

The poem begins in 'transrealmic combat', since the son is undoing his father's work. At the end, Kinnell recognises he has won, in defeating his father's purpose. Yet it is a hollow victory, for he doubts he will ever straighten out the 'nail' between them.

Part III of *Strong Is Your Hold*, 'When the Towers Fell', deals with the events of 9/11. Such an enormity is still difficult to treat, even for a poet accomplished at writing on important themes. The poem had its origins in counselling sessions with the poet's New York students, in the aftermath of the terrorist attack.

This, the book's longest poem, opens with a paradox: familiarity leads us to see what is now absent. This is testament to the sheer scale on which the twin towers was built. The poem is a cumulatively powerful, rhetorical and lyrical sequence. Firstly, the poet imagines those inside the towers 'calculating profit and loss' and vividly describes the destruction the hijacked planes creates. Then he focuses on the lucky few who escaped the violent deaths of those inside the building, and the rescue attempt seen in an 'electric glare' from his apartment. His attention turns to the grief-stricken relatives standing with photos of the missing (again the paradox: to be here is to be lost); the ceaseless replay of the terror; its context ('a small instance in the immense/lineage of the twentieth century's history of violent death'); the contaminated air; those faced with the inevitability of being burnt alive. At length we are led to Whitman's words

> *They themselves were fully at rest – they suffer'd not,*
> *The living remain'd and suffer'd*

and finally the inescapable image of the towers firstly transformed into the destructive path of a raging god, then being reduced to a black hole

> infinitesimally small: mass
> without space, where each light,
> each life, put out, lies down within us.

It is a powerful ending, invoking religion, science and humanity. The poem's use of French, German and Polish quotations ('We're digging a grave in the sky there'll be plenty of room to lie down there,' Celan) add to the sense of hopelessness. Yet the most significant allusion is, perhaps, to that great New Yorker, Kinnell's master, Walt Whitman, who saw, suffered and bore witness to the horror of the civil war, whilst being sensitive always to its heroisms.

Part 1V of *Strong Is Your Hold* takes the form of a short series of elegies and remembrances, most memorably, 'How Could She Not' , which imagines the day of a friend's death and 'Promissory Note', which celebrates Love's (temporary) triumph over death:

> I will cross over into you
> and ask you to carry
> not only your own memories
> but mine too until you
> too lie down and erase us
> both together into oblivion.

The final section of Galway Kinnell's new book deals with physical love. "Shelley" illustrates Kinnell's theory (explained on the tape) that in art the 'absence of feeling for others damages the great work'. The poem deplores the Shelley 'malaise à trois', as well as the poet's early faith in this 'one true/free spirit':

> and in those days, before I knew
> any of this, I thought I followed Shelley,
> who thought he was following radiant desire.

The poem 'Sex' is a fanciful ode to odours, not nearly as quirky as 'Walnut', a meditation on the penis, apparently whilst travelling on the Newark Airport bus ('that lets me imagine what the fuck/ing of buses might be like.') Two further poems are more romantically conventional in their thinking, 'Insomniac' and 'Field Notes', in which the poet's partner is reading Barber's *The Human Nature of Birds* (a title which is surely close to Kinnell's own heart). The collection ends with poems more immediately concerned with mortality, 'Pure Balance' and 'Why Regret?' In the former, the poet is concerned with the absence of certainty in a future (curiously 'exhilarating', as well as worrying). He explores the idea that holding the notion requires 'pure balance', in order to maintain one's sense of self.

Finally, 'Why Regret?' sums up the poet's ethic: clear-eyed love:

> Think of the wren
> and how little flesh is needed to make a song

and ends with

> Doesn't it outdo the pleasures of the brilliant concert
> to wake in the night and find ourselves
> holding each other in our sleep.

I was first introduced to Galway Kinnell's work through the 1964 selected poems, *The Avenue Bearing the Initial of Christ into the New World*. It was a gift from the Anglo-American poet, Michael Mott, who praised Kinnell to me for the natural authority in his verse. That is still very much in place, after a lifetime's work. The hold remains strong.

Duncan Sprott

Time-travel

James Harpur: *The Dark Age,* Anvil Press, 2007, £7.95
James Harpur: *Fortune's Prisoner - The Poems of Boethius's* The Consolations
of Philosophy, Anvil Press, 2007, £8.95

I have a hunch that most people invited to read a book that included thirteen sonnets on obscure Irish saints and a seventeen-page poem about St Symeon Stylites, would run away screaming. But this is the scintillating territory James Harpur's fourth collection, *The Dark Age,* inhabits, and I urge you, gentle reader, not to flee so soon.

In Harpur's *A Vision of Comets* (Anvil, 1993) it is the poems that involve the past – Greek or Roman myth and history, the Middle Ages – that stand out as his particular interest and strength, and show his deep feeling for the world of antiquity. In *The Monk's Dream* (Anvil, 1996) he begins with Bede and proceeds by way of the death of William Rufus, and a sonnet sequence built around the death of his father, to Gilgamesh and the death of Enkidu, and to Lazarus. The cover of *The Monk's Dream* is black, with a medieval personification of Death – skeletal, holding bow and arrow. Harpur, like Webster, seems to be much possessed by death, with one foot in the pagan past and the other in the Christian. In *Oracle Bones* (Anvil, 2001) his mood is less funereal, but no less historical, with Harpur donning a dazzling succession of masks and mouthpieces: a retired augur, an Assyrian extispicist, a priest at Delphi. In 'Dies Irae' a Dark Age cleric tries to reconcile his mission to save souls in a sinking world with his own sickness, physical and spiritual – a theme that will recur in *The Dark Age.* The same cleric is made to say, 'With my trained imagination/ I bring the dead to life' – words that might very well be applied to Harpur himself. The first three collections bear witness to Harpur's enduring preoccupation with Ireland, and with higher things: he wrestles with the riddle of eternity, looks for the divine light, worries at problems of belief and unbelief, unravels the riddles of the past.

On the cover of *The Dark Age* is a painting by David Inshaw, with exploding fireworks and a lunar eclipse – the sun peeping out from behind the dark moon. It's an apt image, for Harpur's recurring concern in this volume is with darkness – the cloud that separates humanity from God, for example – and with light. Inside the book Harpur sets off some metaphorical fireworks of his own.

To imply that Harpur only has time for the past, however, that – like Poor Jim Jay, he is 'stuck fast in yesterday' – is, of course, quite wrong. In the delightful 'Alien', the poet addresses his infant daughter as 'Dear little traveller' and 'A small unearthly being', an 'alien' like himself. He asks her:

Did you shake off my shyness, hermit ways,
And curse an absent God and pointless life
And wonder why we brought you to this place?

He muses on her future, wishing:

May you adapt and breathe the oxygen
Of this new world, pick up the signs and codes,
Human disguises, masks I tried to learn.

Be blessed to find a kindred alien –
Watch out for eyes, and smiles, and chance remarks
In crowds or somewhere like a lonely mountain

And maybe in the future, the stars uncurtained
On a summer's night you'll show the one you love
The shining home you lost, where I've returned.

Harpur alludes, here, to the book of Hebrews, where people are 'aliens' or 'strangers.' His epigraph, from Henry Vaughan, is: 'My soul, there is a country/ Far beyond the stars' – a country which Harpur revisits in *Fortune's Prisoner*.

'On Reaching Buddhahood' begins with : 'I'd longed for it for years: the holy hush' but ends with bemused disappointment, for Nirvana is not yet attained:

Instead, I find I've gained the Buddha's belly,
And I meditate, cross-legged, on lust and bile
Or watch, serene, the *maya* of the telly

Forgetting if I can the looking glass
And Buddha's balding pate, unholy arse.

The Dark Age begins, appropriately with the Irish weather: 'Roscommon Rain' is a fine example of Harpur's superior craft and almost forensic observation of the natural world. The darkness continues with a moving triple villanelle entitled 'Stroke', about the poet's dying mother.

Then the light shines through the dark, with a baker's dozen of punchy sonnets about Dark Age Irish saints. In 'Brendan' the island of the saints emerges from 'Black fog as light, its shore of powdered gold'. Brendan hears the voice of Judas 'above the raucous ocean' saying: 'Hell is stasis, keep heading for the sun/ And when you reach the light, sail on, sail on.' Harpur's saints exist in vividly drawn landscapes, noisy landscapes. In 'Patrick's Return', for example, he conjures a picture of 'Soft rain soaked fields of stationary bulls/ Where gangs of crows were cackling like the druids/ Who came to curse me, clacking jaws of skulls.' In 'Kevin and the Harpists' a vision of angels play such sweet songs brought from paradise: 'We wondered whether it was we who'd died/ Were being welcomed to the other side.' Harpur succeeds in making these half-forgotten heroes of antiquity live, capturing glimmers of old light for a new dark age. These are necessarily partial portraits, fragmentary, but they have the feel of bright miniatures painted inside the initial letters of a medieval manuscript – vivid pictures that also happen to talk.

In 'James', which concerns the arrest of Jesus in the Garden of Gethsemane, we have a tantalising fragment of Harpur's recently completed work, *The Gospel of Joseph of Arimathea* (Wild Goose, 2007), which will repay seeking out for its fresh angle on the life of Christ.

'St Symeon Stylites' is an arresting piece of ventriloquism using the voice of the pillar ascetic, who took up residence atop a stone pillar in northern Syria – subsisting on a diet of dried peas. The poem's four sections correspond to the pillars, which were increased in height until Symeon was perched 60 feet above the ground, on a balustraded platform – where he stayed for 36 years. His wish in adopting this bizarre residence was to avoid the crowds who flocked to him for his prayers and advice, but the pillar had the opposite effect, attracting a vast throng, whether emperors, pilgrims or sightseers. In an age of licence and luxury Symeon stood for virtue and selflessness in so striking a fashion that nobody could fail to notice, and there were many conversions. Fertile ground, then, for Harpur, who has performed a miracle of his own in imagining the ancient world through Symeon's eyes. The result is graphic, sharply observed: we feel the heat, sense the saint's swimming head, the physical privations. Harpur aptly calls Symeon's platform a 'stage' – this is the saint as entertainer and performer – a kind of Dark Age David Blaine.

Harpur's Symeon, though bathed in sunlight, begins in the dark, no closer to God for all his climbing closer to heaven. He says:

How much higher must I climb
To see you, or even just the angels?
I doubled this pillar's height
To glimpse your blinding glory...
All I hear is the wind
Sighing and groaning...

Harpur's epigraphs are from Sartre: 'Hell, it's other people' – and Milton: 'Which way I fly is Hell; my self is Hell', Symeon himself says, 'Forgive me Lord, I think I hate my neighbour... I know I hate myself'. But as the poem progresses his attitude changes:

I pray for them by day, by night...
And so exorcise my hate for them
My hate for me.

By the end 'a surge of joy, of love' has filled the saint; a 'wave of love flowed up to me/ So tangible I could have jumped/ and stayed afloat' and his abhorrence of the crowd has vanished:

> Each one of them is Christ
> Walking alone through fields of wheat
> Or by the sea of Galilee.

On some level the saint on his pillar is a metaphor for the poet in his ivory tower, who has renounced all thought of worldly wealth; who is somehow set apart from the crowd yet meant to be addressing that crowd. Another species of alien.

Next come two poems from Harpur's work in progress *Voice of the Book of Kells*. Scribe B says, 'I crave the light for copying' – a reminder of the preciousness of light in the past. In *Verbum* the scribe speaks of 'travelling inward all the time.' Harpur's own travels are often inward, time-travel, travelling of the soul, upward, ever upward.

The Dark Age ends with the wonderful 'The Monastic Star-Timetable', in which a medieval monk watches the night sky, using the stars as his clock:

> On the holy night of Christmas
> When you see the Dragon above the dormitory
> And Orion poised above the chapel roof
> Prepare yourself to ring the bell.

He dreads the darkness that represents separation from God, yearns for divine knowledge, asking, 'Lord, how long before a star expands inside me/ Flooding my soul and flesh with gracious light?' He ends poignantly:

> So many nights I've waited for eternity
> Listening for music, looking for meaning,
> But all I've felt is the dark between the stars,
> My heart, beating like a bell, the phrases of mortality.

*

In the introduction to *Fortune's Prisoner* Harpur mentions his fascination with 'notions of fate, fortune, free will, chance, coincidence,' notions that bulk large in Boethius, who rose to a high office at the court of Theodoric the Great, in Rome. Fortune favoured Boethius at first, but his luck ran out c524 when Theodoric imprisoned him, accused of treason and of practising 'magical arts.' Boethius passed the time in jail at Ticinum (Pavia) writing the *The Consolations of Philosophy*, a work that alternates prose and verse, describing how the soul attains through philosophy to knowledge of the vision of God. Boethius's themes are the nature of justice, the problem of evil, and the workings of Fortune and free will. It takes the form of a dialogue between Philosophy, personified as a woman, and the incarcerated Boethius.

Harpur has plucked the 39 poems from *The Consolations of Philosophy* and allowed them to stand alone. They begin with Boethius's distress at his imprisonment. The poems are about God and love, the falseness of earthly riches, the fleeting nature of human honours, the ascent of the soul to the realm of light, the slipperiness of fortune, the laws of chance. They also explore the subject of mental and emotional captivity – people who let greed and lust dominate their thoughts will be unable to raise them up to the divine light. The body is like a prison for the soul – whose true home is the celestial realm of light, from which it came, and to which it longs to return.

Boethius says the soul needs to keep to the 'path towards the sun' and resist the temptation to look down at earthly things. By breaking free of the snares of the world and putting on Philosophy's wings, the mind can fly up to heaven – travelling through the ether and return to its rightful home. What puzzles Boethius is how people of impeccable moral worth are persecuted while evil-doers prosper. One of Philosophy's answers to this conundrum is that Fortune herself dishes out good and bad luck at random. The trick is to reject Fortune's system of values altogether: if you've enjoyed good luck, then you must *expect* the turn of Fortune's wheel – the crash is inevitable. Nothing lasts for ever, for:

Fortune revolves her wheel as wilfully
As water surging up and down a creek:
Swatting once-feared monarchs cruelly

Raising the vanquished... only for a while.
She's deaf to cries, untouched by human grief;
The groaning she provokes just makes her smile.

It's her hobby – how she proves her power
Impressing people with the marvellous trick
Of conjuring gloom from joy within an hour.

The poems point out the worthlessness of human values, the futility of human achievements: the soul must return to the transcendental realm: true wealth is in the dazzling light of heaven. Appropriately, the cover illustration is taken from a 15th century illuminated manuscript showing Boethius with the Wheel of Fortune, king at the top, about to fall, peasants below, about to go up in the world.

In these two books, then, Harpur leads us into the difficult territory where words cease to be of use. His triumph in *The Dark Age* is to make the darkness shimmer with light. An epigraph, from Dionysius the Areopagite, sums it up: 'We pray that we may come into his Darkness which is beyond light, and, without seeing and without knowing, to see and to know that which is above vision and knowledge.'

W S Milne

'We have earth to wrestle with'

Grey Gowrie: *Third Day, New and Selected Poems,* Carcanet, 2008, £9.95

The quality which strikes one on reading Grey Gowrie's *New and Selected Poems* is that of balance, a fine positioning of poetic form with significant content, a rendering of private concerns within a public life. The main drive of his aesthetic is to find 'the stillness' in the midst of 'the worldly weather' of his extensive travels and within the turmoil of his political and commercial lives, the 'vain commotion' of the age with all its aleatory realities and cachinnations. His intention (and his achievement, as I would acclaim it) is to hold this balance, silencing all that is fraudulent and bogus in the world, within the poem's composed frame, its inspiration – 'the wind breathes past the curtains and into the poem' he says, and 'consider how the tree holds but does not bruise the earth'. His success is not arrived at accidentally, as if by some polyphonic spontaneity. His art is carefully crafted; it is the result of conscious choice, of making something of 'the dead day', the 'zero echo' of the age. He works, he says, 'faithfully, line by line' to get the tune of the poem right:

> I try to give shape to thought and please the eye as it travels down the page.
> But music means more to me; a poem starts with a tune and all these poems
> are written to be read aloud; or even muttered aloud: *sotto voce.*

Now, this is all very well in theory (his credo holds close to that of Basil Bunting, for instance), but does it work in practice? Well, the answer is, emphatically, *yes*:

> Child, cultivate words against your wish.
> How else shall the day be done, the day recaptured
> when the whole garden was rapt and the good sun
> found its inhabitants dancing?

– as fine an evocation of innocence as you will find anywhere in modern literature, I would argue, the tone holding a deliberate 'exact and contemporary balance' against the world's 'shrill voice'. Amongst the mayhem, he writes elsewhere, 'A few constants hold', like poetry:

> Each time the tide comes in I'll marry you
> again, Sorrowful. Wait till the moon lies down,
> Sorrowful. We laugh ourselves to sleep
> with a pint of applejack. Tomorrow morning,

what if the ocean has withdrawn forever
and the sea serpents come tumbling round the house
for care and cookies? Come close to me.
Turn over, then. Treat the poor monsters kindly.

The strength of his style is there for all to see, a gentle, laconic lyricism that carries great emotional weight. The declarations of love are made against the certainty of mortality's 'cold stone', our 'essential life' pitched against the fact that we are passing 'parcels of shadows' eaten up, often, with jealousy, spite, malice, the opposites of love:

Clouds: a low ceiling
for ten miles until South Mountain
liberates blue again to make the horizon.
I miss you, would swap words for a wind
to blow it all away and bring you
home. No one knows where you've gone...

The book evinces wide and eclectic reading, but the poet's voice and technique, from the beginning, are both mature and distinctly his own. They bear the stamp of his own personality, his own character. The poet's phrasing is also precise and memorable. He says of the sixties, for example (with a backward glance at Wordsworth), that 'it was electric to be alive', evoking scrupulously the off-balanced, haywire rhythms of rock music, and with that all the easy morals of the age.

Gowrie has written of modern American poetry that it excels in the conversational lyric whilst at the same time revealing the exasperated psyche of the age, and the North American influence, the timbre particularly of Lowell and Berryman, I would argue, is clear enough in his own poetry where the mind's torsion, its 'shape', 'its wavelike arabesque', encounters a myriad of marital, geographical and mortal divisions:

Where is love? morality?
Two by two they are twining
a wavelike arabesque
white as the vacant, turning
scallop that brought her here. They fix the horizon.

The world has become an ocean:
shoreless, but held together
by a girl whom stars put
out of reach of worldly weather...

Gowrie revels then in the weave and twist, the dance of the poetic line, the shape of the lines on the page, and the music on the ear, but this formality is only the surface revelation of a deeper impulse, that of an intensely thought-through philosophy of life. In his notes to the book he says that his political hero is Edmund Burke, and on the strength of this volume one can perhaps see why. There is a similar emphasis on establishing truth on the basis of unbiased opinion, mature judgement, and an enlightened conscience, all within a spirit of peace, repose and 'principles purely pacific'. This considered equanimity (but not complacency, Gowrie is never complacent – 'You would be startled / at the force of my dislike for our lives' he says at one point, in a Flaubertian tone of disgust) in the political arena sits equally with the philosophical, where the exemplar is Bernard Williams, both writers believing in clearing up confusion, and seeking out the clarity of the 'geometer'. They both hate utilitarianism (especially in its insouciant Benthamite forms) and stress notions of inner necessity, authenticity, and self-expression, endorsing D H Lawrence's dictum 'Find your deepest impulse, and follow that':

If big themes are tragic, happiness
blooms in small corners: sunlight on a dress
moving in from shadow; flood water; a call
to capture the unfolding sensuousness
of white nymphaeas or purple iris;
absurd pleasure at the steamy pile

of straw christened by horses and settling in
to rot by the compost heap, good as a win
at the races, and, best of all, the bright
certainty that in the end sins are forgiven
or rotted down themselves, season by season,
and we have laughter while we have the light.

That last line is written in the face of what Nathaniel Hawthorne called 'mortality's gripe', a fact faced up to in the courageous sequence on the poet's own heart transplant surgery at Harefield Hospital, *The Domino Hymn* (first published by Agenda Editions and The Greville Press). (The notes tell us that 'a "domino" transplant is when you receive a heart from a living donor who has in turn undergone a heart-and-lung replacement from a dead one', a very intricate procedure indeed.) That sequence of poems renders movingly and sensitively (without any self-pity) the mundane and terrifying trials of E Ward, the Operating Theatre, Pharmacy, Outpatients, Radiography, and X-Ray, sometimes with the black humour such places require (see especially the elegy for Scott Everitt, 'Postscript: The Magus'). The primary themes in this sequence are courage in facing illness (the author's own, his witnessing of others' in hospital, and that of the sufferer's relatives), the precision and skill of the medics tending the sick (especially the surgeons), the necessity for hope in all of this, the marvels and terrors of modern medicine, and the necessity of enjoying the transience of things. There is some deft play on literary euphemisms and clichés, such as 'the torn heart', 'an imagined heart' and 'a change of heart', all transformed into a grimmer and more desperate context by the patients' awaiting transplants, playing off the artist's concerns with those of the scientists possessed with 'Newtonian…precision'. What can be seen as merely a kind of literary conceit or mundane phrase (e.g. 'a change of heart') in fact becomes a technical possibility, a type of miracle almost (there is some play with religious language too in the sequence, as in the title, but this I feel has a more sardonic tinge to it). Gowrie's respect and admiration lie mainly with the other patients, his own family's tenderness, and the professionalism of the medical staff caring for him. The poet's 'sparks of perception', his consciousness, take all of this in and shape it into brave poetry. Out of the night-vigils, the anxieties, the systole of sleeping and waking, pain and its relief, death and life, through 'the sub-aqueous world of care', 'the drowsy syrups' of the painkillers appeasing death, the poet's spirit baulks imminent death, hoping to live a little longer, an exemplar of all of our lives. Only recently, sitting in an Outpatients section of a hospital I noticed leaflets of poems in racks for patients to read to while away the time. The thought occurred to me then that the NHS should incorporate in future some of *The Domino Hymn* poems in the publication. Without detracting from the reality of illness, the sequence also praises the human spirit in its determination never to give up hope:

A last summer
of life, or at least misgiving
that leaves will billow again for the great
eye. How they enfold
even a hand held high against the light
this bed side of a window – blue veins
with green gradations beyond them, an admonition of green
which only the sun on a white rose by a brick
wall undermines to tell a different story.

The gentle, loving lyricism, the laconic lines that carry emotional weight here are typical of the volume in general, of elegies which expose 'each layer of sorrow', and of poems which emphasise the glory of courage and skill in lives beset with transience.

Each shift of perception in a Gowrie poem is accompanied with an exact, correlative step in rhythm, a concord close to that which you often find in a successful film – the poem 'Cull', I think, is a fine example of this technique, like successive 'shots' in a movie. After the hectic catalogue of travels it is a relief to sit with the poet in his Virgilian retreat, far from the city's sirens and 'the mad ways of the self-important', eating now 'a country loaf' after 'the long light of summer'. Here, in the section entitled *Marches*, Gowrie celebrates his convalescence. After 'pain's narrow horizon…your body's / concentration on pain' comes 'the mind's secret: to live, to live', knowing now that 'what kills / is certainty'. The poet is finished at last with the interminable 'brouhaha' of politics, finding 'refuge from the politics of the tribe':

> it's all drift, the green envelops
> the rose with only a memory of sky…

Having looked closely at the 'fabled, dusty/ days' of history, his own and others', 'the tangled skein of skin and broken columns of bone', he looks back on his public life and finds a new and ongoing duty: 'to contrive / a civilisation / and keep it alive'.

The 'new knowledge', the 'new light' of these later poems only shines through because of the deep self-knowledge, the alert self-awareness that 'we have earth to wrestle with', that everything we enjoy has been won at a price, even this retirement. There are few public men of any worth today who can write a line of verse, let alone a book of this magnitude. The only regret for me is that to write *The Domino Hymn: Poems from Harefield,* and *Marches,* Grey Gowrie had to endure twenty-six years of almost complete poetic silence. That was a loss for him, surely, and what is more, a loss for us. Happily, though, the silence has been redeemed. Let us hope there is more poetry to come.

Belinda Cooke

A Felicity of its Own

Peter Robinson: *The Look of Goodbye: Poems 2001-2006,* Shearsman Books, 2008

Gaston Bachelard, in his *Poetics of Space,* offers us a formula for poetry at its best when he argues that 'poetry possesses a felicity of its own, however great the tragedy it may be called upon to illustrate' and Peter Robinson's latest book, *The Look of Goodbye* edges us into just such an aery realm, capturing life's darker sides – fragmentation, loss, pain of exile and anger at world events, yet all conveyed with a satisfying sense of a job well done. At the same time, we also see him edging back from the abyss with a voice that, with the illusion of casualness, accepts and appreciates the pleasures inherent in being able to cast a poet's eye over the material world and everyday events.

This substantial collection covers the work of six years and provides a fairly chronological creative diary, with some thematic rearrangement, taking us from early impressions of the new millennium, through the poet's final years in Japan (Sendai and Kyoto) before relocating to England in 2007. The title conveys the physical and mental landscape of departure from Japan interwoven with various other farewells of people and places referred to throughout the book. Such perceptions, though, are hard to pin down as is made clear by the extended use of conditional forms: 'as if', 'perhaps', 'it might be', along with titles that are often so fragmentary – 'Naturally Enough' 'What Have You' – that one feels one might throw them up and allow them to attach themselves randomly to the welcoming poems below. This all suggests that memories don't so much happen as 'maybe happen', offering possible versions of events.

The experience of exile, on the other hand, is less ambiguous, and is clearly conveyed in a cold light. One can't miss the irony in 'Alien Registration': 'Dr Robinson you need to review your alienation card', and in 'As Like as Not' where he states: 'Where it's like our real life were over:/we're living a posthumous existence', while 'Transit Lounge' is an unbearably accurate description of that in-between state of necessary flights – the awful tedium, 'in the limbo of now'. Nor does exile necessarily draw fellow victims close to one another, with the 'compatriots', in 'English Abroad' dried up inside, unable to communicate or draw on a shared culture:

> who'd like to commiserate, but
> the language just rummages inside them
> as if it were fretting to find a way out...'

Moving into the second section, loss increasingly dominates. In 'The False Perspectives' 'Everything is sloping off anywhere else'. Lost loves, old haunts or locations are now obsolete or have disappeared. In 'Closure' (with its suitably double-edged title) the extended metaphor of the seashell is beautifully executed providing multifarious sea associations that allow the reader to share in the journey into the ghost world of the past:

> And I see how the vacant ex-restaurant
> through its cloud of chalk
> is like nothing so much as a seashell
> in which you catch talk
> that talked and went so far with distant
> wave-forms broken on the shore
> of others' mind like swell, swell
> echoing from the years before.

Repeatedly we see the search for signs, markers, or shifts in the weather with little expectation of finding anything tangible because of constantly changing viewpoints. There is also some serious pessimism going on in places, such as the slightly humorous, self-mocking reference to the self as landscape in 'York Notes': 'you hardly recognize / your self, it is so overgrown', or the bitter-sounding lines in 'Stranded': 'out of love with all humanity /starting from myself…'

Yet there is also an acceptance of this world as given, rather than a raging against the dying of the light. One of the ways Robinson conveys this is by interweaving the motifs of urban refurbishment and changes in the weather or shifts in the landscape. By so doing he works with the reader a little, for he appears to underplay nature's traditional role of providing solace – such as in 'The False Perspectives': 'like that faulty landscape / with a crack in it' – only subsequently to reinstate its restorative role. Take the relaxed, affectionate tone of 'After Words': 'because I've no quarrel with the badly-abused / landscape as such' and, no matter how abused, it can be renewed: 'It's like the visible world had reopened, / refurbishments complete'.

Though Robinson doesn't work in Technicolor, any affirmation is conveyed as a kind of awe that results from him bringing the poet's eye and ear to the material world, providing a perception that is necessarily complex, evoking not just the present but imaginative associations and memory also, as in 'Languages of Weather':

> I listen for the sound of a voice
> as for a passing, brief sensation
> in the languages of weather…

In reading Robinson's poetry, blink and you may miss it. A piece that could almost act as his poetic manifesto to the passing moment is 'What Lies Sleeping', a tribute both to loved ones and life's transient occasions:

which is how unutterable meaning
makes itself felt now a loved one
nods off on the train
as features are shedding defences
to tired eyes or, again
a life's glimpsed with no stances,
without self-presentation –
this truth never hidden from the senses;
it just needed underlining.

These lines are astute both in the accuracy of how a face appears when not alert as well as in highlighting the psychological complexities of body language; the word 'stances' jumps out from the poem because of its careful usage here. All-in-all the poem provides a fine example of how Robinson creates poetry from life's non-events, as in 'The Better Halves' where we find him 'at the non-event of a five-tier / pagoda undergoing restoration, gazing at the impact, the fact of it'.

There is ample evidence in the collection of Robinson's use of wordplay, deployed to reinvigorate jaded language, transforming it into something complex and often paradoxical. Take the example of 'Brief Visitation' – a visit either real or imagined – where the phrase 'or else I'm listening, lost for words,' conveys both amazement and fumbling incoherence, thus juxtaposing the mind of the younger and older speaker in the poem. It goes on to provide a lament for the addressee's imminent departure, from the moment, the memory and ultimately the universal departure to death, affectingly conveyed via plain, transparent diction:

when sooner or later, go you must –
and you're leaving very, very soon,
you again, if only just.

Robinson finds a certain joy in the nuances of language and at times will have a little fun with it. In 'On the Mobile' he first draws attention to the humour in a young girl's overheard phrase: 'I've got to give him time to fall in love with me', but by the end of the poem he has taken us to a completely different place where Robinson both recalls his own youth, his exilic life by means of an echo from 'Ode to a Nightingale', and then, repackaging the phrase, provides an imaginative leap to optimism on behalf of humanity:

I'm back to some Luna Park, or Disneyland forlorn,
seeing coach windows fill up with her voice
as she gives him time to fall in love
and we pass flaked bridges, pubs and villas...
It's almost like being reborn.

The Look of Goodbye is a substantial volume by any standard, over 132 pages, but, because of Robinson's multi-layered treatment of landscape, memory and language, we are invited into a text that is even weightier. This is a collection that needs to be treated with a good deal of respect before one even begins to come to terms with its measure of what Bachelard called 'a felicity of its own'.

Michael Tolkien

Who Can Follow with the Eyes of Sense?*

Anne Beresford   *Collected Poems* (1967-2006), Katabasis, £14.95

Anne Beresford has been noticed in various directories and critical journals but seldom accorded detailed critical attention even for her outstanding recent collections: *No Place for Cowards* (1998) and *Hearing Things* (2002). The 2006 *Collected* now enables us to appreciate the correlated spiritual journey of nine major collections from 1967, as well as some notable new poems. Rather than outline all its complex and varied aspects or assess the work in relation to contemporary achievements, I will examine some of its intrinsic poetic methods and qualities.

This essentially 'contemplative' poet says in the closing words of her 350 page book that she leaves 'the final sentence to the earth.' Not a sentimental or hackneyed idea that unregenerate nature has all the answers, but signifying a consistently 'grounded' outlook, a refusal to have recourse to the esoteric, to cool detachment or otherworldly wishful thinking. The natural world is constantly acknowledged in specific terms as an inevitable part of awareness; but it is never given abstruse or fanciful motivations. As in the prose fiction of Susan Hill, natural phenomena are intense presences that communicate wordlessly but can never be ignored. In 'Letter from the Dead' (*Landscape with Figures*, 1994), the one who revisits offers no illuminations, only an urgent plea that someone still living should relish the world's vitality while she can.

The diverse content of the *Collected* surprises the reader into feeling that human experience in all its repressed psychic corners, superstitions and its delusive hopes and ambitions is somehow touched on. Preconceptions of logical exposition and narrative coherence must be cast aside. The hiatus, or potent unsaid, is frequently used like the tactical rests, without which music would be the poorer, and the result can be a remarkable counterpointing of subjective reflection and stark, unavoidable facts. Starting points may also take the reader off guard: the modest recurrent scenarios of kitchen, garden, village, church often conjure up a variety of perspectives at many levels. The whole collection also establishes a sense of unity with its internally consistent 'world' of references, images, recurrent objects. These are subsumed and drawn upon to give a feeling of continuity. This also applies to a wealth of tales generated by revisiting myth and historical anecdotes: metamorphosed characters and conflicts recur in several books, and interact on one another.

Centres of consciousness are decisive. Particularly in the earlier books the persona whose awareness dictates the poem's development tends to be passive,

---

* Title of a poem in *Hearing Things* (2002)

moved by forces, events, people (primarily masculine and 'monolithic' in behaviour and attitude) who have control over material circumstances and 'externals', unaware of and insensitive to the inner, evasive meanderings of consciousness and imagination.

In later collections this kind of narrator often feels more combative but the sense of frustration continues to suggest the spirit's longing for freedom and expansiveness, a theme that gives rise to many of Anne Beresford's most memorable poems. In one of several reflective monologues set in mythical Hades (from *Footsteps on Snow*, 1972) Eurydice complains of being crushed by divine edicts that ignore the individual's psyche and predicament. 'Bye Laws' from the same book expresses similar constriction in a playful satirical glance at the omnipresent intrusion of petty rules. It begins with an invitation to walk with a mysterious lady who embraces a unicorn and talks of her life being embroidered in sunlight; but you cannot join her: no one may walk on the grass. Then each less and less colourful attempt at imaginative growth is stifled by trite negation until one must conclude: 'there are all makes of cages/even one like a chair/we can be quite comfortable/it is forbidden/to lean out of the window'.

More subtle but still in this vein are two arresting poems from *Sele of the Morning* (1988). 'The Mill Owner's Wife' purports to be a Victorian Tale. In fact the wife's austere, cheerless account of the forbidding environment, her husband's regulated material kindness and her longing for a softer climate suggest more than disappointed incarceration. It is easy to be absorbed by the literal truth of Anne Beresford's direct, unadorned tales; but in this one, as in so many, the understated implications of an asphyxiated spirit wait patiently to be heard, like their narrator. So also in 'The Fallow Land', a plea to someone close and loved to value and savour, and therefore share, the subtle, nourishing details of the here and now. The restless partner is told: 'No words reach you/no raindrops touch you/ you have taken the white road/ turned aside to the fallow land/and it is permitted to weep/while learning to count by years not days.' Emblems are interlaced here, but as with the 'Victorian tale', readers are given room to find their own level of response.

Arguably such poems are ultimately more sustaining and more indicative of the entire canon's poetic strengths than experiments with more direct autobiography set in specific circumstances, such as a series in *The Curving Shore* (1975) which attempts to come to terms with social changes and threats, formative friendships and arresting moments, all from a confused past.

However, that early collection highlights another adjunct of the confused, ruminative narrator: a limboid state of mind, sometimes reminiscent of *The Waste Land*, but without its sardonically despondent voices. 'The Awakening' imagises the after-death reminiscence of figures who have lived out lives as unfulfilled as those depicted above, now in a vapid no-man's-land where a regimented cycle conforms '... to current patterns/walking in yellow lighted streets/ absorbed by our own footsteps/with no experience of joy/and suffering second-hand....We are here in line./It is sufficient.' A predicament conveyed later in the specific, yet nightmare setting of a hotel in 'Night Life' (*No Place for Cowards*, 1998). The inmates are there but not there, like the old French lady who 'offers me a box of half-eaten chocolates/then she adjusts her hat/and seems to evaporate/between two beds and a table.' Part of the appeal here is ambiguity: is it the story-teller or the one observed who is lost between worlds?

Using an apparently routine domestic incident, 'Home Visit' from *Sele of the Morning*, 1988, shows in the context of a one-way dialogue between patient and doctor, a similarly 'lost' state of mind. What is the use of medicines to cure incoherent longings, to make up for the fleeting moments of joy? All this is asked in a manner which suggests the frustration of incoherence. Another instance of this poet's dexterity with broken, faltering monologue. And in every collection we are given hints about kinds of early conditioning that promote such rootless meandering. A notable example is the ironically entitled 'Diploma' from *Songs a Thracian Taught Me* (1980). A certificate for life is earned by the absorption of negative comments about a potentially lively and exciting world, about petty *dos* and *don'ts*, about your ignorance of facts. Characteristic of this poet's subtlety is how an apparent series of childhood memories is told in the confused, haphazard manner in which a child is influenced. Not surprisingly the unremarkable man who emerges promises his wife 'things/which in the end/amounted to misunderstandings.'

Should we infer from these subjections of the passive and intuitive to a world demanding action, enterprise and regulation that Anne Beresford adopts a 'feminist' stance, even though her typically open and elusive manner is in itself the reverse of dogmatic? As a deeply reflective woman writer she articulates a female sensibility, often with attractively barbed humour, implying more than the literal surface of what's depicted, as in this excerpt from 'Letters to Constantine' (from *Sele of the Morning*, 1988):

Some women
are left washing up at weddings
when the family
holding champagne glasses
pose for the festive photograph.

Dizzy, tired out
by the noise of over-excited children
they stand at unfamiliar sinks
and dream of space craft

arriving on the lawn
filling the garden with silent music
exotic flowers and gentle shadows.

Shadows of dreams only
for these women also know
the outcome of weddings…
later at home they remove
their straw hats
and veil their eyes.

That last phrase has moving overtones about the need to repress opinions and insights. But there is no suggestion here or anywhere else that the 'feminine' with all its physical, mental and social ramifications, is the ultimate answer to a history of male dominion and insensitivity, or that the male rôle should be supplanted. Once again though, we feel how the reflective and imaginative aspect within us all is obliged to go to ground and *veil* itself. However, this poem is one of several which focus on conflicts arising from a variety of tensions between the sexes.

I have quoted the only light-hearted moment from these *letters*, a linked series of darkly contemplative pieces in a disarmingly forthright style, conveying a woman's diurnal loneliness during the long absence of a loved one. It is one of many instances where Anne Beresford intensifies a woman's inner life by seeing it lived indoors and looking out, a framework that makes for some of her most engaging poetic drama. The outside is merely a repository of memories, 'natural' presences with their own purposes, or full of items the persona longs to share.

Enclosed is the first autumn leaf
from the ornamental cherry tree
first in the garden to redden and fall.

Night has left behind strange powers –
disturbed, something inside me is crying.
Sun shines on the yellow daisies
pears drop from the old tree
and the wind is gentle.
Whose shadow on my door?
Who spoke my name?

The sequence in its entirety is reminiscent of Tennyson's Mariana poems with their power, as the critic Lyall commented, to suggest 'the correspondence and interaction between the mind and its surroundings, between the situation and the subjective feelings.' 'Relict' (from *Landscape with Figures*, 1994) goes further by conveying the empty domestic routine of a woman drained of purpose and abandoned by a male partner. A well-worn subject is given new life by an unsentimental faithfulness to small objects with their implied bleakness and by a positive moment where an unfaced truth and its consequent emptiness are confronted.

More dramatic but still anchored in palpable emotional and physical conditions is 'Roman Comedy' (from *The Curving Shore*, 1975). One of many vivid dramatisations of the lot of historical figures, it depicts the final crisis of Julia, daughter of the Emperor Augustus, imprisoned for immorality, variously married off, then exiled to die of starvation. Unaffected pathos is created by the interweaving of a torrid setting, ill-assorted memories, the guards' confusion, and semi-delirious monologue. Two juxtaposed poems from the 1994 book are also indicative of a balanced and inclusive attitude to feminine adversity. 'Pysche', among several explorations that take advantage of the wealth of implications in the Cupid/Psyche myth, shows the woman as victim of circumstances beyond her control, yet weighing up her experiences with acceptance. 'Yes that was when she became fully conscious of her plight/and wondered where Amor was/or if he had ever been …/ And later still/when she wept over her cup of nectar/ knowing she would remain/an unknown thread of silk/among the gods.' Then, from modern history, we encounter 'Sarah Coleridge Speaks'. In clear, direct terms an unhearing husband is addressed by the woman who shared without acknowledgement the life of a man who philosophised, made grand poetic gestures, an exhibit visited by admirers who ignored her, and yet in his private moments was consumed by neuroses and terrors that plagued her. She concludes with an inconclusive memory which implies a future with no change:

> And when your friends
> brush past me in the kitchen
> impatient, sneering,
> I relive the time when, far off in Germany,
> your work, your genius undisturbed
> by messages of grief,
> I rested my head
> against the empty cradle.

Even more forthright and uncompromising is 'The Mothers' (from *Hearing Things*, 2002) At one level it is an ironically authoritative appraisal in quasi-biblical tones of womankind as blackened, traduced, even mythologised by male dogma. ('The root of all evil,/she destroys all she gives birth to,/she is the curse of men/and seemingly her children.') Such irony and the disarmingly tender but still double-edged conclusion subtly redeem the poem from feeling like invective or harangue. 'Meanwhile she begs to be re-housed,/her position reassessed./ Having met her personally/I know her to feel lost, confused/and contrite.'

This detached, layered technique points to another decisive facet of Anne Beresford's poetic approach to a wide diversity of human experience. Her spare narrative exposition punctuated by pregnant silences and hiatuses makes for a universal, scaled-down intensity with the timeless resonances peculiar to myth and legend. Though this facilitates her many inspired explorations of Greek myth already alluded to, there are fine poems in this manner with no specific legendary context where time, place and context are left open. Two early poems, 'First Dance' (from *The Curving Shore*, 1972) and 'The Courtship' (from *Songs a Thracian Taught Me*, 1980) might be dreams, fantasy or episodes from the repository of legend, and yet there is a vivid and convincing immediacy of experience. 'September Fable' from the 1980 collection is a simple tale suggesting the intrusion of violence and a hectic time scale divorced from a seasonal pattern into a settled rural way of life, as soldiers seek out a small farmer for official execution. The poem's close fabric defies quotation but notice the pathos distilled into the man's last moments:

> Come morning he stands
> with dew on his feet
> by a grave dug as carefully
> as his asparagus bed.
> 'Bury me here alongside
> my carrots and strawberries.
> I am your man.'

And similar to this quiet hint at the futility of judicial murder is another legend-like depiction of stealthy change in an isolated community. 'Collage' (from the 1972 collection) introduces mysterious cloaked presences who stir up nervous disintegration among people prone to superstition and draw a child into their influence. This implied loss of a simple, unsophisticated way of life is worth more than any environmental hand-wringing or verbal assault on faceless bureaucracy. It is a haunting, half-articulate tale that suggests confusion, helplessness, and something irreversible:

> It was the child who broke the spell
> crept out one morning
> to search for primroses
> forgot the grey shapes
> half hidden by the trees
>
> One of us saw him
> running breathless
> down the avenue
> towards the downs
> a last speck of white.
>
> Why? cried his mother
> banging her head against stones
> why? she wept
> into her hands…

Equivalent work in the later collections is more matter-of-fact and confiding, though no less arresting. One from a series of such poems in *No Place for Cowards* (1998) is 'The Uninvited.' Its wild horses of mythical vigour and agility feel like an emblem for morally unregenerate, untameable forces that cannot be ignored as they charge across conventional, comfortable barriers, notably from a wilderness into a garden; but within the subtext there are questions about the conflict of the material and spiritual, taking responsibility for actions, acknowledging the world in all its often repellent complexity. ('To enclose them/in promises of heather-covered moors/proves useless,/to plead work or declining years/only laughable./ They trample on skeletons/not understanding bones,/they know nothing of reality, nothing of evil.') The creation of animal legend without anthropomorphic taming down or sentimentality is also achieved in the moving yet witty monologue, 'Heron' (*Hearing Things*, 2002). An authentic bird in all its habits and behaviour, it emerges as another of many figures in these poems whose appearance belies their significance and who are enlightened by apparently unspectacular experience: 'and though I could tell you tales/which would rival the Arabian Knights-/for I have witnessed and heard strange things/when waiting patiently, half-hidden in nettles/or reeds, by an out-of-the-way stream-/my nature is solitary and quiet./ Read what you can of my secrets/ in my long-winged flight across your path.' Note how the final injunction typifies this poet's delight in a conundrum, which challenges the reader to think emblematically.

Complementary poems in the same book carry further this mythical imagising of dimly-grasped forces, forgotten or sanitised in a world absorbed with one-dimensional 'realities'. 'Two Figures and a Baby' sketches a gruesome nocturnal rite with overtones of black witchcraft, performed by figures that almost merge with their natural surroundings and make promises of revelations, all observed with scepticism by onlookers, who nevertheless admit the impact on themselves and their surroundings. 'The Chariot', in contrast, adapts Elisha's witnessing of his father Elijah's apotheosis by means of whirlwind-driven fiery chariot and steeds (2 *Kings*, ii). Set in a brightly illuminated landscape, it suggests a mystical, elevating experience with the terrors of transfiguration, a moment of revelation awaited, its scale never anticipated. Drama builds up through a companionable, confiding presence reminiscent of Christ on the road to Emmaus, peaks with the approach of what might be cloud, chariot or wall of fire, and the overwhelming revelation that we are part of an imponderable whole. But then the narrator is 'alone between sea and heather,/holding a cloak of darkness in hands/which seemed suddenly alien.' Once more he's confronted with the limits of being human and living out the allotted span. Is such commerce with the transcendental too costly? Like other poems referred to this is not conventionally 'spiritual'. It derives from an awareness of the conflicts that arise from our place 'on this isthmus of a middle state', caught between aspirations and earthly roots.

'Rootedness' is a constant feature of what might be called poems that are concerned more specifically with a spiritual journey, though it is to some extent a misleading subdivision, since every poem in the *Collected* is part of a lifelong tentative enquiry into what makes us human and how we live poised between various needs and appetites. Which is no doubt why an attractive hallmark of the more 'metaphysical' poems is their comprehensiveness, a refusal to allow artificial and misleading divisions between the material and spiritual, the symbol and the symbolised, 'real' and 'unreal'. The earliest collections are apt to be preoccupied by memories, often fragmented and confused, that hint at wider, indefinable realities; but in *The Curving Shore* (1975) a sense of 'pilgrimage' begins. The soul's life is a haphazard journey requiring full engagement with the world as it is, but towards a gradually emerging goal. Accompanying it, but taking all kinds of elusive and unpredictable forms, there is a presence who tests, guides, reassures, as in the 'The Comforter': 'Days drop with the leaves/are trodden into the earth-vanish. When? I ask him. Now?/ he ruffles my hair with long fingers./He waits./High time to start back, a long walk,/and much will have changed.'

In a sense the poetry is also on a pilgrimage: it takes many years to arrive at a fully convincing medium to express this inner life and quest. Throughout, the true measure of meaningful vision is 'humanity' in all its physical and mental complexity. 'Christ Tempted by the Devil', from the 1975 collection, makes this clear with its deliberately misleading title, briefly digesting the forty days in the wilderness to conclude: 'the real test would come/when the drops of sweat/fell on rough grass/the cicadas singing out the desolate night/while his friends slept.' But the point is more arrestingly conveyed in 'Leiston Abbey' from *Songs a Thracian Taught Me* (1980), indicating that Anne Beresford's most disturbing and memorable poems surprise us out of easy, blinkered contentment with surfaces. Two people visit ruins in a meditative, prayerful mood, and notice a rabbit carved in stone. Aesthetically pleasing, it adds to the sense of peace and stillness, its folded paws merging with greenery; and then: 'The stone moves gently/as though a heart were beating quickly./ And bending down I see that the stone/is alive and suffering./This is its sanctuary./ Nothing makes sense/ with the heavy clouds spitting rain/onto the rabbit, its eyes obliterated/by the large swellings of diseased flesh.' Such insistence on inclusive reality is found in another context in the same book. 'Elusive Love Poem' addresses the 'Master of Disguises' as 'near' in a dirty train full of ill-assorted people, and not because the narrator is actually on a pilgrimage. 'All passengers pale and anxious./The effects of hard winter?/ Industrial turmoil?/We are sceptical pilgrims/knowing well that the world has not/promised anything to anybody./ Your hand presses my heart –/the falcon does not struggle when caught./Your words are always with me./One day I will sing unrestricted.' Without the acceptance of the here and now and how it is peopled, and the unconditional love this must generate in the heart, there can be no comprehensive, 'unrestricted' celebration.

Anne Beresford's more directly theological poems, though often intended to relate to contiguous, contrasting pieces, are sometimes less convincing than those which dramatise an indirect apprehension of the numinous in unlikely places. Yet some of these reflections have the sinewy compactness of R.S.Thomas's verse: direct but leaving a sense of unplumbed mystery; peculiarly abstract and specific all at once. Two poems from *Landscape with Figures* (1994) stand out in

166

this respect. 'Omens' digests with an undertow of wit the Old Testament history of Yahweh the tormentor, a theology which results in subtle spiritual paralysis: 'but Yahweh's head is balder/his breathing slower, heavier/his rage is calculating/ For the first time prophets raise their heads/anxious/silent.' So, too, in 'The Surprise' the divine manipulator is caricatured: 'And God said:/Let them be pushed/through a corridor/into the light/ready/to be pushed/through a corridor/ into the dark/.../Hope shall be their despair.' Two gnomic poems in *Hearing Things* (2002) are just as laconic but far-removed from this biblically portentous intonation, and they present stylistically and tonally distinct answers to such perversely one-dimensional theology. 'St Francis on the Mountain' suggests by means of the contemplative's ambiguous perceptions that truth is an amalgam of contradictions and the perception of it only earned by strenuously passive acceptance. The imagery and diction are geared with precision to voice this hard-earned insight: 'The more he felt, the clearer he saw/how the world became a whirling fire/and the pain of detachment a union/with what had always been.' In 'Destiny' the meditative spirit is reassured by gentle implication through images of drifting into and merging with a flourishing landscape, that there will be no intervention by some alien force, since the comprehensive quality of reflection is what moves the soul forward. Another way of suggesting that the individual, not some supernatural ogre, determines his/her spiritual destiny.

Two poems from *No Place for Cowards* (1998) with a narrator confiding in the individual soul, are a variation on this idea. 'Crossing Over' combines quietly intractable images of the physical world with a strange angle on near-death experiences that result in a new scale of perceptions and reactions. 'Washed Up' envisages a sea/swimmer experience to present this in-between world, or even the final passing away with its reluctance and sense of being caught between impressions. Two excerpts mark out delicacy in depicting the unknowable with what I can only call convincingly contrived lack of specificity.

How had it come to this
how could he have imagined
when manoeuvring seas
heavy or placid –
his natural habitat–
that he would land up here?

– – – – – – – – – – – – – –

His body becomes unfamiliar
dry, colder, he can feel it wither
his eyes
dimmed
survey a lost world
and he swallows its beauty
as he would a shoal of fish.

Perhaps the revisiting of biblical tales and episodes is an adjunct of all these explorations. Poems of this kind, whether early or late, are well-crafted and colourful, but they tend to feel too contrived and certainly less 'universal' than writing in a more broadly 'mythical' mode. The problem for today's reader is manifold. Either the context and its diverse interpretations are inaccessible, as the bible is no longer a common repository of reference, or for the initiated such monologues may feel too refined and sophisticated in tone. However, there are exceptions. In 'Murder' (*Hearing Things*, 2002) a disinterested voice comments on Cain's feelings over his treatment of Abel. It makes this moment feel formative of the human conscience for all time. 'Cain pale with distress/pondered on the word 'sin'/not sure of its meaning./And words which had not been invented/grew up in the soil he had tilled/ nourished by blood and bone.' Likewise 'Scenes from St. John's Gospel' in *New Poems* have the same poignancy, allowing telling detail to speak for itself in the spirit of the gospel narratives, yet implying a sense of revelation and of a presence that transforms. Qualities particularly present in reflections on Magdalen, the woman by the well at Sychar, and the woman taken in adultery ('In Flagrante Delicto') who finds herself in the town square

> which smells of animal –
> where she'd been dragged,
> now stood there
> wondering what the man –
> with dirty feet –
> was writing in the sandy soil,
> wondering if death was nearer than she'd thought.
>
> And then silence.
> The two of them suddenly alone
> sun very hot for the time of day.

To return to 'pilgrimage', there are two revealing poems at the beginning of *No Place for Cowards* (1998): 'February for the Crazy Pilgrim' and 'The Crazy Pilgrim in Conversation'. These assert the mutual vibrancy of body and spirit, distil Anne Beresford's attitudes to deceptively acceptable divisions between levels of experience, suggest what her work has amounted to and where it must lead.

> I'll not creep through each day
> head bowed, feet tentative
> Away with amulets/sprigs of mistletoe
> white heather
> there's no place for superstition…
>
> It is remarkable
> to conceive a desire for a new life

when the present one is only slightly worn
but I am fearful of losing myself
losing the world would be no loss
but imagine losing oneself
imagine looking in the mirror
 and not being there.

There is no quick fix and we must face up to contradictions. The term 'crazy' has significance similar to that in W.B. Yeats' *Words for Music Perhaps* (1932), a series of lyrics uttered by Crazy Jane, crazy in the sense of being finely cracked through the wear and tear of experience, as well as dementedly frank. Part of one of her dialogues with the bishop is most indicative: 'Love has pitched his tent in/The place of excrement./ For nothing can be sole or whole/That has not been rent.' There's no room for over-refinement, no point in not squaring up to who you are and what you experience. Hence 'no place for cowards' and as for *Hearing Things*, its title poem set disarmingly in a garden, warns us about 'overfabrication': allow what comes to you to form the poem, which does not mean to abandon your art, rather to match what's written with the quality of experience. So it is by a process of 'realisation' or 'fulfilment' rather than by what critics love to call 'development' that the last two published collections include more direct engagement with the seamier side of human behaviour and experience.

Perhaps the most outstanding of these are informed by an acute but never despondent sense of mortality. To mention just a few (three of which envisage male protagonists) indicates their range of subject matter and technique. The tale of a faux pas by 'George Eliot's Piano Tuner' is told in a brisk form that feels as tight-lipped as those who observe the events. There's humour, implicit pathos and a sharp glance at bourgeois preciousness that shows more concern for removing vomit from silk wallpaper than for the lot of one 'probably dying of TB/ or mortification.' 'Elgar' combines a fragmented style with mundane details to identify with the composer's inclusive artistic impulses. His creative spirit and the emotional, practical realities of his life are fused into a memorable portrait. The quasi-musical finale, following the death of his wife, interweaves nostalgia and living objects:

he walked in late autumn
under the trees in brown afternoons
thought of the soft skin on her neck
where her necklace lay.
Those words never spoken.

A last adagio orchestrated in his brain
not meant for human ears,
celebrated by trees
the copper of beech

knotty trunks of oak
vibrating in wild winds
blown from nowhere.

'Death on the NHS' employs dry, restrained humour to rein in felt but unspoken frustration. The health machine feels like a faceless juggernaut with its own detached programme, as suggested in this densely packed metaphor: 'The end was a shattered lamp/paramedics trampling broken glass/and kindness underfoot.' Officialdom displaces feeling: 'You can't see the dead without an appointment/ and with one you must wait/but not here/half in, half out of a busy ward/with telephones ringing/nurses scurrying and raised voices.' As in the Collected's best meditative writing we are disturbed but allowed room to supply our own details. In 'The Sale of Mr Buzby's House' we encounter just one example of this poet's talent for expressing bereavement in its many aspects. Here one is moved not just by the breaking of long attachment to various items, but by the way this is reported in a sympathetic yet matter-of fact voice, which hints that the recipient of the news, or we ourselves, realise how little the narrator understands, even in the restrained closing lines:

Did I tell you about the piano?
Once, he played me a nocturne,
D Flat major, he told me.
I listened as the sun dipped into night
and I wept a little
at the closing bars.
His fingers were so delicate.

Such a gentle threnody, and yet the style works quietly below the surface with the metaphor of diminishing light and the final metonymy for the fragile gift of life.

The informing spirit of this whole collection is openness and heartfelt response to what happens, whether or not it is palatable or 'convenient.' 'Angels' (*Hearing Things*, 2002) is indicative. They are not shining presences but unlikely bearers of unexpected blessings to which you may or may not respond. ('Only afterwards a smile or a word/suddenly becomes illuminated.') Similarly, the contiguous 'List for the Gardener'. He never comes, his physical appearance can't be recalled or predicted, and the list of disorder grows, perhaps another emblem for patiently awaiting the clear path of illumination. But the conclusion is especially apt: 'We'll make a new list to leave on the kitchen table/Then someone will find it and say:/ Is this the beginning of a new poem?' Poetry like angels consists of apparently off-beat concerns and encounters. Anne Beresford has gauged with increasing subtlety what kinds of insights these may provide.

Benjamin Bird

'The virtue of the mind'

The status of mind in George Oppen's *The Materials, This In Which,* and *Of Being Numerous.*

Critical work on George Oppen is united in noting the importance of the interconnected themes of the accuracy of perception and the existence of reality to Oppen's poetry. Yet, critics have differed significantly over the degree of certainty and stability that Oppen attributes to the relationship between consciousness and the world of objects, with which so much of his poetry is concerned. Commentators have frequently attempted the difficult task of summarizing Oppen's complex approach to these issues. Edward Hirsch, for example, suggests that Oppen's work questions whether 'the poet can transcend his own subjectivity to see things as they really are' and concludes that Oppen's is a poetic oeuvre of 'the isolated mind' (Hirsch 170). More recently, Peter Nicholls has argued for the opposite position, that Oppen's discovery of Jacques Maritain, in the years before his return to poetry, provided him with 'a certitude of the interiority of the human being, and its importance; a certitude that between man and the world there is an invisible relationship deeper than any material interconnection' (Nicholls 15). David McAleavey, meanwhile, asserts that it is 'Oppen's very unwillingness to valance any set of assumptions about the mind and the process of the world which informs his work. Because his skepticism is immense, conclusive speech is difficult for him' (McAleavey 382).

These critical positions are notable for their insistence that Oppen maintains a relatively stable position on mind in his later poetry. Like McAleavey, I accept that the evidence of Oppen's poetry forbids the conclusion that he adopted a single, dogmatic position on mind, but, by contrast with McAleavey's belief in Oppen's thoroughgoing 'skepticism', I argue that his work is permeated by an anxiety about the ontological status of mind, which causes him to oscillate between often radically different positions on the intrinsic nature and capacities of consciousness. This uncertainty in Oppen's poetry is typical of the emergent postmodernity in which the later part of his career was situated and is intimately connected to his political views and his relationship to political action. His work often implies that political action only becomes feasible if, as he told L.S. Dembo, one believes 'that consciousness exists and that it is consciousness of something' and, consequently, it often demonstrates a near obsessive concern with the grounds for belief in the reality of consciousness and the accuracy of perception (Dembo 163). Although Oppen rejected the idea of overtly 'political poetry', or 'poetry as being politically efficacious', his work demonstrates a need to establish the possibility of a progressive politics, by convincing himself of the innate substance and strength of the mind that must engage in such activism (174).

These concerns make his oeuvre particularly apposite to the atmosphere of scepticism about the reliability, and reality, of consciousness that has characterized the postwar era. During the almost thirty year hiatus in Oppen's publishing career, numerous theories emerged that reduced the human mind to what John R. Searle has called 'publicly observable mental phenomena' and neglected the fundamentally subjective nature of consciousness; that, as Searle points out, 'its ontology is a first-person ontology' (*Rediscovery* 4, 17). Proponents of artificial intelligence argued that computer technology might simulate or replace human thought; increasingly sophisticated neuroscience explained thought with reference to the activity of fibres and neurons in the brain; the behaviourism of B.F. Skinner, with its emphasis on 'observing and describing' behaviour at the expense of experience, became the dominant method in American psychology (Smith 270). This philosophical milieu provided fertile territory for Oppen's wish to explore the 'political efficacy' of consciousness itself. Such widespread distrust of human perception enabled, and challenged, him to test what he told Reinhold Schiffer was his 'realist philosophy and approach', which 'means that it's impossible to doubt the existence of the consciousness itself' and its access to the world; that 'it carries in itself and by itself the fact of actualness' (Schiffer 18).

In the same interview, Oppen declared that poetry served him as 'a test of conviction' or 'truth' and that, 'within the writing of the poem…you discover what you believe and what you don't believe' (20). Oppen's three collections of the nineteen sixties, *The Materials* (1962), *This In Which* (1965), and *Of Being Numerous* (1968), serve precisely as such 'tests of conviction'. They constitute a kind of trilogy on the reliability of perception and the reality of consciousness and, although these questions are explored in Oppen's subsequent collections, his discussions there do not go significantly beyond the contents of these books. The title *The Materials* refers to the objects of perception, but also to the concatenation of mind and body that constructs the human subject. It is the implications of these 'materials' for the nature of existence and of consciousness that form the basis of Oppen's explorations in this collection. *This In Which* refers directly to the felt interiority of consciousness and the potential for insularity and isolation, if mind proves incapable of reliable perception. *Of Being Numerous* responds to this terrifying possibility of isolation, and the doubt that it creates about the existence of mind and self, by exploring whether identity might be found or constructed in a sense of communal solidarity that transcends the apparently intractable mind-world relation.

'Image of the Engine', the second poem of *The Materials*, broaches one of the most controversial questions of postwar philosophy of mind: the ontological relationship between mind and machine (*NCP* 40). The wry cranial metaphor of the opening line, 'Likely as not a ruined head gasket', implies that, given the purely physical basis of consciousness, it may be considered comparable to any mechanical device. Oppen pushes the analogy to an extreme point, raising the possibility that the machine shares a quasi-spiritual level of intuitive understanding with humanity, that 'from the cooling steel' may emerge 'A still and quiet angel of knowledge and comprehension'. Yet, section two expresses dissatisfaction with this notion, asserting the 'image of the engine / That stops' to be a 'definition of mortality' and declaring 'We cannot live on that' (40). The poem's final section opens with the quotation '*Also he has set the world in their hearts*', introducing a pervasive theme of the collection, that, in spite of feelings of alienation, consciousness remains capable of communion with the world. The lines that follow, 'From lumps, chunks, / We are locked out' are ambiguous in the context of what precedes them, but may be read as articulating the alienation from matter that attends the idea of mind as computer, or mere mechanism (42). As Searle has argued, the computer is ignorant of the outside world and treats signifiers as isolated counters that refer to nothing (*Minds* 371). He contends that

> What it does is to manipulate formal symbols. The fact that the programmer and the interpreter of the computer output use the symbols to stand for objects in the world is totally beyond the scope of the computer. (371)

The poem ends with the image of humanity's 'beautiful bony children' abandoning 'The lost / Glitter of the stores' and engaging in a quest for 'Earth, water, the tremendous / Surface'. This pursuit of nature leads to strong affirmation of the link between inside and outside. Sifting the contents of 'Earth' and 'Water' leads to an unexpected inward journey and the epiphanic discovery of the 'heart thundering / Absolute desire' (*NCP* 42).

The Materials contains a number of poems that assert precisely this link between subjectivity and external object, which is often experienced as a dialectical process of production, in which mind and world both undergo significant change. 'Product', for example, concludes a depiction of Oppen's beloved New England boats and the 'dry tools / And the dry New England hands' that construct them, with lines that refuse even to distinguish between inside and outside: 'What I've seen / Is all I've found: myself' (61). 'Sara in her Father's Arms', similarly, compares the child to a 'violent, diligent seed' and wonders 'What will she make of a world / Do you suppose, Max, of which she is made' (51). This mind-world relation seems to go somewhat beyond what Oppen called his 'realist' approach and accords with his belief, which he also conveyed to Schiffer, that 'one's subjectivity is also encountered, not found'; discovered through a productive partnership of interior and exterior (Schiffer 19). In Oppen's work, this notion of interdependence has ineluctable political implications. The title of 'Myself I Sing' might suggest solipsism, but, in fact, addresses the responsibilities of the individual for the community and the indissoluble bond between them (*NCP* 56-7). The line 'Pioneers! But trailer people?', with its allusion to both Whitman and Cather, is devastating in its juxtaposition of the American tradition of pastoralism with a degrading level of poverty, from which the national literature has often shied away. Oppen describes in elliptical terms what may be the purchase of a 'A pocket knife, //A tool', from such a 'trailer' person, an incident that leads, in almost Wordsworthian fashion, to philosophical meditation on the relationship between them. The emotional impact of the encounter leads Oppen to reassert the interdependence of world and subjectivity, declaring that 'I think myself / Is what I've seen and not myself'. Yet, nevertheless, the tool salesman suggests to him the image of 'A man marooned' who 'No longer looks for ships, imagines / Anything on the horizon' (56) and, momentarily, causes him to wonder anxiously if humanity is 'Incapable of contact / Save in incidents' (56-7). The poem closes with an assertion of unity that seems part confident belief in the mind's access to the world and part urgent response to the same call of 'conscience' that made Oppen a political activist (Dembo 174).

> And yet at night
> Their weight is part of mine.
> For we are all housed now, all in our apartments,
> The world untended to, unwatched.
> And there is nothing left out there
> As night falls, but the rocks (*NCP* 57)

Such references to 'the rocks', or 'rock', are numerous in *The Materials* and are often emblematic of the ineluctable 'actualness' of reality and the harsh challenges it poses. At the end of 'Myself I Sing', the image also seems to convey the harsh ambivalence felt by the poet, in recognizing a shared humanity, while remaining impotent to effect meaningful economic change.

'Population', the third poem of *The Materials*, ends with a similar reference to rock, this time in the form of an allusion to T.S. Eliot's *The Dry Salvages*. Oppen's description of the 'Populace' finding 'the rough deck / Inhabited, and what it always was' recalls Eliot's assertion of the subsistence of certain aspects of mental and emotional life in section two of that poem (*NCP* 43). Describing what he calls 'moments of agony' as 'permanent with such permanence as time has', Eliot compares the mind's anguish to a rock that, 'On a halcyon day', 'is merely a monument', 'but in the sombre season / Or the sudden fury, is what it always was' (*Salvages* 29). Oppen eventually reinterprets Eliot's dark warning of the persistence of mental experience as a source of comfort in a postmodern environment, in which consciousness is often experienced as fragmentary or unreal. However, 'Population' begins in a mood of near despair, comparing our contemporary state to 'a flat sea'. 'Here is where we are', the poem laments, 'the empty reaches / Empty of ourselves'. In this forbidding environment, a vacuous sense of self is compounded by a mind that appears vulnerable to collapse: the following stanza reads, 'Where dark, light, sound / Shatter the mind born / Alone to ocean'. Oppen once noted in a letter that 'There seems to me no problem for an artist more difficult than separating the brute ego, the accidents of the ego, from the self which perceives' (*Letters* 56-7). Allowing for the replacement of the term 'ego' by 'mind', this poem appears to be attempting something very close to this 'difficult' separation. Indeed, the way Oppen follows his reference to the 'Empty' self with lines describing the destruction of the shattered 'mind' suggests that the poem may even posit a causal relationship between these entities; explaining the apparent hollowness of contemporary subjectivity by the vulnerability of 'mind'. 'Population' ends in a way that anticipates the later concerns of *Of Being Numerous* imagining the alienation of the community redeemed by the fact 'we are / A crowd, a population, those / Born, those not yet dead'. Eliot's threatening 'rock' becomes the reassuring presence and accessibility of other human subjects. A sense of mind and self as unreal is ameliorated, if not wholly banished, by 'finding / Incredibly under the sense the rough deck / Inhabited, and what it always was' (*NCP* 43).

In interview, Oppen makes clear that the phrase *This In Which* is a direct reference to consciousness (Dembo 63). It is drawn directly from 'Psalm', which depicts 'wild deer' and repeatedly draws attention to their reality, in exclamatory lines such as 'That they are there!' Its final stanza reads

> The small nouns
> Crying faith
> In this in which the wild deer
> Startle, and stare out. (*NCP* 99)

Oppen comments that the poem concerns the 'act of faith' that constitutes belief in the reality of consciousness, that he is emphasizing 'this in which the thing takes place, this thing is here, and that these things do take place' (Dembo 163). As the title suggests, the collection is more firmly anchored in the interior space of consciousness and the book shows greater concern than its predecessors with examining a wide variety of psychological experience in American culture. It also appears more prone to the anxiety that the mind may be irrevocably isolated from the world. 'Psalm' is rare, in this volume, in affirming the reliability of consciousness. 'Giovanni's *Rape of the Sabine Women* at Wildenstein's', for example, limns a notion of mind as self-destructive, yet incapable of engagement with reality and impotent to affect the nature of being. Oppen describes one character in the painting as offering

> shelter
> From the winds
> The winds that lie
> In the mind,
> The ruinous winds
> 'Powerless to affect
> The intensity of what is'

In the remainder of the poem, he seems to allegorize consciousness as a 'little boat', stranded 'At sea', and speculates that his increasing alienation is structural; that selfhood is situated 'Beyond the heart, the center of the thing / And cannot praise it / As he would want to' (*NCP* 112). In any case, the 'act of faith' that he has insisted underpins his belief in consciousness is less evident here: he emphasizes the 'long helplessness' of the mind's 'boat' and notes sorrowfully that

> one needs such faith,
> Such faith in it
> In the whole thing
> more than I,
> Or they, have had in songs (113)

Several poems connect this alienation with the technologies of contemporary capitalism or the excessive individual wealth that the system generates. The volume's first poem, 'Technologies', takes an ambivalent view of its subject. Its comparison of the emergence of various technologies to 'a sort of summer', in which 'the hard buds blossom / Into feminine profusion' conveys an initial sense of such technics as a fertile addition to civilization (93). Yet, the wording is strikingly close to that of Heidegger's essay 'The Question of Technology', in which he refers to those technological inventions with their intellectual roots in the Renaissance, as having burst 'into bloom' in modernity (Heidegger 11). As Oppen has made clear the importance of Heidegger's thought to his work, the similarity is unlikely to be coincidental and, in light of Heidegger's hostility to twentieth-century technology, the reference suggests, at least, a degree of scepticism towards these contemporary 'blooms' (Dembo 169). Moreover, the 'feminine' technics are associated with a distorted and limited consciousness, what Oppen calls 'the little core of oneself', or 'The inelegant heart / Which cannot grasp / The world' (*NCP* 93). The second half of the poem warns explicitly against the destructive potential of technology. It hints that, under its new technocratic regimen, the 'business //Of the days' will 'distract' from intellectual life, before, rather dramatically, imagining the technological foe

> Arriving
> Out of uncivil
> Air
> Evil
> As a hawk (94)

By contrast, 'The Guest Room' perceives excessive wealth as an impediment to a meaningful relationship between mind and world. Its title connotes impermanence or vagrancy and, accordingly, it begins by warning that 'There is in age / The risk that the mind / Reach / Into homelessness, "nowhere to return"'. The juxtaposition of this prophecy of mental isolation and rootlessness with a violent rejection of 'the noise of wealth, / The clamor of wealth', as 'the voice / Of Hell' seems to imply a causal link between the two (107). The connection is confirmed within a few lines, when 'The great house / With its servants' is described as 'safe harbor / In which the heart sinks, closes now like a fortress' (107-108). Oppen offers the possibility of what Heidegger would call a 'saving power', in the form of 'The virtue of the mind', which 'Is that emotion / Which causes / To see' (107). In interview, Oppen has distinguished between 'the neurosensitivity of the eye and the act of seeing', which he associates with 'tremendous emotional response' and stated that 'those who lack it I despair of. And that's when the poems sort of stagger now and then, when I talk about despair' (Dembo 173). 'The Guest Room' contains just such a moment of 'staggering' and 'despair'. The mention of 'that emotion / Which causes / To see' is followed by the stammering lines 'Virtue...// Virtue...?', which, in their hesitancy and shocked repetition, appear mimetic of Oppen's horror at the absence of such redemptive 'emotional response' in the homes of the wealthy.

Norman M. Finkelstein has argued that, in this volume, Oppen's belief in perception is undercut by the 'obvious inadequacies of language' (Finkelstein 365). However, I read Oppen's recurrent references to language as the displacement of more fundamental doubts about the capacities of consciousness, which he sometimes seeks to ameliorate or rationalize. 'A Language of New York', for example, opens with discussion of the sense of unreality that attends contemporary capitalism and the scepticism it creates regarding the mind's ability to grasp or penetrate the concrete, but shifts into a meditation on the linguistic, before dropping its doubtful tone altogether. It begins by addressing New York as 'A city of the corporations / Glassed / In dreams' and associating it with a suspicion that 'the mineral fact' of these structures is 'impenetrable / As the world, if it is matter / Is impenetrable'. Its second section remarks on the participants of this forbidding system: the 'shoppers, / Choosers, judges', whose sensibilities appear largely deadened. In Oppen's words, they

> develop
> Argument in order to speak, they become
> unreal, unreal, life loses
> solidity, loses extent (*NCP* 114)

This 'unreal' loss of 'solidity' is very much like the experience of the schizophrenic, as described by Deleuze and Guattari. Their notional child of capitalism lives at one remove from reality, with a psychical life organized by 'the code of delirium or desire', which 'proves to have an extraordinary fluidity' (*Anti-Oedipus* 15). Like Oppen's somnolent victims, whose lives lack 'extent', this 'capitalist being' imagines itself as 'a body without organs' (10), caught within a system where 'There is no such thing as man or nature now, only a process that produces the one within the other' (2). The passage is an example of what Oppen has called 'my idea of categories of realness', which he explains as a 'sense of the greater reality of certain kinds of objects than others' (Dembo 167-168).

Yet, in 'A Language of New York', Oppen quickly retreats from this scathing attack on contemporary consciousness. He reminds himself of the army life he spent with his supposed social inferiors, who were often 'more capable than I', and questions his right, in such a context, to 'talk / Distantly of "the People"' (115). Moreover, he abandons discussion of the mind, taking refuge in the notion that language is to blame for the sense of unreality and alienation that he perceives around him. In section four, he states that it is 'Possible / To use / Words provided one treat them / As enemies', before redefining them as

> Ghosts
> Which have run mad
> In the subways
> And of course the institutions
> And the banks.

Rather than confront his daunting anxiety that consciousness may be incapable of responding to the abstractions of postmodern capitalism, Oppen concludes that the most pressing problem may be linguistic. This presents him with a far more manageable difficulty: after all, language is his own area of expertise as a poet and a space in which he can at least construct a substantial response. Of words, he suggests hopefully that 'If one captures them', 'proceeding / Carefully they will restore / I hope to meaning and to sense' (116). By the final sections of the poem, Oppen avoids the question of consciousness altogether, preferring to refer directly to the 'actualness' of reality. Section six is addressed to his daughter and asserts the diachronic existence of 'a brick / In a brick wall' (117) that 'was waiting here when you were born' (118).

In 'Five Poems About Poetry', Oppen seeks an evolutionary explanation for the weaknesses he observes in consciousness. In the fifth of these poems, 'From Virgil', he hints at the destructive effects of untrammeled self-interest on the mind, declaring that

> Mind
> Has evolved
> Too long
> If 'life is a search
> For advantage.' (104)

In his letters, at this time, Oppen demonstrates a similar scepticism about the direction of mental evolution and expresses doubts concerning the capacity of consciousness, in most people, to develop at all productively. After the publication of *This In Which*, he wrote that 'It is really true that evolution has gone too far', and continued, 'The evolution of the mind…is simply not viable without a conscious effort, a conscious invention on the part of the mass of people which seems simply impossible' (*Letters* 130). The twin determining factors of capitalism and natural selection also undermine Oppen's faith in the agency of consciousness, causing him to ask, without offering a reply, 'At whose behest does the mind think?' (104). The first poem of the group, 'The Gesture', takes a similar view of the corrupting effects of capitalism, insisting that the question 'How does one hold something / In the mind which he intends / To grasp' has become inseparable from the inquiry, 'how does the salesman / Hold a bauble he intends / To sell?'. The following poem, 'The Little Hole', is among Oppen's most damning commentaries on contemporary consciousness, in its suggestion that the human mind has been deprived of autonomy to the extent that the senses merely lay the human subject open to the machinations of a hostile reality. As Oppen has it, 'The little hole in the eye' 'Has exposed us naked / To the world' (101):

> Blankly the world
> Looks in
> And we compose
> Colors
> And the sense
> Of home (102)

Like Deleuze and Guattari, Oppen seems to depict a being that 'experiences… nature as a process of production' (*Anti-Oedipus* 3) and has become unable to distinguish between the 'self and the non-self', or the 'outside and inside' (2). The final poem of the collection 'World, World – ' responds in a way that anticipates *Of Being Numerous*, by seeking to overcome or transcend the limitations of contemporary perception through human solidarity. Oppen dismisses those that 'will not look' and 'are not pierced' by their fellow man, insisting that 'One cannot count them / Tho they are present', and defines his aspiration, in these unpropitious circumstances, as 'the act of being / More than oneself' (*NCP* 159). The precise nature of this seemingly laudable aim is left notably vague, especially in terms of how such self-transcendence and intersubjectivity are to be achieved, in the context of thoroughgoing doubt about the mind's abilities. It is an unresolved difficulty that lies at the heart of Oppen's next project, and his last poetry collection of the 1960s, *Of Being Numerous*.

Of Being Numerous attempts the challenging task of formulating a response to the despairing scepticism that pervades large parts of *This In Which*. It foregrounds its relation to the previous volume, by including a number of extended quotations from it, many as full sections of the collection's eponymous poem. These excerpts are often those most associated with the suspicion of consciousness that dominates that text. More than one is taken from 'A Language of NewYork', including passages preoccupied by the unreality of 'A city of the corporations' (164) and the enervated existence of consumers that 'loses solidity, loses extent' (170). Such absorption of large portions of *This In Which* signals acceptance of many of its premises. Indeed, Oppen acknowledged that the isolation of mind and self was the starting point of the collection. For him, these poems are concerned with 'the learning that one is, after all, just oneself and in the end is rooted in the singular' (Dembo 172). In fact, if anything, in this volume, Oppen's expressions of distrust of the mind become more explicit. In section twenty-six, for example, we read of

179

> The power of the mind, the
> Power and weight
> Of the mind which
> Is not enough, it is nothing
> And does nothing
> Against the natural world

Moreover, the 'rock', which often symbolized the reassuring veracity of reality in Oppen's earlier work, has now become 'The fatal rock / Which is the world', affirming the inadequacy of mind confronted by dangerous reality (179). At times, the poem laments the insularity of the mind, which, it implies, must inevitably lead to social fragmentation. In section five, for example, Oppen writes of 'consciousness / Which has nothing to gain, which awaits nothing, / Which loves itself' (165).

Yet, in this volume, Oppen is unwilling to accept the pessimism implied by such a dismissive view of consciousness and seeks refuge in an ethic of human communality, in which distrust of mind might be dissolved in the alchemy of intersubjective union. As he told L.S. Dembo, in 'Of Being Numerous' he wrote 'a whole poem to establish, if I could, the concept of humanity, a concept without which we can't live' (173). Oppen takes as his starting point the story of 'Crusoe' and interprets the fictional sailor's desperation for social contact as exemplary of the human need for fellowship. Oppen emphasizes that the isolation he explored in *This In Which* is ultimately intolerable for the human subject. He states that

> Obsessed, bewildered
> By the shipwreck
> Of the singular
> We have chosen the meaning
> Of being numerous (166)

and goes on to raise the possibility that excessive solitude may exacerbate a sense of alienation from mundane reality, speaking of 'The unearthly bonds / Of the singular' (167).

In spite of the poem's obvious horror at 'the shipwreck / Of the singular', the phrase 'Being numerous' is a strikingly ambivalent working definition of community. It implies coexistence, but does not necessarily include meaningful contact between its participants and suggests that what Oppen calls the 'concept of humanity' is as yet only an abstract notion, which has still to be formulated or proven. The philosophical difficulty at the heart of the poem's project is whether human relationships are feasible, given the flawed consciousness that Oppen has suggested lacks reliable access to reality. Indeed, as the poem goes on, it becomes clear that much of the social activity Oppen describes is actually motivated by the mind's despairing need to confirm its own existence and that of the body. In section fifteen, a 'Chorus' chants plangently 'Find me / So that I will exist, find my navel / So that it will exist'. Several of the poem's middle sections describe a similar contradiction between the will to discover the reality of mind and self in communal relations and a collective scepticism that seems insurmountable. In section seventeen, Oppen discovers what he calls 'Anti-ontology' 'in the subways' (172) and portrays an anonymous character (himself?), who 'wants to say / His life is real', but is surrounded by an uncomprehending environment, in which 'No one can say why' (173). At times, Oppen suggests that the failure of a communistic ethic is assured by humanity's unwillingness to confront disagreeable realities. In section ten, he promises to 'listen to a man' (167), 'tho he will fail and I will fail', before reaffirming that 'He fails, that meditative man! And indeed they cannot "bear" it' (168), a reference to Eliot's suggestion in 'Burnt Norton' that 'human kind / Cannot bear very much reality', which lays blame for humanity's collective withdrawal from reality and one another on its innate moral weakness (*Burnt* 8).

In the second half of the poem, the insoluble nature of the poem's conceptual contradictions becomes more acutely apparent. Oppen frequently asserts the importance of community and our ability to 'know' one another, before retreating into doubts concerning the extent and value of this knowledge (*NCP* 187). In section twenty-six, he suggests that we experience an intuition of our individuality, but that we also sense the reality of our interconnectedness and that therefore 'We want to defend / Limitation / And do not know how' (177). He goes on to aver that

> Of Lives, single lives
> And we know that lives
> Are single
>
> And cannot defend
> The metaphysic
> On which rest
>
> The boundaries
> Of our distances.
> We want to say
>
> 'Common sense'
> And cannot.' (178)

Yet, in spite of this intuition of psychical union, Oppen suggests that the mind remains insufficiently powerful to enact or experience the underlying unity of human life. However, distaste for his conclusion causes Oppen to evade any explicit statement of this. Instead, he suddenly drops the subject of individual and community and displaces it with remarks on the mind's alienation from the natural world. His remark on the insufficient 'Power and weight / Of the mind' is only in the context of the 'Behemoth, white whale', with which it is inadequate to deal. The section ends with a bald and plangent assertion of our ability to perceive nature clearly, but makes no connection between this apparent clarity and the problem of interpersonal communication. Oppen merely notes, with some bewilderment, that, in spite of our seeming estrangement from one another, we see 'the pebbles / Of the beach', 'clear as they have ever been' (179).

The pattern of assertion and withdrawal becomes more pronounced in the poem's closing sections. Section thirty-three exults 'Which is ours, which is ourselves, / This is our jubilation' (183) and section thirty-six, similarly, asserts that

> For us
> Also each
> Man or woman
> Near is
> Knowledge (185)

but immediately wonders dolefully whether this 'knowledge' might only be 'of the noon's vacuity' (186). Section thirty-seven maintains that the 'links' of community remain 'Of consequence', but the following section questions even the possibility of one human subject gaining meaningful knowledge of another, opening with the claim that 'You are the last / Who will know him / Nurse', before retreating, first, into self-contradiction, 'Not know him', and then into rhetorical questioning, 'How could one know him?', and settling for the rather empty observation that 'You are the last / Who will see him / Or touch him, Nurse' (187). The poem ends inconclusively, seemingly with the acceptance that its aspirations towards a collectivist ideal can only be enunciated with numerous qualifications and, as yet, unanswerable queries. Oppen admits that the text's ambiguous ending is indicative of his ambivalence about 'the concept of humanity' he elaborates.

What I hope to have shown in this essay is that, rather than being a skeptic about the relation between mind and world who, McAleavey suggests, refused 'to valance any set of assumptions about the mind', throughout the nineteen sixties, Oppen is deeply conflicted about the status of the mind and its relation to the world and is seeking to reconcile mutually exclusive positions on the subject (McAleavey 382). I believe the evidence of these three collections is that this insoluble problem caused Oppen to oscillate violently between radically different views on the nature of mind and, as a consequence, on the possibility of human solidarity and collectivism. Oppen acknowledged as much to Reinhold Schiffer: on the relation between mind and the world of objects, Oppen admitted that 'It's ambivalent all through the poems. They even directly contradict each other. It's the situation we're in' (Schiffer 16). Perhaps the most important finding of this article is the relationship it posits between Oppen's view of the status and reliability of perception and his ceaseless political anxiety about whether some form of communism might be feasible. His desire to answer the latter question in the affirmative repeatedly causes him to affirm the efficacy of consciousness in direct contradiction of his own assertions to the contrary. It is this irreducible tension that renders George Oppen's poetry of the nineteen sixties so endlessly troubling and absorbing.

Works Cited

Deleuze, Gilles and Felix Guattari, *Anti-Oedipus: Capitalism and Schizophrenia* trans. by Robert Hurley, Mark Seers, and Helen R. Lane (London: Athlone Press, 1984)

Dembo, L.S., 'George Oppen', in *Contemporary Literature*, 10 (1969), 159-177

Eliot, T.S., 'Burnt Norton', in the *Four Quartets* (London: Faber and Faber, 1946), pp.7-13

Eliot, T.S., 'The Dry Salvages', in the *Four Quartets* (London: Faber and Faber, 1946), pp.25-33

Finkelstein, Noman M., 'The Dialectic of *This In Which*', in *George Oppen: Man and Poet*, ed. by Burton Hatlen (Orano, Maine: University of Maine Press, 1981), pp.359-73

Heidegger, Martin, *The Question of Technology and other Essays*, trans. by William W. Lovitt (New York: Harper Torchbooks, 1997)

Hirsch, Edward, "Out there in the World': The Visual Imperative in the Poetry of George Oppen and Charles Tomlinson', in *George Oppen: Man and Poet*, ed. by Burton Hatlen (Orano, Maine: University of Maine Press, 1981), pp.169-180

McAleavey, David, 'Clarity and Process: Oppen's *Of Being Numerous*', in *George Oppen: Man and Poet*, ed. by Burton Hatlen (Orano, Maine: University of Maine Press, 1981), pp. 381-404

Nicholls, Peter, 'George Oppen in Exile: Mexico and Maritain', in *The Journal of American Studies*, 39 (2005), 1-18

Oppen, George, *New Collected Poems*, ed. by Michael Davidson (Manchester: Carcanet Press, 2003)

Oppen, George, *The Selected Letters of George Oppen*, ed. by Rachel Blau DuPlessis (Durham: Duke University Press, 1990)

Schiffer, Reinhold, 'Interview with George Oppen', in *Sagetrie*b, 3 (1984), pp.9-23

Searle, John R., 'Minds, Brains, Programs', in *The Mind's I: Fantasies and Reflections on Self and Soul*, composed and arranged by Douglas R. Hofstadter and Daniel C. Dennett (Frome, Somerset: Penguin, 1981), pp. 353-73

Searle, John R., *The Rediscovery of the Mind* (Cambridge, MA: MIT Press, 1992)

Smith, Laurence D., *Behaviorism and Logical Positivism: A Reassessment of the Alliance* (Stanford, CA: Stanford University Press, 1986)

I have images -

a cypress,

by a broken wall.

Johnny Marsh VII

Louis Armand

Calvary at Midnight

Having travelled the old routes, the anxious ones, their
questionable deviations, cold-water hotels, bordellos

and fit-up joints. Arriving one day, thirty years late,
recounting obscure crimes, passing off little forgeries

to gain time, pieces of notoriety among the inept,
the credulous or beatific – for the sake of a life beyond

whatever merely depicts it, or one last desperate
howling laugh into the dark? Of course, you have

become used to such scenarios, which are dependable
as a wallpaper's repetitions, pulling us away

from a room's hard edges or from that thing glimpsed
through thick glass, familiar yet maladroit as the hidden

family idiot. A thing which conjures up ideas of
inert flesh seen not animated, existing there only to

sour in the eye, like a love that even the most determined
adversary is unable to claim without giving in.

How will all of this appear in broad daylight? Waking
from the sort of sleep that can't ever be psychoanalysed,

forbidden worlds, an island in the mist. There will
always be something left to doubt – hunched over our

soup and bread, breathing it in, as if to recover some
disavowed intention to have lived and acted otherwise.

Sonata and Interlude

Once again, flowers. They want to destroy me,
they're pleased. On the table there's a drawing
I've begun – it begins with a line and then
branches out. 'I cut you, cut you, all of you.'
Mouth and stamen and rush of cold water.

And autumn is already beginning, this morning
at four o'clock. Their bouquet resembles a
mirror with a serrated metal frame – this is why
I can't bear to stay in. Also of wax, dough or
cooking fat. I was at the station yesterday evening,

facing them but refusing to talk. Oh, your letters
are terrible, so sad. A long, pernicious, narrow,
dark stem – a story – a table by a lake. Geneva.
You can always find some cause to suffer for.
Shapes flatten and spread in the dense two-

dimensional atmosphere, like a stain flowering
on a tablecloth beneath a toppled vase. They
look so pleased, lying among their handiwork.
The weather makes an appeal to urgency,
clearing everything away, smudging out.

Windows thicken like blotting paper. A stoppage
before the onrush – a sickness of repetitions.
The glass, you can see, has a crudely pigmented
hole where the vestiges grimace. In the ungarnered
immediacy of a gesture wanting to be forgot.

D.W. Brydon

Elegy

It is wrong to write a poem
when someone dies. To replace them
with a permutation of words. It does not
immortalise them. They do not
breathe again when the poem is read.
They are dead.

There are not enough spaces between the words
to echo silence. The page looks
too alive. I need to
rip up the sentences until it is impossible
for anyone to understand.

Old flame

Two automata drinking in the sun –
synapses, axons and neurons.
The filaments of your eyes
light up. Data from the newspaper
is reassembled in an exchange.
Your gentle audio stream
switches my pupils to widescreen.
The distance across the table
and surrounding white noise
hinder transmission and reception.
My CPU is struggling with the signals.
Your gaze is magnetic. Current rushes to my cheeks.
Your arm is a crane: biceps contracts, triceps
relaxes. The glass rises then docks.
Two clocks
valves and blood
are no longer keeping time.

David Burns

Baccalat

Item, when it (cod) is taken in the far seas and it is desired to keep it for 10 or 12 years, it is gutted and its head removed and it is dried in the air and sun and in no wise by a fire, or smoked; and when this is done it is called stockfish. and when it hath been kept a long time, and it is desired to eat it, it must be beaten with a wooden hammer for a full hour, then set it to soak in warm water for a full 12 hours or more, then cook and skim it very well like beef.

Anon, from *Le Mesnagier de Paris*, c. 1393

He felt the jagging signals up the line
and settled pull by pull to their resistance,
the deep-weight sawing drag on salt-sore hands.
Hauled blind at first
then, through the thick green lens and dancing light
saw dark shapes splintered and remade,
a twisting underflash of white
and they came whole,
shedding the last of the sea,
each frenzied arch a forceless flex on air.
Tossed down to drum and quiver,
they stilled and dulled in drifts against the boards.

She split their guts and threw them to the gulls.
Winds that Arctic pack had iced and sharpened
scoured them where she racked them up in pairs,
sucked their liquids out and back to sea,
sculpted wood-hard forms in parchment skin:
a tail, bent in its final flick,
a fossil turn that curled through one cracked fin.

Cod, torsk, morue; baccalat, salt-cod, stockfish.
Stacked until the mast grew from their mountain
and sent off on a dead migration
to soak in earthen crocks of strange soft water;
reforming flesh, unlocking their salt essence
for mouths long from Löfoten.

Last Open Day at the Mill

Pitching his voice easily over the dank slap and dry grind
he showed how it all came to him and from him
at that single stance:
the line up through the floors to the rattling hopper,
wheels and levers rodded to cogs and sluice,
a chute at his side spilling flour
into the slow fill of the bag.

'The bell on the hopper rings when the grain's finished;
can't run the stones dry, or they start to spark – it explodes,
flour dust in air. There's a few mills gone like that.'

A man for all mills he was
and all he'd collected was laid out under new dust
for him to choose what to take – a gallery of wear:
a pitchfork, all wood, all one,
glossed from a million passes through warm hay;
black basalt bearings
that older mills had spun on and shone for seasons;
stones, on stones, on stones,
from the cold mass of querns
to slivers ground out of their weight.

We turned at a new clatter, saw the wedge dislodged
from its joint in the off-square frame
and the miller already swinging himself up the ladder.
'Whole place'd shake to bits, left to itself,' he drove it back in,
'mostly I feel them slip before they fall. That stream,
it pushes much more than the wheel.'

We went out, across the glide of the leat
and round to the spray of the tail
where rows of stumps braced
against rows from millers before him.
'Elm,' he'd said, 'gets tougher as it gets wetter.'
The pull of the water out through the long pool
drew us with it, down to a quiet reach.
Staring into our reflections you said
it felt like the earth was turning
under the still stream
and you pulled at levers in the air.

Patrick Carrington

Marielle's White Shirt

They saw the neon palm, heard
salt air whisper a gypsy's promise
to tame their nightmares, shrivel
the bad dreams small.

Five for foreign-eye crystal
to read their wrinkled scars, ten
for tea leaves or tarot. The future
was cheap, draped in Persian print
and rhinestone, but prophecy
glittered from her like diamonds.

For butter and eggs, she stepped
from trailers of vagabonds into summer
sun, from campfires where guitars play,
where tomorrow is serenaded and sold
to anyone willing to pay for its lies.

But autumns on the boardwalk
were different, all plywood and time.
In a white shirt, she walked by the sea
that was more her father
than the one she never knew.

Always, she went to the clutch
of the water, its old eyes, knowing
the arms and stares of other men
were tricks of her own dishonest craft.

Even when the sea gave her nothing,
deserted with ease and no word
of farewell, she stayed. Because
she could not abandon the storm
that created her, or a love
as pure as her fallen cloth.

The Elders

When drought came to San Joaquin,
they say the sun died at dusk
just like the unpicked fruit.
It would leak its last wrinkled light
on migrants walking with hoes
and shovels shouldered, and then

fall, dark and dead into the Pacific
like a dry berry to ground.
The elders knew it was time then
to care. Old men pointed to sea
to buoy the boys, talked of boats
bursting with albacore. And when
mission bells filled the valley
at night, they spoke of Christ
and resurrection and new light.

Long before dawn, the abuelas
with eyes bright as Spanish song
baked jeweled king's bread though
Christmas was worlds away. They
spit-polished blue Talavera plates,
overflowed them with huevos y chorizo
and heavy grapefruits halved. Wet,
and as pink as sunup over High Sierra.

Laura Ciraolo

Reverberations of Ghosts

I kept my brother's voice
trapped in a machine
so I could hear him speak
to me out of the past into real time

reverberations of his life
resonating in the timbre and tenor
of his voice, of what he did not say
between the lines and the openings

interstitial, interspace, intervals
surrounding subliminal particles.
His voice detonates in orbitals
where electrons disappear

at the moment of measurement.
His voice echoes in the vacuum
filling oblivion beyond the luminous
bodies flung across the universe.

He continues to speak
into the silence that is here
where he used to be
where he was erased.

Stewart Conn

Mull of Oa

The beach at Kilnaughton, on Islay, possesses 'the singing sands'. A monument erected by the American Red Cross commemorates those who died when two US troopships were torpedoed off Oa, in 1918.

On checking my rucksack I discover
I've forgotten my binoculars, and curse
my carelessness. But this releases me

to see what I please. Not till I draw
close does a great woodpecker askew
a telegraph-pole (a first for Islay?)

become a junction-box. A standing-stone
is archetypal bull, all brow and shoulder;
another an old woman, back bowed.

Seal turns to rock or vice-versa. A pair
of acrobatic sea-eagles metamorphose
into kites held by surfers in the Bay,

a lesson in grace and muscularity.
Further peopling the place, there appear
at dusk almost tangible presences:

near the ruins of Kildalton chapel, a cross
intricately carved by a sculptor from Iona,
and a glistening sky, its mauve and silver

a selkie's skin trailed across the horizon.
The uncanniest saved for last: from
the rocks at Kilnaughton, as a steamer

changes course off the Mull of Oa,
I hear not sands singing, but the sighs
of the drowned, perpetuated in still air.

Belinda Cooke

Three Translations of Marina Tsvetaeva

i

I am glad, that you are not sick because of me,
and that I am not sick because of you,
that the heavy earthly ball will never
slip away beneath our feet. I am glad
that we can joke around, can be relaxed
and not play around with words,
and that we don't go red with embarrassment
if we so much as touch each other's sleeve.

I am glad also that before me
you can comfortably embrace another,
that you do not want me to burn
in hell's flames because I do not kiss you.
I am glad you don't call out my name, my dear,
night and day – in vain –
that there in the church silence
they will never sing alleluia over us.

I shall always be grateful that you,
unknowingly, love me thus:
for my night-time peace,
for the rarity of our sunset meetings,
for not walking with me beneath the moon,
for the sun which is not above our heads,
for the sad fact that you are not sick because of me,
and I am not sick because of you.

ii

Yesterday he still looked me in the eyes,
but now it's all turning to one side.
Yesterday he sat with the birds –
but now all the larks have become ravens.

I am stupid and you are clever,
you're alive but I'm struck dumb.
O women's cry throughout the ages:
'My love, tell me what I did to you?'

Her tears are always water and blood –
in tears of blood and water she washed herself.
Love's not a mother but a stepmother –
expect no justice, no generosity there.

Boats carry the loved ones away,
the white road leads them away...
and a groan is sent up the length of the earth:
'My love, tell me what I did to you?'

Yesterday he still lay at my feet,
compared me to a Chinese dynasty,
then opened out his two little hands:
life has turned out like a rusty kopeck.

And now accused of infanticide
here I stand, unloved and weak.
Still from the depths of hell I ask you:
'My love, tell me what I did to you?'

I ask the chair, I ask the bed:
'Why do I suffer and struggle to live?'
'He stopped kissing – he broke you at the wheel:
to kiss another,' they reply.

He taught me to live in the heart of the flame,
then threw me onto the icy steppe.
That's what you, lover, did to me!
Now tell me love what I did to you?

I know I'm right, there's no point arguing,
I'm no longer a lover that's quite clear.
You can be sure when love departs
death the gardener comes near.

It's just like shaking a tree –
in time the ripe apple will fall...
For everything, everything forgive me
my love – that ever, ever I did to you!

                    iii

It's time to remove the amber,
it's time to change the words,
it's time to put out the lamp
over the door...

Katherine Dimma

Proust's Wisdom

Epigraphs for writing
in quiet rooms. The bluest curtain
against the palest wall. The pillow
I make my home. The safe weather
of the closed window. There are those
who think Proust was mad when he took to his bed.

These are people who have not loved. Nor lost.

Reliquaries

She took his name down from the sky
where it had been too long.
Let us not lie and say there is any other subject.
Let us not pretend.

Like a reliquary of loss – each burnt-out cathedral
holds blackened saints, broken words, and gold.
From the downed, another meaning comes.

We must know how to look at things:
The moon was once a grave for silent gods –
But oh what cataracts there did weep.

Angela France

Learning to Play the Violin by Holding a Bow

This is the bow. The sprung strength of its ruddy glow
is Pernambuco wood; it holds the filtered light of the rain
forest, the depth of the canopy's shade. It is strung
with pale hairs from thoroughbreds; each as poised
and high-stepping as the notes you reach for.

Your right hand must be relaxed, confident,
your thumb pressed against the mother of pearl
to feel the waves' pulse in its lustre. Curl
your fingers over the stick; each one feathered
away from its neighbour and firm in its intention.

This arc, from left shoulder to inclined chin, would be filled
with gleaming maple and spruce. Practise the space, the balance
against your collarbone, the line from shoulder to thumb
where the neck will rest. Arch your fingers over,
train them to be particular, precise, to yearn for
the vibration of string on ebony.

The luthier knows music is held in the bow; let your hand
find it. Taste the control of a sure sweep forward,
the caress of pulling back; feel the song's shape
swell in your hand, the ache of the pale hair for strings.
Move always from your centre to master the owl's dark swoop
if you would release the lark ascending.

George Gömöri

Daily I switch languages – call them masks:
At times a mask can feel like your own skin.
At other times, the spirit has to struggle,
Saved only by the tongue it calls its own.

The mysteries of life, of the universe,
I can describe in English now, although
In my mother tongue alone I can stammer out
The words that compose the sunset, make it glow.

Translated from the Hungarian by **Clive Wilmer** *and* **the author**

Mill-time

> '*The mills of God grind fast*'
> *– Sandor Marai, 23 October 1956*

The mills of God grind fast
the mills of God grind slow
for who can tell
whether it's long or short
that half-life those 33 years
before justice stubbornly hoped for
something at once too little and too much
was finally done … the flour, at any rate –
ground exceedingly fine
by the mills already mentioned –
was sprinkled over our heads in the mean time
and by the time we were able to bury our dead
our hair had imperceptibly turned to frost

Translated from the Hungarian by **Clive Wilmer** *and* **the author**

Fake semblances of Odysseus

Fake semblances of Odysseus, we wander over the planet
while at home our Penelopes, formerly smiling,
have suddenly gone serious
and taken to the weaving of winding-sheets…
It's winter now, our galleys are burdened with frost,
an evil north wind wails over grey seas,
the stars, moreover, are so inhumanly abstract.

We did not stay behind with the lotus-eaters,
were not broken apart by Charybdis and Scylla,
but are consumed with the consciousness
that, look, the struggle is not yet over
and at home the suddenly serious Penelopes
are weaving shrouds, funereal winding-sheets.

Famous Achaeans, what was the worth of your empty chatter?
Did you make sacrifices to Poseidon
the dull-brained but mighty? Have you ever been able
to challenge him with brave deeds? Did you ever do so?
You have given us food, but otherwise there is nothing
but nimble words to lament or juggle with –
that's all you've been able to do,
famous Achaeans.

Fake semblances of Odysseus, we wander over the planet.
The sea is weaving a winding-sheet of our sighs.
The past is sunken in fog, thick fog hides Ithaca's fate.

Translated from the Hungarian by **Clive Wilmer** *and* **the author**

Harry Guest

The Custard Mountains

A burst of atmospherics like
black sparks of sound flecked the suave Third
Programme voice. I'd lugged my sister's
heavy blue wireless upstairs. Gales
scraping The North Sea dashed salt rain
against the panes. The boy I used
to be had just heard of Lorca.
That week's *Radio Times* promised
half an hour of his poems read
in English. My obedient ear
managed to trace 'a line of light'
drawn above 'the custard mountains'.
I saw them vividly as heaped
and treacherous – a quaking ridge
whose sheen and softness must have lured
unwary pilgrims to their high
yellow horizon. Did they sink?
Could they return? What lay beyond?
Maybe a sulphur plateau? Lakes
of liquid gold? Or a forest
with foliage of saffron flame?
No spurts of image mattered since
that shiny dollop of a range
existed in a poet's mind
and was its own conviction – not
only that time listening alone
to words in my cold bedroom but
as fodder for bewildered dreams.
The printed page years later proved
how he'd limned a sky of Spanish
brilliance to form a backdrop
for some 'clustered mountains' and those
vulnerable lemon-coloured
mirages vanished for ever.

Rahul Gupta

Lyrics for Lutemusic

Maiden, be kind;
Do not dally
With me in my folly,
As if love were loaned:
Maiden, be kind.

Lady, be mild;
Reward me courtesy
For all my chivalry,
Be not so self-willed:
Lady, be mild.

Mistress, be sisterly;
Upon your breast
Let me rest, at least,
Cradle me tenderly:
Mistress, be sisterly.

Muse, be less cruel;
Take this the heart
Of your own poet,
Leave me my soul:
Muse, be less cruel.

Goddess, be good;
Accept my prayers,
Teach me thy praise,
Drive me not mad:
Goddess, be good.

Imprimatur

A Skaldic Sonnet

Her image emblazoned in his dazzled gaze,
He feels over her a blindman's hands:
Spelling her profile in the lines of his palms,
Her silhouette's pattern in the caress
That imprints her embrace in his fingers' ends –
Braille inscribed in the whorls of his thumbs,
Hieroglyphic nerves have learned
By heart, enciphered on members and limbs
That reverberate the echo of her frame:
A syllable throbbing in loins, lips, brains,
Impressing her mark, her motto and emblem,
Her own likeness limned in his form;
Her signature set by the seal of her kiss:
Seeing eyes read her name in his face.

David Hale

July 1st

The humid air is full of remembrance,
ash flags hang at half mast. At the wood's edge
we fashion a looping limb into a ladder,

split it lengthways with maul and froe,
exert pressure on the slightest of cracks.
As we chamfer ragged edges, talk turns

to Mametz and Theipval – the generation
cut down there, like the forests given over
to make planks, beams and posts – the vast tonnage

of timber swallowed up along the Somme.
Many from these wood-filled marches,
the red horseshoe stitched on their backs:

bodgers, wheelwrights, hurdle makers,
their names recalled on churchyard plaques,
who when not felling, fighting or laying

corduroy roads through seas of mud,
kept their fingers busy making the furniture
of trench and dugout, rough-hewn ladders

like my own to replace those shattered
on stormy days. This my first, made in the time
it took them to make dozens. And in this making,

this use of simple tools and coppiced ash
from woods they knew so well, we come
close to crossing each other's paths

this hot summer morning, where limestone
turns to chalk, cornflower to poppy,
our thoughts from thunder to distant guns.

Red horseshoe is the insignia of the Gloucestershire regiment

Hunter

for no apparent reason starts to laugh
as he tells me his dream of making books
near the end of our daily paragraph,
fragments of parsival and captain hook,
snuff movies, the mail and mickey mouse, glued
onto wedges of used sandpaper:
of cutting out cornflakes packets to use
as covers, binding fantasy in landscape
as he searches for the story that will
help him escape the shackles of his own
story – a mass of disordered detail
set in care, custody and children's homes,
in which those without faces or with masks on,
behave without any sense of reason.

Alyson Hallett

Hartland Quay Cliffs

I arrive and the arms of the cliffs encircle me.
Night stars netted in strata
a million bell-like waves sunk
in their fabric of stone.

I swim out to sea and they watch me.
Hidden eyes blinking through faults,
hidden hearts beating an avalanche
of rocks to the beach.

I sleep on the sand and they dream me.
Cast skeletons in my feet,
carve gills in my neck,
chisel fins from my spine.

I sing and they orchestrate me.
Language deserts the word
and we revert to howl, croak, hiss.
Cliffs kiss and adore me with their old stone lips.

Stroke

Asthore,
　　　my darling,
　you are split in two. One of you
　　　　　　lies in a hospital bed
　　　the other has fled to the stars.
You are both ill and astral now,
　　　　　　locked in a diary of days
　　　translated by light. Blue light, you say,
　　　　　blue light. Asthore,
　　　　　　　　　my darling,
　　there is no mistaking the relation
　　　　　between sidereal and sideration –
　the first relating to the stars,
　　　　　　　the second a stroke, sudden paralysis.
　Patient in your hospital bed
　　　　the blighted body relies on drips and drugs
　whilst that other you
　　　　　　relieves itself of gravity, of flesh,
　　　and meteors into the sky.
　　　You are a storm of heavenly light,
　　　　　　　　　mother,
　body and ghost conjoined.
　　　　　　You cannot fasten a shoe,
　cannot summon the strength
　　　to lift your arm,
　　　　　　but a different constellation burns in your brain
　　　　　　　　and bows it, bends it
　　　　　　towards the light. Blue light.
　　　Asthore, my darling, my mother,
　　　　　as you wake day by day your light
　corrupts the commonest things – this bread, this tea,
　　　　this programme on television.

Simon Jackson

My Fever

For Jana

Confined to bed, sheets sticking
like shrink wrap to my fevered skin.
The sun seeps through heavy curtains.

The sweet sharpness of peppers, hung in chains outside
to make *ajvar,* or *kiseli paprika*
and keep us the whole winter fills the room.

Mushrooms are drying on the straw
and my mother's voice rises from the thick-walled kitchen.
She brews clear broth to raise me to health.

I know you're dead. I know this country
doesn't even exist any more,
yet the smell of fresh linen and *rakija*

rubbed onto my boyish breast
enwraps me more convincingly
than this new land or fat duvet that weigh upon me now.

Baba putting wet oats in my socks
to take away the fever,
and you, scolding her home-spun remedies.

I feel my mother's hand, warm and dry,
passing across my fevered forehead
and know all will be well.

Chris Jones

Cyprian

Who would think it worth the trouble
of ploughing waste rubble
and tilling the saline crust
of sun-leached Paphos dust,
so the share, dragging a scar though Earth,
shed sudden scarlet tesserae in the dirt,
spilling a rivulet of shards, tiles and glass
into bleached sullen wilderness?

And then what? Gather in this harvest
of sacrifice and savagery, inbred incest?
How would you restore the jigsaw seeds?
Make sense of the scattered pieces
of unearthed, murdered Ikarios
skin-flayed Marsyas
or the carrion-gnawed organs
of the dismembered Orphic corpse?

Fawzia Kane

Tantie Diablesse warns against doppelgangers

Doppelgangers are a strange species,
Slowly, they'll come to you
                    whispering

we were born where dark and light meet
                yet never touch,
then one day westbound winds
cast up silver nets,
               and pulled us from the stars.

Their smiles hide claws; these mimics
steal livelihoods, break spirits,
                   they bring days of the dead
to your wedding feast.

                You'll fall gently
into their lies, while accepting their offerings:
sugared bones
            on gilded trays,
pumpkin seeds, beaded rubies
strung on wired lace,
                drawn and woven
from the very bolts they will use
to fix your face over theirs.

Waiting your turn

it was before the days of Enzyme-X
so white socks would be boiled
in a saucepan on the stove

and Mammy would pour milky
sweet tea into your cup,
straight from hugup land;

it would be quiet, because everyone
else was old enough to go to school
where salt prunes were handed out

to bring home; and Pappy was with
Uncle Hacket and Uncle Brim, in
the oily refinery where the river

had *so much crude on dat water*
it could ketch on fire anytime, fellas!
(and it did, one hot night)

there wasn't any wrought iron
burglar-proofing in the house then,
so the morning light would be buttery,

without spider shadows, the colour
of ripe mangoes from our tree
whose branches were so cradling

you could climb to its top and
point out hump-backed mountains
in Venezuela, far away, behind the sea.

Robin Laffan

Reminders

A glass in the fridge nestles
among old cheeses
and crumpled lettuce
waiting to remind you
of your tablets,
two with every meal.

A single shoe
carefully positioned
on the sideboard,
next to the telephone
whose signal you often missed
winking its need to talk.

A pen balanced on the arm
of what was always your chair,
points with determined precision
at the folded newspaper,
rcminding no-one now,
of the unfinished crossword.

Siren

Where does the feeling come from
on a day like this, when a grey curtain
enfolds the bay, and unseen,
the lighthouse bewails its blindness,
warning away leviathans,
who inch forward upon the sea?

Where does the wind come from
that sweeps gently about the pale
stone church, tugging at my coat,
as if to tempt me away from work,
to a hidden meeting on the beach,
beneath the rising water?

In the lee of the church tower,
beside the newly repainted statue
of the grieving Madonna and crucifix,
I turn my back on the granite wall
to look into a cataract-eyed day,
and listen for the call of the lighthouse.

Christopher Locke

End of American Magic

... These are not the roads
you knew me by
– Adrienne Rich

You don't rise to shock
the windows closed, thunder
kicking darkness in all
its awkward falling. You
don't rise to curse the sink,
water dripping like coins
plunked one wish at a time.
You don't rise to escape
your dreams, leaving them
to dissolve through bed sheets
like salt. You don't rise
to blind yourself with rage,
the mirror flagrant in its double
vision of loathing. You don't even
rise to check your children, their young
lives troubled by what you say or
choose to leave out. No, you rise
because your brother could not,
two years drowning in the country
of methadone, privately
deconstructing himself one
mouthful at a time, until
the weight of all that guilt
became a vision of hanging:
learning his bodyweight
would need ten feet if he
were to do it right. But
the rope's coarse answer
never found flesh, and he
sleeps now fourteen days
sober, his voice again
human. So now you divorce
sleep to embrace everything
you've lost, sit at the dining
room table disheveled and stunned

by life, celebrate the lit columns
of daylight pronouncing themselves
above the redundant houses in
Florida, the hem of the wind's
silk robe dragging slightly
across the lake, and three glossy
ibis silently passing, birds you
just learned the names of yesterday:
you and your daughters rising
from the pages of Audubon amazed,
imagining the animals' sharp voices –
that their outstretched wings were
real enough to touch.

Gill McEvoy

Visit From a Long-eared Bat

Fierce winds have flung you in from the night,
hurled you against the lit veranda wall,
a spatter of black mud. You cling.
We greet your strange arrival with delight.

I see the fish-hook on your wing,
the thin vanes on its leathered fan
as you splay it out, then draw it in,
your soft wax melting in and out of shape.

Your ears, black spathes of arum,
shiver to the echo of a moth in flight.
You've moved right round; now, upside-down,
could plummet any second

like a fat ripe plum,
splatter on the stones below,
stain them with the seep of
sloe-dark blood.

The night is lashed by wind,
clouds claw across the moon's white face –

a moth blows in and batters at the lamp;
your sudden shadow shears my head.

Lucie McKee

Light Change

Fights continued. Sure of their truths they seared
and salted each other's wide wounds to clinch
the teaching. She found weaknesses to lynch
with mob action of eye-paint, teeth, words feared.
He played the grand vizier with his sharp beard.
Iron bands of logic made them each flinch
with pain of life denied. There was no inch
supplied. No relief, no concord appeared.

What made them change, then, one snowy evening
when the light seemed to cast oriental
depth and ochre stillness. Branches etched black
in a harmony that was interesting
and rearranged and, somehow, parental,
though nothing was exchanged, or taken back.

Standing Elsewhere

Ecstasy is something I must keep
for myself, here on the rat surface
of November. Dark mountain peaks
cut into an expiring sky, broody
gray everywhere, stillness, the air
so cold it's close to flint, close
to the smell of a musket just shot
in a local replay of the local battle
of the Revolution. There is nothing
to support me in this emptiness,
this drop to black and white life
I could call despair save that I am
left alone to the sheer transport
of my own elation which I've kept
secret in a tree like any squirrel,
but, I take this moment to fly
elsewhere from the bare branch.

Abby Millager

Fata(l) Morgana

Sun's last shrapnel savages trees, steel
twists as leaves. I try

to shake it off but you
are not here. You are altitudes away, grains

of desert sand
lain end to end.

        I search for you

in the humming rocks. They pulse
against the outer facts of their shells, against

the trill of your bright armament. Sun
glint ejects from the muzzle's strobe, sniffs

its prey, turns
to *fata*(l) *morgana.*

        Illusion. Mirage. Gravel
        catches my chest, travels

an undone road. How long can you breathe in
insurgent water? Flanks fray. Froth

creeps up the ripped river's clear
and present fingers

that press oblivion
into your throat.

Let me be

your moss helmet, your forest charm, your
perpetual coat. And you –

you be immortal, you song, you rhythm, tides high –
expanding – you

salt sea rain
always comes back to.

W S Milne

The Highland Clearances

The wind is a singing voice down the dark glens
Where no ear hears, and where no echo lives.
The wind blows through the empty shielings,
Stirs the grass, and the odd drifting leaf of autumn.
All those singing voices gone into the chorus of the winds!
Lost on the mountain-tops, or drowned in ditches,
Or singing the Gaelic still across the waves.

Walking the Grampians

The marram-grass in the dunes rustles.
On the mountain paths our boots crush the roddenberries.

The peewees call in the late evening frost.
Clouds are at rest like stilled doves.

The gloaming gathers in the eyes of the lochs,
And the evening-hour settles in wreaths of mist.

(The night awaits morning's impress.)

Dyce Churchyard

Pass by. They are buried.
All the lovely faces

Flowers in the ditch.
Fanfare, and silence.

They have gone
Into the blind night

Beyond these stones.

(A cloud glides across the sun.)

Ray Racy

Body and Soul

Hell's harridans torment the soul
For all the love one never had.

The young in one another's arms
Exploit the sport of selves entwined
In trust and roguish ravishment,
As breast to breast and thigh to thigh
Their secret zones are tightly twinned
In cataracts of delight.

Yet lust makes no amends
For decades of despair,
Nor can a body's tactile bliss
Compensate the aching void
That mocks the heart's paralysis.

Only love's manna heals the soul,
Completes the consummated dream,
Binds love and passion in a magic spell
And conjures an epiphany.

Peter Robinson

Clear as Daylight

'The dancers, faces oblivious & grave, –
testing testing
the dancers face oblivion and the grave.'
Geoffrey Hill, 'After Reading *Children of Albion* (1969)'

Reading in an early dawn –
I'm distracted glancing over
edges of slim volume pages.
The words, too fathomable words,
cross patios, backyards,
outliving children of Albion
who face death now, as best they can,
and the first birds sing.

To identify with where we live,
I read us into things
like the cut of some diamond red brickwork;
though, try as I might,
dripping tap and leaky cistern
gall me to the quick,
like one swan biting at another's neck
as if we'd never learn.

But even the things I'm reading
strayed among wild rhubarb
are moving over surfaces
of cloud types, sun- and storm-light,
that heat has flaked to pieces
and they're sublimed, resentment-free,
like purgatories in others' verses,
to skies filled with activity.

Like a Foreign Country

That much would have to be explained:
how cloud-roofs at dawn
were burned off by a July sun
and showers washed out washing day,
how identity theft protection
or laundry would get done
when there was the tax disc to display.

It was time, time to cultivate our garden
where blades of whitened grass
hid creatures still alive
beneath their mossy stone
or in a creosoted shed
with ivy bursting through its boards –
still lives of paint cans and so on.

That much had been left behind.
Cloud-diffused sunlight would soothe
my jangled nerves. You'd find
it was like our daughter's school report:
me too, I'm happy as can be
expected, coping well
with moving … in a foreign country.

Days gone, terraces, terra incognita,
were like our faces redefined
at a bathroom mirror when it's cleaned;
for time had taken its advantage
over us, the gained
and lost perspectives realigned.
That much would have to be explained.

Peripheral Visions

Catching a stretch of dawn skyline
revealed by raw spaces between
lopped-off poplar trunks
pillaring an overlooked villa's avenue,
I turn and in the window
(like a hinged mirror) notice you –
for though a perpetual hum
of lorries on the ring-road reaches my ear,
we can see them now
as they rev out through our *periferia*.

Yet now that I've caught my reflection
and yours reappears in the glass
where Daphne's wild arms used to wave,
I see it's like this any time
we're arrived from elsewhere and are lost
by slip road, truck park, bypass.
Signposts have too much or no sense at all,
like an eyeful of how things appear
when we're not used to them …

Yet now that this reflection
glimmers in our rear-view mirror,
I see it's like this any time
we're arrived from elsewhere foxed
by a new gyratory system,
or half-erected towers and cranes –
for the town's a rash of roundabouts
and we'll be lost once more
among growth rings, ripe stains
of year after year after year.

E.M. Schorb

Old Icarus

Grandchildren turning
their faces from
drooling kisses
to avoid
what you have
become:
teeth like graveyard
stones, sunken cheeks
pockmarked
(where once,
as a boy,
the feathers went),
wens, wild hairs.

The wax your father poured
has melted
and the feathers,
plumes he placed so carefully,
flew, fell,
and you fell
into the sea
but did not drown,
owning a future,
as you did,
long enough
to hug your grandchildren
close and have them
turn away.

Robert Stein

The Dutch Pietists

Thus the ecclesia of the true converts – this was common to all genuinely Pietistic groups – wished, by means of intensified asceticism, to enjoy the blissfulness of community with God in this life.

M Weber: *Die protestantische Ethik und der Geist des Kapitalismus*

Rammed the wooden shutters tight against the day –
Not the light of God.
Desiccated, unstalked, smoothed down cut apple-pieces,
Held each thin eighth like the wafer on the tongue.

Blessed is the clean, the whole,
That which is made my own.
I would succour, I would savour the very breath of God.

At night, as they prayed,
Fingers and knees on the floor,
They felt the sea somewhere chafe against the land,
The transparency of water being the eye of God,
The keening wind as the unspeakable language,
The clamour of His wild hair against each mouth,
The press of absence which is greater love.

The Visit – c 1938

She has come with a present for me.
She has come to thank me and
The dog leaps, leaps at her in the blue room.

In the blue, or lilac room, perhaps, the dog is sitting in a chair.
It barks. She has come with something large, peculiarly large, wrapped and tied.
It is a hidden thing.

                I am in the room, waiting,
Or am just coming in
Happy – no, frightened – to see the dog yapping
At this unknown woman burdened with her secret
And the dog sniffs at her –
My mother who has come without a present.

I run to my brother because I am frightened of her.
I am in the chair crying because she has not come back.

The room is blue, the room is dark.
I am listening to the blue fading on the walls.

My mother is hiding somewhere in the room from me
And the secret of her death is covered –
No, the piano is covered over completely.
It is all black. The dog growls at the carpet,
Paws away at the room, digs, digs and I forget.

Andrew Waterman

Close-Up

When twilight comes it pulls the mountains near.
Keeping going, picking up after falls,
fording the rivers, had been enough to push
horizon on before me, keeping distance.
Now as a shiver passes through the grass
it closes in, looming, and no way of telling
what, if anything, might lie beyond it.

*

New-built, and fit for all its purposes:
spotless corridors ramify, lifts purr,
to where things happen, beyond the waiting areas
saccharined with wall pictures, fish in tanks.
A woman recalls sweets long gone, liquorice twist,
bulls'-eyes, flying saucers, 'the Coronation
there in black-and-white on a twelve-inch screen.'
And one by one we are called, some wheelchaired on,
some helped by steadying arms.
                                                    'State of the art,
all our equipment here,' they tell me
as flat on my back I'm slid within
the CT scanner's glimmering tunnel, fearing
that if this thing the biopsy found inside me
has spread, this suave machine won't fail to find it.

*

'Look! – snowdrops!' cries my sister by the river
past Pull's Ferry, 'you could say
a drift of snowdrops.' Delicately surmounting
wan February grass. A year ago
Veronica rejoiced in them: 'Bucaneve!
Vedili!' – then they were adrift on snow.
Now I kneel to stare at one close-up,
the tiny flower pendant on bare stem,
supplicant, heralding spring's accession
through gold swathes of daffodils to May's
hedgerows foaming with white hawthorn blossom.
Gift annually thrilling, yet at each
recurrence piercingly unique.
That now I can't for next year take for granted.

As if a crash that somehow not abruptly
over carries on, no end in sight
yet caught within it visions of sweet elsewheres
clear of it. Yes, I'll come to Venice,
talk poetry drinking wine by the canals;
and to you in Taormina where
we'll linger in the public gardens among
hibiscus and bougainvillea, hearing
toc... toc... toc... from the tennis courts,
balls flying to and fro, voices calling the score.

*

As just one rotten apple in the barrel
corrupts the whole, this cancer in my... No,
that's cliché... Nor does biology know
moral categories. So let's say
a pearl, occasioned by one speck of grit,
expanding in layers round it...
                                        I'm away
inside my head, as head-and-shoulders clamped
to a narrow table by the Perspex mask
they beam the radiation through
my throat.
            But neither will that image do:
the pearl protects the mollusc, doesn't kill it...
Trying words for this shifts it to a plane
where I embrace it...
                        'As spores inhabiting
an organism reproduce to spread...'
Hoping their rays will zap the bastard thing.

*

The view from here pulls far things close and clear:
short-trousered, Elastoplast on knees, and hair
incorrigible, a bunch forever vying
come to the stream. Rope slung over a bough,
each swings, lets go, makes it to the far side
no worse for a grazed palm or shoeful of water,
myself among them, and pushes on,
gobstoppers bulging cheeks, snapping off shoots,
whooping, reckless, vanishing
into forest... Careers, marriage, divorces,
and, these overcome, what's still to come.
Deaf to my warning cry, 'Mind how you go!'

Gerald Wells

On the Move

Recollection, like the grainy
Shots from old film, is diffuse:
Maybe there was mahogany
Behind fittings of brass.

But no hope of sleepers on a train
Cobbled from anything not wrecked
In those early months of peace. None
Of that's important, just the fact

It runs at all, its glass-reflected
Faces staring back from continental
Darks of that long anticipated
Night – bearing him, an incidental

On the run, the never-arriver
Needing movement for the sake
Of moving, heading anywhere…
Destination another state

Of mind; his skill – not requiring
The miraculous (wiser than most),
Needing space to take fresh bearings,
Unload a drill pack's weight of angst.

Station stop and a border guard
With dogs, spectral in first light –
There's the sound of a sleepless bird…
He'll remember that.

Louise Wilford

Clee Hills

The wind nags, up here, above the cloud-line. Fog's
like hiding inside an eiderdown dipped in the sea,
wet feathers on your skin – makes you feel smothered,
snatches at your breath. As if the world ends at your
fingertips. You have to guide yourself by old fence-posts,
feeling out the livestock like a game of Blind Man's Buff.
Eyeless at the edges. No matter how much you rub your sleeve
against your eyes, it won't come back til the fog lifts.
But still, the wind's worse, the piercing groan of it.

The land up here's quarry-scarred – scooped out, piled up,
abandoned. Generations of poor sods worked eight-hour
days, after an hour's uphill tramp, hacking at the dhustone
with 28lb hammers. Sometimes they slept here, days lined up
like dominoes. Old mineshafts capped with brick domes,
not filled in – bubbles in the hillside that could pop at a wrong step.
The landscape slips and slithers. Stumps of pylon footings
like old men's teeth, spoilheaps like scaly breasts,
the flimsy needle of a radio-mast poised to scratch the sky.

Great granddad was a face-man on the Clee.
The wind carried the crunch of the crusher down the hill.
His son farmed this moonscape, taught my mother,
aged two, to ride a horse, the stirrups dangling, straps
rolled up so she could get her feet in. Pools of black tar
left over from the workings caught the sheep
like birdlime. We're hardy here, but even now I
still find wind-dried sheep bones on the flanks and in
the crevices. The rain paints the sky grey as pewter.

No one leaves the Clee Hills. There's generations here,
each knowing every other. The fog that seeps into our
skin, seething like freezing steam, sticks us to these bleak
slopes. Sometimes, you look down at the clouds below,
a white-grey ocean of curving mist caught in a still-shot
as if time has stopped. You hear only the wind's eerie
whistle. A sheep's bleat. Your heartbeat. You could drift over
that sea, canvas sails wind-filled. You could climb the hill's
rigging to the crow's nest and watch the white-grey waves.

Pat

The chalk rolls with a rising cadence,
in an itching scramble across the desktop;
it picks up speed, launches itself,
smashes in a tiny detonation of dust,
splits on contact, a debris of frosted rubble.

I remember your porcelain skin:
flawless, powdered like sugared marsh-
mallows, the plump cushions of your
cheeks sinking into unaccustomed hollows,
a bruise of fear beneath your eyes.

I lit a candle for you in Sacré Coeur.
I tried, in that city you loved – surrounded
by blue and gold icons, white stone like
alabaster, flawless – to conjure your face
from the crowds of faces. My feelings strayed.

But now, for a second, you're there – in the
flakes of teacher's chalk – and I stumble on
a sudden sob I have to change to a cough,
remembering how you split, cracking on the
instant of impact against your own dust and dreams.

Rik Wilkinson

The Children Lost

Art has no power to trace the lines removed;
The child, the children lost in forest rides.
No measure maps the ley-lines of those loved
Among the sweeping pines, the tall green brides;
Leys that would move the fork, my hazel wand,
Are deeply buried in the sensual ground.
What running laughter killed, from woodland pond
The impassioned hunter called – but never found.

Striding the candled room, turned heel to wall,
Face turned upon face, flames mirrored in the flame,
The future throws long, barren shadows : all
Behind, the crowded yesterdays to blame.
  My mind is filled with brutal briar in flower;
  A tangled stream in bloom, a ruined Tower.

I had images -

I remember the church,

Musicians,

Shadows.

Johnny Marsh VIII

Two Chosen Broadsheet Poets

Agnieszka Studzinska and Nadia Connor

Agnieszka Studzinska was born in Poland, and came to the UK when she was 7. She is now 33. She lives in London and works as an English teacher. She has an MA in Creative Writing from the University of East Anglia, and is working on her first collection entitled *Snow Calling*, like the poems chosen here.

Snow Calling

i

Winter opens to snow
            blinds the field –
branches splice like roots in a landscape

dead with beauty –
            the timeline of a train
slips through it like a cold vapour –

our faces steady themselves in windows,
disappear into the air of passengers

smeared across them like graffiti
            like something –

I listen to the snow calling

as it settles on wood rising in water,
            a signature of footsteps in ice.

*

Her sickness is a necklace of sores around the jaw line
clicks of air at the back of her throat
            sentences between dying and death –

she prevents her escape from herself
by the wool of blanket or time –
            she is a wooden petal sundered

234

tells me *you are my medicine* –

her glance almost too clear – too lambent for this world,
we sit there untranslatable like absence
                    listening to the snow calling.

                    *

I stand in the garden at midnight, you sleep upstairs
snow becoming your breath as if the invisible is made visible –

now anything feels possible – even a snow owl
in this backyard, feathers like snow preying on my voice,

coating with papery breathlessness
like echoes of drunken villagers returning

home – they cut a silence with boots
a day's work in their mouth

years in their hands gloved with weight –
the owl's wingspan like a cloud flying above their heads.

                    *

We lose each other in speech, a speckled language of childhood
its tongue turned to a pebble
                    the pebble skimming the surface of water
water breaking into shavings of cyan
                    snow light at an angle saying more than we can –
the snow owl holding this light   us inside it –

blanched by the moon and the workings of distance.

                    ii

I heard it – a faint quail of something unborn
        clouds growing in ache
the callous of air at midnight   warming
as the bonfire in its gallantry gets taller and rounder,
swells like a yell – the seconds stock-still,

235

we stood there cowed – divided
                    snow calling   spring
the wind bit harder, uncoupled each root from its body
unearthed memories of being little and looked after,
swept chairs and a table over – the walnut tree wide-eyed
self willed, its branches waving to the anthem of nature,
                                          I am gripping tighter –
                    snow calling
a garden spins in its own generative grammar,
we are all waiting – wet with wind
                          wishing
for the wind to blow another hundred wishes –
unbury the almost buried,
branches   bone-black
smouldering as the wind hushes a struggle,
                          wishing
for it to stop.
                And both of you
in deep sleep elsewhere in your skins   out of reach
my very own two wishes –
you have given me something to live for, she says as if prolonging the end.

An Observation on Figs

Sycamore figs distended
 in a family garden –
we picked them this morning
or should I say
you picked them
in your determination,
& resilience against the fractured
branches of your own being &
I watched you
vanish between these branches
& emerge like a swimmer
out in the green tarns of foliage
& shout something about
finding or damage –
& detain your breath once more &
dive into the loose light
of your life & this first summer
alone, without him –

gulp for air as you re-emerged
releasing more figs,
seeds of unwanted independence –
& not knowing where to put all this
or to whom you should give all this
& why this new light
makes you feel invisible?
Between the skin
of fruit and pulp,
you tell a daughter
not to depend
& choose cautiously
as you disappear into the contradictions
of what is whole
& what is left behind
on the branches
that you emptied.

Nadia Connor is twenty years old and lives in Sheffield. She is currently reading English at Pembroke College, Cambridge. This is her first publication.

the artisans

too long winter, we are quite   o you
    alive through the unbedded smoke   star
the deepening scar-marks   of my door
  the long walk home   you with your
      walk home unending   limp eyes
              your pleading
you are keeping well in my cellar   *mother immaculata*
  you are brewing up our stolen times   *on the floor*
(we have stolen others)   *come tongue me*
      and when i   you your most heroic-
    breathe   fanciful
our harvest of sighs, of quiet wingings *come lay me to rest*
the breathless cadence   *find my*
  of want   sealess death
      i am in love only with winged things   prosaic
thin faceless ones   forgetting
    o pure   (we are in lieu of ourselves)   its caresses
and i hate your true voice
i hate   *you who is responsible*
    you who takes me to your breast

desirelessly chalking your   and pink days
possessing limbs so unstartled –   on cliffs
calm in their own wide wake   risking everything
(i have given up my ghosts   to stand above your own
for red lipstick and your dry smiles   poetic death
i have given up my books)
      unchancing it
so this story's yours   while by the knives
     this dividing   you secretly are weaving
though i would change in any way
though i would paint myself   your narratives
and pay   like smoke
    to endure your pleading fingers   between the rocks
bleeding myself into the sink   *madonna bewitch –*

238

sister

double-winged

the blossom's fist
      is a tentative balance, unbloomed,
            as you, out-leaning, trembling

with poise struck your dancer's
         star to behead it:

resting here, unkissed,
your arms full of roses,
the exploding mouth of the Camellia
(yes, desperate to be kissed)
will undo you as i
am already half-undone by you,

      sun-bitten, unshy, flaring forwards
beneath the haloes
and the untongued Honeysuckle's arms.

Lyric

Sleepless with secrets
where shall we shed ourselves
but in the night's fold
where kisses stiffen
and prospects blow
from my window like roses –

we are folded into each other
like petals, like the habit
of an old rose, a condensation
of curves netting distancelessness;
the old possession.
From unshut eyes

love weeps burdenless
like wax into alien sepulchres.
The windows open on little stars.
Beneath the woven fold

you're sleepless and undreaming;
your face is white; you sit up weeping.

This is the calamitous silence
after all things explode:
the blue minute,
hysterics all done down;
our things
unfolded as snow:

your watch; my heart; the dead shreds.

Carnations

She pressed my flowers between her sheets.
Long fingers, barely daring
a touch not made deft
by the quiet detachments
of craft would take
the heads from my carnations,
arrayed on tables,
desks, in untimely utterances

of pure frivolity;
the last laugh
before the end had started.
Her hands came clear
as any artist's:
unkempt and up close,
seasick with breathing,
pressing painted mouths

amid my dictionaries
of quotations, facts,
slipped in between the leaves
with dry pinched fingers,
two a page, the clumsy pairings
of love. Over sestinas
and sonnets, definitions, doubts,
the flowers keep their memoranda,

hanging still as kisses
in the paper's dry museum,
the pursed lips of time.

A book to protect.

There is often a book,
not so much text
as talisman.

Johnny Marsh IX

The Thomas Hardy Poetry Competition 2008

In memory of James Gibson

This competition was sponsored by **The Thomas Hardy Society** in association with *Agenda* and judged by **Bernard O'Donoghue** who was born in County Cork, Ireland and is a Fellow of Wadham College, Oxford where he teaches Medieval Literature. His *Selected Poems* came out in the spring of this year.

Poems had to show some affinity with the work of Thomas Hardy in terms of subject matter, theme or technique.

First Prize: Sheila Smith

Sheila lives in Nottingham and her poems have been published in several journals and anthologies. Shoestring Press published her chapbook, *Chalk and Cheese*, in 2001.

Burial

The shiny brass and varnished wood
which has nothing to do with you,
yet haunted me as a revenant would,
the shiny brass and varnished wood,
in the black rain as I lonely stood
to board the train, taking me to
the shiny brass and varnished wood
which has nothing to do with you.

Mourners trailed over the graveyard grass,
wet, and crushed from last night's gale.
I let the family and coffin pass as
mourners trailed over the graveyard grass.
Sun lit a gate where a roan horse was,
a robin's song fell shrill and frail.
Mourners trailed over the graveyard grass,
wet, and crushed from last night's gale.

As though my heart had found its king,
and lodged where it had always been,
when I stood at the earth's black opening
as though my heart had found its king
my flowers flew like a bird's wing
to your breast. The throw quick and keen,
as though my heart had found its king
and lodged where it had always been.

Second Prize: **James Simpson**

James lives in Hayshott, West Sussex. A collection of his poems, *Hunting the Wren*, with artwork by Carolyn Trant, came out from Actaeon Press in 2007 as a limited edition. In 1999 he received a Jerwood Foundation award for his poetry.

Woolbeding

It is like the scene in the oil painting.
a mother and her daughter
walk into the night;

the light from the cottage windows
behind them,
two glimmers of an oil lamp.

And so it is when the world marks time
some light remains;
from candles at the carol supper,

of sheep on a hill
above the church
blinking at the gold cupped moon;

from slow progress
across fields
sorting potatoes and stone.

There is still a light from the window
but it is diminishing now
only our voices gather in the dusk.

Third Prize: **Jane Croft**

Jane's background is in education in schools here and overseas, and as a part-time tutor for the Open University. Apart from poetry, she writes non-fiction articles and novels. Her first book, a historical romance, comes out n America next February and in England in September 2009.

Frost

We turned the horses out at fade of light
And saw the moonrise on the meadow's crest
As brilliant stars announced the coming night
And fiery gleams sank slowly in the west.
On hill and hollow frost had lain all day
Thick-furring turf and tree and hawthorn hedge
With ice, and bound like iron the rutted clay
And rimed the furrows at the pasture's edge.
Its beauty held us and we lingered yet
Both careless then of time, the passing hour
That brings the silent blight; the unseen threat
Whose stealthy touch destroys the budding flower.
The carefree day is gone that found us there:
Mere shadow, glimpsed like breath in frosty air.

Notes for Broadsheet Poets

Caroline Clark was a chosen young Broadsheet poet in the previous *Lauds* issue of *Agenda*, Vol. 43, Nos. 2-3 and has work forthcoming in *The Reader* and *The Frogmore Papers*. This year she has had several poems shortlisted for the Plough Prize and the Mslexia Poetry Competition. She comes from Lewes in Sussex and now lives in Montreal. She is currently translating essays by the Russian poet, Olga Sedakova. New poems of hers can be seen in Broadsheet 11 www.agendapoetry.co.uk

The following essay by Caroline Clark links to Greg Delanty and his dialogue, to his many voices, his incessant reading of poetry, indeed of any poetry he can lay his hands on. It also links to William Bedford's essay on Geoffrey Hill and Paul Muldoon: 'The Fascination of what is Difficult' in this Greg Delanty 50th Birthday issue of *Agenda*, Vol 43 No 4 / Vol 44 No 1.

What Lies Ahead

You cry into your hair at night, despairing. You write in your notebook a command, a prayer: 'Give me a mentor, the kind that will rip up my work in disgust knowing I can do better'. It seems to you that mentors are a thing of the past, of literary salons, letter writing. I'm writing here to myself, let's say of six years ago, a twenty-five year old. At that time I was mid-way through spending almost all my twenties in Moscow. I had come back to the UK for a year to do an MA in Modern European Literature. I was soon to write my dissertation on Paul Celan and Osip Mandelstam, who were, I see now, to become mentors of a kind. The words of true mentors tend to stick with you, even if you don't want to hear what they are saying or don't know why their words should resonate so deeply. I want to tell you here about some of those words that have stayed with me, that have helped me to understand poetry – how to read it and how to write it. In short, Mandelstam taught me the importance of drafting and Celan taught me the importance of going deeper, the need to step beyond. But 'in short' won't do – it's the getting there that counts. This too I picked up from them.

I was initially drawn to write about them together because of a conception of poetry they both shared. It was one that I found irresistible, perhaps because it formulated so precisely for me the driving force of poetry:

> The shipwrecked sailor throws a sealed bottle into the sea at a critical moment, and it has his name in it and what has happened to him. Many years later, walking along the dunes, I find it in the sand, I read the letter, I learn when it happened, the testament of the deceased. I had a right to do this. I did not unseal someone else's letter. The letter sealed in the bottle was addressed

to its finder. I found it. That means, then, that I am its secret addressee.[1]

A poem, being an instance of language, hence essentially dialogue, may be a letter in a bottle thrown out to sea with the – surely not always strong – hope that it may somehow wash up somewhere, perhaps on a shoreline of the heart. In this way, too, poems are *en route*: they are headed toward.[2]

I'll steal the next few sentences from my dissertation: Mandelstam, a generation older than Celan, had the first of the above passages published in 1913, while Celan delivered the second statement as part of his address on receiving the Bremen literary prize in January 1958. The generation's difference between them is evident even here, with the decidedly more traditional prose style of the elder poet and the more difficult, idiosyncratic style of the younger poet. The case for linking the two poets has a firm, if at first seemingly thin, foundation in this shared metaphor, but we shall see how deeply it concerns their poetic conceptions and how significant it is to their poetry...

You can see how I meant to go on. Part of my task was to adopt an academic tone. Now I'm starting to fill in the non-academic gaps, so to speak. Let me take a word I use there as my starting point: difficult. I was aware that their poetry was considered to be amongst the most 'difficult' of the twentieth century, but perhaps not as aware as I could have been. Thankfully so, I say now, as I would have probably panicked in the headlights and frozen. Poetry is difficult, I'd always told myself. It's the most difficult thing I can occupy myself with; it doesn't come easily (but when it does!). That said, I would advise my former self to take less seriously the idea of difficult poetry, and in its place take more seriously the actual reading of poems, the actual writing of poems.

What stayed with me – well after lines of their poetry, quotes from their essays and speeches, dates and historical facts had faded away – was this idea of the elemental directedness of poems. Their words revealed to me the core dynamic of a poem. I felt this could be summed up with one word: towards. Towards what? Towards the reader, the future, the past, words opening towards each other. Celan goes on to say: 'Toward something open, inhabitable; an approachable you, perhaps an approachable reality.' I already felt, but had not formulated, what the two poets were saying: the poem is sent out to someone, but no one in particular, in the hope of a response. The poem is oriented by hope. I felt the immediacy in this statement and the implications of my picking up and receiving their poem-message. Mandelstam writes: 'There is no lyric without dialogue';[3] Celan, a generation later, says poems are 'essentially dialogue' – I felt I might one day establish my own dialogue with them. A poem to which I often return, which

---

[1] O. Mandelstam, 'About an Interlocutor' in *Selected Essays*, trans. S. Monas (University of Texas Press, 1977): 59

[2] P. Celan, 'The Meridian' in *Collected Prose*, trans. R. Waldrop (Manchester: Carcanet Press, 1999): 35

[3] O. Mandelstam, 'About an Interlocutor' in *Selected Essays*, trans. S. Monas (University of Texas Press, 1977): 62-63

perhaps above all others of Mandelstam's has remained with me is 'The Horseshoe Finder'. In it I have a strong sense of this movement towards – progression, transformation, a searching out. On first reading it I was particularly struck by the decidedly more modern, more Celanesque sounding final section:

> Human lips,
>> which have nothing more to say.
> Retain the shape of the last word spoken
>
> …
>
> What I say now, is not said by me,
> but is dug up out of the earth like grains of petrified wheat.
>
> …
>
> Time cuts through me like a coin,
> and there is no longer enough of me left for me.

Mandelstam speaks of the 'uncanny shiver of joy' one might experience as a reader when a poem reaches out, 'when one is called unexpectedly by name'.[4] It was with a certain joy that I learnt Celan had felt called upon to translate this poem. He had answered Mandelstam's 'message in a bottle', entered into that so hoped-for dialogue which I saw now could be truly realised: in his translation was the most authentic of poetic encounters.

Of course as someone whose greatest desire was to 'write poetry', the hope offered by this dynamic 'towards' corresponded to my own: to make contact, establish dialogue, find a reader. I knew too it would be difficult. Here's where some advice from an insightful mother of a friend came in: just do it. In his essay 'Conversation about Dante' Mandelstam says that poetic material 'exists only in the execution' (this last word *ispolneniye* translates also as 'performance', 'fulfilment', 'rendering', 'enactment'). In other, more homely, words: poetry exists in the doing – in speaking it, in reading it (and as I also understood, in composing it). It is a phrase I often use to push myself on – to read more aloud, write more. I felt I was woefully lacking in education though. I took Mandelstam's lament over the lack of the 'cultured reader' personally. In his essay 'Attack', he speaks against the incompetent reader who cannot be relied upon to properly understand the text. What is needed is a responsible and responsive reader, one who turns the relationship between reader and writer into a two-way exchange. Celan perhaps calls for such a responsive interlocutor in the opening of a poem:

> Sprich auch du,
> sprich als letzter,
> sag deinen Spruch.

---

[4] ibid 60

Speak, you too,
speak last,
have your say.

Although I felt wildly lacking in education and 'culture', I was sure I could as least
be responsive and responsible. As for the rest, I'd tell myself: less of the panic and
just get reading.

Mandelstam insists that poems cannot be paraphrased or retold. They are
what they do. This helped me immensely with that cruellest of questions I was
sometimes asked: 'what do you write your poems about?' How I hated that
'about'? I would substitute it for 'towards' and risk ending up in semantic knots.
It's simple, as I took Mandelstam to be saying, with poetry there is no 'about', it's
all in the doing. Read it and see.

Or with Celan, crack it open and see. I read in awe as Celan would crack words
open to reveal new depths, forge new joins. I would study how the words in
his poems would not stand alone but would be in constant communication or
tension with the others – one word engendering the next. Through him I gained
a stronger sense of the potential locked in words; I caught a flash of what happens
when grammar is followed to its logical conclusion:

> In der Mandel – was steht in der Mandel?
> Das Nichts.
> ....
> Im Nichts – wer steht da? Der König.
>
> In the almond – what is there/stands in the almond?
> the Nothing.
> ....
> In the Nothing – who is/stands there? The king.[5]

Here unfolds a new universe in which the newly substantivized 'nothing' (now '*the
nothing*') pulls logic in a seemingly paradoxical direction: nothing is made into
something, crack it open, what do we find there? Celan is unrelenting in how far he
strives to push language, with every word allowed to exert its full pull. In his speech
'The Meridian' Celan talks of a 'step beyond' which is part of all art, a step away
which must lead to 'that which is most one's own'. Poetry takes you on a path away
from yourself, by doing so there is the promise that you can 'set yourself free'.

Celan pushes and pulls the word and grammatical logic over astonishing
distances; language, the reader surely feels, astonishes him. It is as Mandelstam
says in his essay 'The Morning of Acmeism': 'The capacity for astonishment is the

---

[5]An attempt at a literal translation. The verb 'stehen' literally means 'to stand' but is also used in
expressions which mean 'to be', so we can read the line either as 'there is nothing' in the almond or
'nothing stands' in the almond.

poet's greatest virtue…Logic is the kingdom of the unexpected. To think logically means to be perpetually astonished.'[6] A term Mandelstam uses to describe the Acmeist movement works well for Celan's lyric: organic. His is a word which is alive, ever responding, ever resisting, in motion. As Celan says, the poem is underway. Indeed if the state of being oriented 'towards' is vital, so too is the opposing movement 'against'. In this state the poem (indeed, the poet too) must experience or endure all that it encounters. Celan's reality-bound poems are ever in a state of flux, towards-against. Was I allowed to be influenced by these poets whose fates were so different to mine? Whose struggles were incomparable with mine? One thing was clear: they were showing me how hard a poem needed to be worked at, worked towards. I very much took on Mandelstam's idea that the poet must master the skill of tacking. As the sailor must navigate against the wind and tides, the poet must work through drafts overcoming resistance encountered en route. Taking the 'oblique' approach is how the artist must proceed. I would have to learn not to be so eager to seek out the end of a poem, but learn to work through more drafts, dig deeper.

Nadezhda Mandelstam describes how her husband had once sought to destroy various versions of the same poem, but then later came to value this drafting process, and began to preserve similar poems which had arisen from the same impulse. Again, I return to 'Conversation about Dante':

All nominative cases should be replaced by datives of direction… Everything is turned inside out: the substantive is the goal, not the subject of the sentence.[7]

To anyone unfamiliar with grammatical cases, the meaning here may not be immediately apparent. For me, a student of Russian and German with a desire to write poetry, I felt I had struck gold. Mandelstam here calls for Dante's poetry to be understood in the dative, to be set in motion by the reader rather than be fixed in place. The dative case is that of direction, it is the state of being oriented towards. The nominative case is that of arrival, of stasis, of being equated to the substantive. Mandelstam scorns the tendency to view art as if it came 'ready-made' and he insists on the importance of drafts. Here he ranks the approach, the journey, the draft above the arrival, stasis, completion.

On first reading Mandelstam's words that drafts should never be destroyed, I tried to obey in awe and mild terror. Along with misconception of 'difficult'

---

[6] O. Mandelstam, *Selected Essays*, trans. S. Monas (University of Texas Press, 1977): 131 *Acmeism* was a school of poetry whose key members included Anna Akhmatova and Mandelstam. Their major concerns were to depict the concrete world of everyday reality with brevity and clarity, with the precise and logical use of the word. They took a stand against the mysticism, and lack of interest in the concrete and the human, of the earlier generation of Symbolists.

[7] O. Mandelstam, 'Conversation about Dante' in *Selected Essays,* trans. S. Monas (University of Texas Press, 1977): 44

poetry, I also had a tendency to isolate single sentences as imperatives issued in the sternest of tones. With some poets' statements on poetry this takes no greatly exaggerated sense of solemnity: that sternness is truly there and also a lack of generosity of spirit. Rather than reading this as a dictum 'never destroy drafts', I see now he was saying that the draft cannot be destroyed, it is integral to the finished poem. Even a single phrase you write – perhaps don't even write down but hear, turn your attention to for a moment and then let go – hasn't given up the ghost for good, it may resurface in a poem when you least expect it. It takes a great deal of willingness to work through, rather than around, those things which initially seem unsayable. Now in my present work I sometimes recognise the kernel of a past poem I tried to crack years ago but abandoned in an early draft. This is most heartening – to feel that something you once found so difficult now seems less so.

Mandelstam's praise of the dative condition helped explain why I so disliked that question 'what do you write *about*': it was demanding that I define something that I was working towards, that I put my work into the nominative case, set it in stone. Of course I could say what 'themes' I was interested in, but I always felt I was betraying myself somehow. I had less trouble playing the 'about' game, once I learnt to play along. You could say I learnt to take myself less seriously, but perhaps I just learnt to take the question less seriously. Indeed if I knew what a particular poem was to be about I wouldn't be writing it, as many have said before. But whether something may have been said many times before is not important. Everything there is to say about poetry has already been said, including this statement itself. But when you are able to say it in your own words, have worked towards a particular discovery through your own experience, you have earned the right to dare to repeat all those gone before. So I would advise my past self not to be afraid of repeating what great discoveries have already been made, but instead go ahead and discover them on my terms:

> Everything that has been will repeat itself anew,
> Our sweet joy is all in the moment of recognition.[8]

When I left university it was with the anticipation that something new lay ahead. I have since found it more realistic and fulfilling to return to things newly rather than seek out something brand new and shining. I return to books I read for my studies but now without the secondary literature, to look at them newly, read the work of poets without the ulterior motive of proving a thesis, of setting their words in stone.

I'll end with the same words I used to close my dissertation, a short quote from Emmanuel Lévinas: 'Poetry is ahead of us'. It is a quote from Lévinas commenting on Celan's speech 'The Meridian'. I use it in my dissertation to support my

---

[8] From the poem 'Tristia' by Mandelstam.

conviction that the poetic word is dialogic, and that poetry is oriented by hope. I'd like here in this non-academic space to openly turn it to my own purposes, direct it to my past self of a few years ago: Poetry is ahead of you, and it's here with you now. Look around.

TRACED IN

FOOTSTEPS

Johnny Marsh X

Louis Armand is a writer and visual artist living in Prague, where he directs the Intercultural Studies programme in the Philosophy Faculty of Charles University. He is formerly the editor of the *Prague Literary Review* and founder of the Prague International Poetry Festival. His books include *Séances* (Twisted Spoon, 1998), *Inexorable Weather* (Arc, 2001), *Strange Attractors* (Salt, 2003) and *Malice in Underland* (Textbase, 2003). www.louis-armand.com

William Bedford first appeared in *Agenda* in 1972. He has published poetry, novels, children's novels, short stories and criticism around the world. His *New and Selected Poems* is due from Poetry Salzburg. He is currently Royal Literary Fund Fellow at Oxford Brookes University.

Benjamin Bird was awarded his Ph.D at the University of Leeds for a thesis entitled *Models of Consciousness in the Novels of Don DeLillo*. He has published many articles and has taught at Leeds and Huddersfield Universities. He is currently working on a book about the influence of Puritanism in twentieth century American fiction

Colm Breathnach was born Cork City in 1961. He studied philosophy and Irish at UCC. He has worked in lexicography and as a terminologist and is now a translator with the Irish Parliament translation service. He is three times winner of the Oireachtas premier prize for poetry in Irish. He has published six collections, the most recent of these being *Chiaroscura*, Coiscéim, Dublin, 2006

Terence Brown is Professor of Anglo-Irish literature at Trinity College, Dublin where he is also a Senior Fellow. He is a member of the Royal Irish Academy. He has published and lectured widely on Irish literature in English and on Irish cultural history. Among his publications are books on Louis MacNeice, on W.B. Yeats and on poetry from the North of Ireland.

D.W. Brydon was born in Edinburgh in 1975. He was a lecturer in mathematics at Hertford College, Oxford before moving into finance some years ago. His poem 'Sleepless' was published in the online supplement to the *Lauds* issue of *Agenda.*

David Burns grew up in north-east Scotland and is a field archaeologist, working in Oxford. His poetry has been published in *Anon*, *Poetry News* and the anthology, *East of Auden*.

Paddy Bushe was born in Dublin in 1948 and now lives in Waterville, Co. Kerry. He writes in both Irish and English, and has published eight collections of poetry, the most recent of which is *To Ring in Silence: New and Selected Poems* (Dedalus, 2008), a bilingual volume. He has also published three books of translations. He has won the Strokestown International Poetry Prize, the Listowel Writers' Week Poetry Prize, Duais an Oireachtais and the Michael Hartnett Award. He is a member of Aosdána.

Patrick Carrington's latest collection of poetry is *Hard Blessings* (MSR Publishing, 2008). He is the winner of the 2008 Matt Clark Prize and Pocataligo Poetry Contest. His poems have appeared in many journals in the U.S. and in the U.K. He serves as the poetry editor of *Mannequin Envy* (www.mannequinenvy.com). He lives in New Jersey.

David Cavanagh's collections of poems include *The Middleman* (Salmon Poetry, 2003) and *Falling Body* (forthcoming from Salmon in the Fall, 2008). His poems appear in journals and anthologies in Canada, Ireland, the U.K. and the U.S.A, including *The Book of Irish American Poetry* and *Salmon: A Journey in Poetry*. He lives in Burlington, Vermont, and is an associate dean at Johnson State College.

253

Laura A. Ciraolo was born in New York City and has lived there as long as she can remember. She's had her cat for 10 years, her husband for 28 years and her car for 21 years, not necessarily in any order of importance. She has poems out now in *Left Facing Bird*, the *New York Quarterly* #63, the *Long Island Quarterly*, *Iota #78* (UK) and *The Centrifugal Eye*. She's had poems recently in *MiPOesias*, *Rumble*, and *Orbis Quarterly International Literary Journal* (UK). When Laura is not reading or writing, she is finishing a graduate degree in Theology.

Michael Collier is the author of five books of poems, including most recently, *Dark Wild Realm*. *The Ledge* (2000) was a finalist for the National Book Critics' Circle Award and the Los Angeles Times Book Prize. He teaches at the University of Maryland and serves as the director of the Bread Loaf Writers' Conference, Middlebury College. From 1977-1981, he served as *Agenda*'s American correspondent.

Billy Collins's 8th collection of poetry is *Ballistics* (2008). He served as U.S. Poet Laureate from 2001 to 2003.

Stewart Conn's publications include *Stolen Light: Selected Poems* and *Ghosts at Cockcrow* (Bloodaxe Books), *L'ànima del Teixidor* (with Anna Crowe/Edicions Proa, Barcelona), and most recently a pamphlet *The Loving-Cup* (Mariscat Press). He has lived for many years in Edinburgh, and was from 2002 to 2005 the city's inaugural Poet Laureate. In 2006 he edited *100 Favourite Scottish Poems* (Luath/Scottish Poetry Library).

Belinda Cooke completed a doctorate on Robert Lowell in 1993. Her poetry, translations, articles and reviews have been published widely. She has one book of poems, *Resting Place* (Flarestack, 2008) and *Paths of the Beggar Woman: the Selected Poems of Marina Tsvetaeva* is forthcoming with Worple Press this year. She teaches English in Scotland.

Anthony Cronin is the author of several collections of verse, including the long poems *R.M.S. Titanic, Letter To An Englishman* and *The End of the Modern World*. He has also written novels, collections of essays, a well-known memoir, *Dead as Doornails*, and biographies of Samuel Beckett and Flann O'Brien. He is married to the novelist and poet, Anne Haverty and lives in Dublin.

David Curzon was born in Australia in 1941. He has a B.Sc. in Physics and a Ph.D in Economics. He worked for many years, 1988-2001, in the United Nations, evaluating the effectiveness of UN programmes. He was also responsible for the development of training programmes on evaluation for UN staff in offices around the world. He has had many books published all over the world.

John F. Deane, born on Achill Island in 1943, has published many books of poetry and has won many prizes and awards. His latest collection is *The Instruments of Art* (Carcanet, 2005). He founded the Dedalus Press in Dublin. He also founded *Poetry Ireland*. He is a member of Aosdána, and this year has been visiting scholar in the Burns Library of Boston College. His latest collection is *The Instruments of Art* (Carcanet, 2005).

Born in Toronto, **Katherine Dimma** holds degrees from McGill University, The School of Visual Arts and NYU. She has been the recipient of several grants and awards, including an Ontario Arts Council Grant and the London Life Purchase Award. In 2004 her chapbook *Wind in the Trees* was published by Nightboat Books. Her poems have appeared in several journals including *Barrow Street, Painted Bride Quarterly, Thin Air,* and *Redactions*. She lives in Brooklyn with a dog named Otto.

Angela France lives in Gloucestershire. She works for a local charity, with disengaged and challenging young people. She runs a regular live poetry event – 'Buzzwords' and is studying for an M.A. in Creative and Critical Writing at the University of Gloucestershire. Her poems have appeared in small press anthologies and a number of poetry journals including *Acumen, Iota, Orbis* and *The Frogmore Papers*.

George Gömöri, poet, critic and scholar, was born in Budapest but went into exile in 1956. He lectured in Polish and Hungarian at the University of Cambridge. He has published eleven books of poetry in Hungarian and translated many Hungarian poets into English. With George Szirtes he edited the anthology *The Colonnade of Teeth: Modern Hungarian Poetry* (1996). Two books of his poetry have appeared in English; a third, *Polishing October*, to be published by Shoestring Press, will be published later this year.

Eamon Grennan's most recent volumes of poetry are *The Quick of It* and *Out of Breath* (Gallery Press), and, in the U.S., *Matter of Fact* (Graywolf Press). He taught for many years in the English Department of Vassar College, and currently teaches in the graduate writing programs of Columbia and New York University. He lives in New York and spends time in the West of Ireland.

Rahul Gupta was born in the Lincolnshire Wolds in 1976 and read English at the University of York, specialising in mediæval languages and literature. He lives in the Cathedral Quarter of Lincoln and has also been published as an illustrator.

Harry Guest is a well-known poet and translator. He is a French and Japanese specialist. Last winter itinerant press brought out his translations of Jean Cassou's wartime sonnets entitled *From a Condemned Cell*. His long poem *Comparisons* is scheduled to appear soon from bluechrome.

Rachel Hadas is Board of Governors Professor of English at the Newark campus of Rutgers University, New Jersey. The most recent of her many books are *The River of Forgetfulness* (2006) - poems, and selected essays, *Classics* (2007). She is currently co-editing an anthology of Greek poetry in translation from Homer to the present day for Norton.

David Hale was born in Scotland and now lives in Gloucestershire. He works in the woodland at Ruskin Mill College with young people with Asperger's Syndrome. He has had poems published in a variety of magazines, and hopes to get his first pamphlet together soon.

Alyson Hallett's first full volume of poetry, *The Stone Library*, came out with Peterloo Poets in 2007. She has also published fiction and drama and established herself as a successful public artist. Alyson has taught courses for the Arvon Foundation and she has just finished a 3 year poet-in-residence post at the Small School in Hartland. Prior to this she was Visiting Writer at the University of the West of England for two years. Full details can be seen on her website: www.thestonelibrary.com

James Harpur is the poetry editor of the *Temenos Academy Review* and *Southword*. He has had four volumes of poetry published by Anvil Press, as well as a book of translations. Other books include *The Gospel of Joseph of Arimathea* and *Love Burning in the Soul: an Introduction to the Christian Mystics*. For more information visit www.jamesharpur.com

Anne Haverty's collection of poems, *The Beauty of The Moon* (Chatto, 1999) was a Poetry Book Society Recommendation. She has published three novels, one of which, *The Far Side of a Kiss* (2000) was long-listed for the Booker Prize. Another novel, *One Day as a Tiger* (1997) was a winner of the Rooney Prize and shortlisted for the Whitbread. Her biography of Constance Markievicz appeared in 1989. She is married to Anthony Cronin and lives in Dublin.

Seamus Heaney won the Nobel Prize for Literature in 1995. He holds many honorary degrees and is a member of Aosdána. His latest collection is *District and Circle* (Faber). *Agenda* published a *Seamus Heaney Fiftieth Birthday issue*, Vol. 27 No. 1 in Spring, 1989.

Gail Holst-Warhaft is a poet, translator and musician who directs Mediterranean Studies at Cornell University. She has published her poems, translations of Greek poetry and prose, and essays on Greece in the U.K., the U.S., Greece, and Australia. Among her books are *Road to Rembetika* (4th edition, 2006), *Theodorakis* (1980), *The Collected Poems of Nikos Kavadias* (1987), *Dangerous Voices* (1992), and *The Cue for Passion* (2000). Her first collection of poetry, *Penelope's Confession*, was published in 2007. Her poem 'Translation' was published in *Agenda* in 2005.

Lia Hills' work has been published, performed and translated in Australia and overseas. In 2007, a contemporary ballet, *Les Portes du Monde*, for which she wrote the libretto in French, was performed in Lausanne, Switzerland. Lia is editor and co-initiator of the poetry section of *Moving Galleries*, a poetry/art project currently displayed on trains in Melbourne, Australia. Her prize-winning poetry collection, *the possibility of flight* will be released in 2008, and a crossover novel is forthcoming with Text Publishing. She is currently translating Marie Darieussecq's novel *Tom Est Mort* to be released in English in 2009.

Jane Hirshfield's sixth poetry collection, *After* (HarperCollins, US / Bloodaxe Books, UK), was a finalist for the T.S. Eliot Award in the UK and named a best book of 2006 by *The Washington Post, The San Francisco Chronicle*, and *The Financial Times*. Her poems have appeared in the *TLS, Poetry London, The Guardian, The New Yorker, Poetry*, et al. A collection of three recent essays, *Hiddenness, Uncertainty, Surprise*, has just appeared in the Newcastle University/Bloodaxe Poetry Lectures series.

Maysa Abdel Aal Ibrahim was born in Alexandria, Egypt in 1961. Between 1978 and 1980, she was a student of Desmond O'Grady, well-known Irish poet and Arabic scholar. She finished her MA on William Carlos Williams in 1982, and her Ph.D on Denise Levertov in 2001. She is Professor at the Faculty of Arts in Tanta University. She is married and has three children.

Simon Jackson was born in Manchester. He worked as an itinerant musician and teacher in Eastern Europe, North Africa and South America during the 1990s and now lives in Edinburgh. *Reflections on Moonlight* won the British Gas Young Playwright Award, *Frankenstein, the Monster's Story* for Theatre of Fire toured Britain, Ireland, Holland and Belgium, and his latest play, *Shooting at the Balcony* is currently being produced for Radio 4. His poetry has appeared in anthologies and magazines here and overseas and an album, *Tomorrow When I Awake as God,* recorded under the pseudonym Torpedo Buoy, is scheduled for release this Autumn (www.myspace.com/torpedobuoy).

Chris Jones is senior lecturer in Poetry at the University of St. Andrews. He is the author of *Strange Likeness: the uses of Old English in twentieth-century poetry* (Oxford University Press, 2006).

Fawzia Kane was born in San Fernando, Trinidad, and came to the UK on a scholarship to study architecture. She now lives and practises as an architect in London. She began writing poems in earnest around 10 years ago after attending Arvon and Poetry School courses. Her work has been published in several magazines, including *Poetry Wales, Poetry London, Rialto, the Shop* and the *Interpreter's House*. In 2003, she was one of the featured poets of the Poetry School anthology *Entering the Tapestry* (Enitharmon).

Brendan Kennelly, the well-known Irish poet, was born in Ballylongford, Co. Kerry and spoke only Irish until his twenties. He was Professor of Modern Literature in Trinity College, Dublin for over 30 years, and has had over 30 books of poetry published.

Galway Kinnell, the influential American poet, was born in 1927. He was the Erich Maria Remarque Professor of Creative Writing at New York University and a Chancellor of the American Academy of Poets. He is now retired and lives in Vermont. His latest collection, reviewed here, is *Strong is Your Hold*.

Adrie Kusserow's first book of poems is *Hunting Down the Monk* (BOA Editions Ltd.). Most recently her poems have been published in *The Kenyon Review, The Harvard Review* and *Best American Poetry 2008*. She is currently Chair of the Department of Sociology and Anthropology at St. Michael's College in Vermont.

Robin Laffan was born in England and lived for twenty years in Wales before moving to Ethiopia for two years and then to Dublin in 2005. His poetry has been published in magazines in Ireland and the UK including *Iota, Anon, Poetry Monthly, Revival* and *Southword*. He is now looking to consolidate his recent work into a collection.

An Irish-American, **Christopher Locke** was born in Laconia, NH in 1968. His poems and prose have appeared in over 100 magazines in the United States, Canada, Britain, and Ireland. Chris has received several awards for his poetry, including a 2006 and 2007 Dorothy Sargent Memorial Poetry Prize, and grants in poetry from the New Hampshire Council on the Arts, the Massachusetts Cultural Council, and Fundacion Valparaiso (Spain). His three chapbooks of poetry are *Possessed*, (Main Street Rag, Editor's Choice Award, 2005), *Slipping Under Diamond Light*, (Clamp Down Press, 2002), and *How To Burn*, (Adastra Press, 1995).

Michael Longley has won numerous awards for his poetry, including the T.S. Eliot Award. Like Seamus Heaney, he comes from Northern Ireland and was born in 1939. His *Collected Poems* appeared in 2007.

Catherine Phil MacCarthy's collections include *How High the Moon* (Poetry Ireland, Sense of Place Award, 1991, a joint book), *This Hour of the Tide* (1994), *the blue globe* (1998), *Suntrap* (2007), and a first novel, *One Room an Everywhere* (2003). She was awarded a bursary in poetry from the Arts Council, in 1994, 1999 and 2007/8. Writer in Residence for Dublin City (1994), University College Dublin (2002), she works freelance as a Creative Writing tutor. She is a former editor of *Poetry Ireland Review*.

Kathryn Maris, a New Yorker now based in London, has published a collection of poems, *The Book of Jobs*. She has won a Pushcart Prize and an Academy of American Poets award, and has held fellowships at Yaddo, the Fine Arts Work Center in Provincetown, and the Hawthornden Castle. Her poems have appeared in *Poetry, Poetry London, The Harvard Review*, several anthologies, and the 2008 *Poetry Calendar*.

Thomas McCarthy was born in Cappoquin, Co. Waterford in 1954. He has many poetry collections published mainly by the Anvil Press, and fiction. He has won many awards and is a member of Aosdána. He lives in Cork City.

Gill McEvoy runs three regular poetry groups: a reading group, a workshop group and *Zest!*, an Open Floor Poetry Night in Chester. She is Artistic Director for *Chester Oyez!*, October 18th-19th, Chester's first celebration of the spoken word. Her work has been widely published in magazines and online. Her pamphlet, *Uncertain Days*, came out from Happenstance Press in 2006. A full collection is due from Cinnamon Press in 2010.

Lucie McKee's poems have appeared in journals in the U.S. and in the U.K., including the *TLS*, *London Magazine, The Rialto, Poetry Review, Stand*. She received *Poetry Review's* Geoffrey Dearmer Prize in 2004. She lives in Vermont.

Paul McLoughlin was born in London of Irish parents. He continues to teach part-time in a comprehensive school and at university, and to play jazz saxophones and flute. *What Certainty Is Like* was published in 1998 by Smith/Doorstop, and *What Moves Moves* (2004) and *Forgetting To Come In* (2007) by Shoestring Press. 'An Interview With Greg Delanty' appeared in *Poetry Ireland Review 90* (2007).

Andrew McNeillie was born and brought up in North Wales. His most recent poetry collection, *Slower*, came out in 2006. His memoir, *An Aran Keening* (2001), telling of his year on Inis Mór in 1968-69, was published by Lilliput in Dublin. The North Welsh prequel to that volume, *Once*, will be published in Spring 2009. He is Literature Editor at Oxford University Press.

Abby Millager lives and writes amid mushroom farms in the Northern hills of Delaware. She was a founding editor of *Diner*. At one time, briefly, she was a doctor. Her poems and other texts have appeared widely in magazines and journals in the U.S.

W.S. Milne, poet and essayist, was born in Aberdeen in 1953. He was educated there, at Corby Grammar School, Northamptonshire, and at Newcastle University where he studied English. A teacher for many years, he is now retired and living in Surrey. He has just completed two works, a trilogy of plays on Mary, Queen of Scots, and a version of Aesop's *Fables*.

John Montague was born in 1929 and has won numerous awards for his poetry. *Agenda* did a 75th Birthday supplement for him, as part of a large double Irish issue, Vol. 40 Nos. 1-3 in 2004. He now lives mostly in Nice, France, and spends some time in Co. Cork each year. *Agenda Editions* brought out his translation from the French of Claude Esteban, *A Smile Between the Stones*, in 2005.

Paul Muldoon, a Pulitzer prize-winner, became Professor at Princeton University in 2007. He is Poetry editor of *The New Yorker*, and an Honorary Fellow of Hertford College, Oxford. His latest collection, *Horse Latitudes*, is reviewed here.

Gerry Murphy was born in Cork in 1952 and resides there now. His latest publication, *End of Part One, New & Selected Poems*, was published by the Dedalus Press, Dublin in 2006.

Desmond O'Grady, the distinguished Irish poet and Arabic scholar, was born in Limerick, Ireland, in 1935 and now lives in Kinsale, Cork. He has published many collections of poetry. His *Seven Arab*

Odes was brought out by **Agenda** Editions and Raven Arts Press in 1990 and his *Kurdish Poems of Love and Liberty* were published by **Agenda** Editions in 2005. He is a member of Aosdána.

Thomas O'Grady was born and grew up on Prince Edward Island. He currently lives in Milton, Massachusetts. By day he teaches Irish Literature and Creative Writing at the University of Massachusetts, Boston. After hours, he plays the guitar in a jazz combo. His first book of poems, *What Really Matters*, was published in 2000 by McGill-Queen's University Press. He has just completed the manuscript for a second book, *Makeover*.

Liam Ó Muirthile is a poet and writer. His latest collection is *Sanas*(Cois Life, 2007).

Leanne O'Sullivan is from Beara, West Cork. She has previously won the Seacat National Poetry Competition, the RTE Rattlebag Poetry Slam, and the Davoren Hanna Award for young emerging Irish poets. Her first collection, *Waiting for My Clothes*, was published in 2004 by Bloodaxe Books and her second collection, *Cailleach; The Hag of Beara*, is due in 2009. Her first work to be published was in **Agenda** Broadsheets.

Louis de Paor was born in Cork in 1961, Louis de Paor has been involved with the contemporary rennaissance of poetry in Irish since 1980 when he was first published in the poetry journal *Innti* which he subsequently edited for a time. His latest collection is *Cúpla Siamach an Ama* (*The Siamese Twins of Time*) was published by Coiscéim in December 2006. A bilingual collection *Ag greadadh bas sa reilig/Clapping in the cemetery* was published by Cló Iar-Chonnachta in November 2005 and reprinted in March 2006.

Ray Racy was born in Manchester on 29 February 1920. His family and he moved to Brazil in 1931. He joined the Royal Air Force in 1941 and flew Spitfires with No. 74 Tiger Squadron. He has a B.A. in English Language and Literature, a Ph.D in Philosophy, and he has had papers published in academic journals. His primary interests are in literature, especially poetry, and philosophy. Other interests include ecology, all the arts, and cycle touring and travel.

Christopher Ricks, literary critic, editor and scholar, is the Professor of Poetry at Oxford, and Warren Professor of the Humanities, Co-director of the Editorial Institute at Boston University. He was formerly King Edward VII Professor of Literature at the University of Cambridge.

Maurice Riordan received the Michael Hartnett Award for *The Holy Land* (Faber, 2007). Previous collections, *A Word from the Loki* and *Floods* were nominated for the T.S. Eliot Prize and the Whitbread Book Award. Other publications include *A Quark for Mister Mark: 101 Poems About Science*, and *Hart Crane* which has recently appeared in Faber's 'Poet to Poet' series. Born in Lisgoold, Co. Cork, he lives in London and edits *Poetry London*.

Tony Roberts was educated in England and America. Since featuring in a Peterloo introductions volume, he has published two poetry collections: *Flowers of the Hudson Bay* (Peterloo) and *Sitters* (Arc). His poems (and reviews) have appeared widely in the literary press. He has just recently taken early retirement from teaching.

Peter Robinson's latest collection is reviewed in this issue. Other recent publications include *Selected Poetry and Prose of Vittorio Sereni* (Chicago), *The Greener Meadow: Selected Poems of Luciano Erba* (Princeton), and *Talk about Poetry: Conversations on the Art* (Shearsman). He is Professor of English and American Literature at the University of Reading.

Fiona Sampson's latest collection is *Common Prayer* (Carcanet, 2007), short-listed for the T.S. Eliot prize. She is the editor of *Poetry Review*.

E.M. Schorb's work has appeared in numerous poetry journals in the U.K., Europe and in the U.S. His third collection, *Murderer's Way*, was awarded the Verna Emery Poetry Prize and published by Purdue University Press.

Harvey Shapiro has published 12 books of poetry. His most recent book is *The Sights Along the Harbor, New and Collected Poems* (Wesleyan University Press, 2006). His *Selected Poems* is available from Carcanet.

Peter Sirr is a freelance writer, editor and translator. The Gallery Press has published his poetry collections *Marginal Zones* (1984), *Talk, Talk* (1987), *Ways of Falling* (1991), *The Ledger of Fruitful Exchange* (1995) and *Bring Everything* (2000). In 2004 the Gallery Press published *Selected Poems* simultaneously with a new collection, *Nonetheless*. Wake Forest University Press published his *Selected Poems* in 2006. He lives in Dublin with his wife, the poet Enda Wyley, and their daughter, Freya.

David Slavitt has published more than eighty books, the latest of which are translations of Lucretius' *De Rerum Natura* (University of California Press) and Boethius' *Consolation of Philosophy* (Harvard University Press). His *Seven Deadly Sins*, a new collection of poems, will appear from LSU Press in the spring.

Tom Sleigh's most recent book of poetry, *Space Walk* (Houghton Mifflin, 2007), won the 2008 Kingsley Tufts Award. His book of essays, *Interview with a Ghost*, was published by Graywolf Press in 2006. He has published many other collections of poetry, and a translation of Euripides' *Herakles*. He has won the Shelley Prize from the PSA, and grants from the Lila Wallace Fund, American Academy of Arts and Letters, the Guggenheim and NEA. He teaches in the MFA Program at Hunter College.

Duncan Sprott's most recent novel is *Daughter of the Crocodile* (Faber 2006), the second instalment of *The Ptolemies Quartet*. He lives in County Cork, Ireland.

Robert Stein's poems have appeared before in *Agenda* (most recently Vo. 42 no. 2), as well as in *Poetry Review, The Wolf, Ambit, Magma, The Rialto,* and *Envoi*. He reviews contemporary classical music for *International Record Review* and *Tempo*.

Daniel Tobin's most recent book of poems is *The Narrows* (Four Ways Books, 2005). Chair of the Writing, Literature and Publishing Department at Emerson College, his awards include 'The Discovery/*The Nation* Award,' The Robert Penn Warren Award, The Robert Frost Fellowship, The Katherine Bakeless Nason Prize, and a creative writing fellowship from the National Endowment for the Arts. He is also the author of the critical study *Passage to the Center: Imagination and the Sacred in the Poetry of Seamus Heaney*. Most recently he has edited *The Book of Irish American Poetry from the 18th Century to the Present*, and several other books. His fourth collection of poems, *Second Things*, will appear in 2009.

Marina Tsvetaeva (1892-1941) is one of the greatest poets of Russia's Silver Age of Poetry. She became an émigré in 1922 but, due to family pressure, returned to Russia at the onset of war with Hitler. Suffering extreme depression and financial hardship, she committed suicide in Elabuga on 31 August, 1941.

Derek Walcott, the distinguished poet from St. Lucia, won the Nobel Prize for Literature in

1992. *Agenda* published a special issue on Derek Walcott, Vol 39 Nos 1-3 in 2003. This included a previously unpublished long poem by Walcott written when he was only eighteen.

Eamonn Wall, a native of Enniscorthy, Co. Wexford, Ireland, has lived in the U.S. since 1982. He is the author of four collections of poetry, the latest being *Refuge at De Soto Bend* (Salmon Publishing,2004). A new volume entitled *A Tour of Your Country* will appear from Salmon in 2008. *From the Sin-e Café to the Black Hills*, a collection of essays, was published by the University of Wisconsin Press in 2000 and awarded the Michael J. Durkan Prize by the American Conference for Irish Studies for excellence in scholarship. Eamonn lives in St. Louis, Missouri, and is Smurfit-Stone Professor of Irish Studies and Professor of English at the University of Missouri, St. Louis.

Andrew Waterman was born in London in 1940. After various clerical and manual jobs, he read English Literature at Leicester University, and from 1968 to 1997 taught at the University of Ulster. He now lives in Norwich. HIs nine books of poetry include *Collected Poems* (2000) and *The Captain's Swallow* (2007), both published by Carcanet. Andrew Waterman is a recipient of the Cholmondeley Award for Poets. His website is at www.andrewwaterman.co.uk.

Gerald Wells lives in Rutland. His poetry and short stories have appeared in many periodicals and various BBC programmes. He has published five collections of poetry and has had work selected for a number of anthologies. He has been a soldier, farmer and lecturer and is now happily retired with time enough to write.

Louise Wilford is currently studying for an MA in Creative Writing at Sheffield Hallam. She has been writing poetry and stories since childhood, and has won several competitions as an adult, most recently the £1000 First Prize in the Writers' Bureau Open Poetry Competition in 2007 and First Prize in the Mike Hayward Creative Writing Competition (second year running) 2007. She teaches A Level and GCSE English part-time.

Rik Wilkinson had no interest in poetry until he was 25. Three years later in 1968 he found himself at The Queen Elizabeth Hall, reading his work alongside Elizabeth Jennings, Peter Levi, John Wain and Sally Purcell. After 1972 little happened until the early 90s when a few poems were published in *Spokes*. Since 2002 he has been published regularly in *Manifold*; and more recently, *Acumen*. He has read his work at several venues and last year was a guest reader at the Torbay Festival. *Acumen* will bring out a pamphlet of his work later this year. You can find him listed on the poetrypf.co.uk website. Try www.poetrypf.co.uk/rikwilkinsonpage.html

Clive Wilmer is a poet and lecturer, who lives and teaches in Cambridge. His most recent collection is *The Mystery of Things* (Carcanet, 2006). He has, for nearly 40 years, been translating poetry from Hungarian in collaboration with George Gömöri, including books by Miklos Radnoti and Gyorgy Petri.

Enda Wyley was born in Dun Laoghaire, Co. Dublin in 1966. She holds an MA in Creative Writing from Lancaster University and has published three books of poetry with Dedalus Press, the latest being *Poems for Breakfast* (2004). Her novel for children, *The Silver Notebook* (O'Brien Press, 2007) was also recently published. She has been awarded The Vincent Buckley Memorial Poetry Prize and has also received several Irish Arts Council Bursaries for literature. She currently lives in Dublin with her husband, the poet Peter Sirr, and their young daughter, Freya.

Jean Cassou's *The Madness of Amadis and other poems*,
translated by **Timothy Adès** (£9.99)
(Bilingual edition: French and English on facing pages)

Jean Cassou, a war time Resistance leader in France, is still somewhat under-appreciated. These intriguing poems represent the body of Cassou's work, following his famous *33 Sonnets of the Resistance* (also translated by Timothy Adès), composed and memorised while Cassou was in prison, forbidden any writing materials.

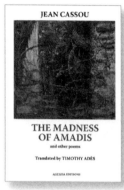

*'Without strain, Adès creates
a perfect mirror for Cassou's language'…*

'He has done the literate British a huge service'…

'Cassou's shade must be glowing'…

'Adès' sensitivity xrays the heart of every poem'.

Harry Guest

Gary Allen: *Iscariot's Dream* (£8.99)

This poignant, multi-layered collection – particularly relevant for our day in its treatment of treachery, and its detailed, graphic rendering of violence as something revolting, not to be mythologised – is the fourth collection by Gary Allen. It is 'thronged with the undead', living ghosts from classical mythology, from the Bible, and from the more recent 'Troubles' in Northern Ireland. Gary Allen, who was born in Ballymena, Co. Antrim in Northern Ireland, uses his childhood memories to give a gripping reality to this book. He has published three very well-received collections of poetry, the last of which, *North of Nowhere*, came from Lagan Press in 2006. He has also published a novel, *Cillin* (Black Mountain, 2005) and a collection of short stories, *Introductions* (Lagan Press, 2007).

'A Courageous and stunning work'…

*'Six poems in, the reader is wrenched awake,
and to the realisation: something very brave
is being done'…*

Ailbhe Darcy in the monthly arts supplement
of *The Newsletter*

NEW TEAR–OFF SUBSCRIPTION FORM

Pay by cheque (payable to 'Agenda'), or
Visa / MasterCard

SUBSCRIPTION RATES ON INSIDE FRONT COVER

1 Subscription (1 year) =
| 2 double issues |
| 1 double, 2 single issues |
| or |
| 4 single issues |
| (The above is variable) |

Please print

Name: ....

Address: ....

....

....

.... Postcode...

Tel: ....

Email: ....

Visa / MasterCard No: ☐☐☐ – ☐☐☐☐ – ☐☐☐☐ – ☐☐☐

Expiry date: ☐☐ – ☐☐

Please tick box:

New Subscription ☐   Renewed Subscription ☐

(or subscribe online – www.agendapoetry.co.uk)

Send to: AGENDA, The Wheelwrights, Fletching Street, Mayfield,
East Sussex, TN20 6TL